THE WARNING DRUM

THE
WARNING DRUM

The British Home Front Faces Napoleon

BROADSIDES OF 1803

EDITED BY FRANK J. KLINGBERG
AND SIGURD B. HUSTVEDT

Publications of The William Andrews Clark Memorial Library

UNIVERSITY OF CALIFORNIA PRESS
Berkeley and Los Angeles · 1944

UNIVERSITY OF CALIFORNIA PRESS
BERKELEY AND LOS ANGELES
CALIFORNIA

❖

CAMBRIDGE UNIVERSITY PRESS
LONDON, ENGLAND

PRINTED IN THE UNITED STATES OF AMERICA
BY THE UNIVERSITY OF CALIFORNIA PRESS

Preface.

T<small>HE</small> COLLECTION *of broadsides here reprinted came into the possession of The William Andrews Clark Memorial Library of the University of California, Los Angeles, in 1930, by purchase from a dealer in London. The entry in the sales catalogue reads as follows:*

"Napoleon's Threatened Invasion of England. Remarkable Collection of Contemporary English Broadsides concerning Napoleon Buonaparte's threatened Invasion of England.

"The Broadsides are mounted in a contemporary folio volume, boards, leather back. 1800–1815."

Inside the front cover of the volume is a notation in ink, of uncertain date and origin, reading "84 pieces." At the time of purchase by the Clark Library the collection was found to consist of 77 pieces on 70 printed sheets. A guess may be ventured that at some prior period certain of the items had been removed as not belonging to the unified subject of the invasion, as do all the now remaining numbers; other conjectural explanations of the shrinkage are possible but less satisfactory.

The dating in the catalogue, 1800–1815, may belong to the earlier history of the scrapbook; at any rate, it does not appear to apply to the volume in its present form. Only a smaller number of broadsides are assigned to a given year; the undated pieces belong, according to inconclusive available evidence, to 1803, and particularly to the summer and autumn of that year, when apprehension in England was at its height. Comparison with tentative assignment by month and year of the individual broadsheets as entered in the catalogues of the British Museum and of the Bibliotheca Lindesiana *supports this view. In the absence of contradictory testimony the assumption may be entertained that the collection was formed by some enthusiast of the school of Pepys and Narcissus Luttrell in the very heyday of the impending invasion and that his volume has come down to our notice with little alteration. If this is so, the corollary may be allowed to follow: the sequence of the numbers in the book represents the planned intent or the whim of the first owner; perhaps nothing more than the accidental order in which he acquired the several pieces and pasted them in his folio. Be that as it may, let the sheets march as when they were first mustered. The editors are willing to follow this course, not only from a proper piety toward the patriotic collector, but also from a prudent desire to avoid editorial hazards. Any departure from the fixed sequence would entail a rationale of rearrangement, either topical or chronological, which it is by no means easy to envisage. Various topical regroupings would be feasible, but no one of them compelling. A strict chronological progress of the entire series, dated and undated pieces alike, would involve niceties of bibliographical investigation which even at best might fall short of certainty. The editor of the "Catalogue of English Broadsides" in the* Bibliotheca Lindesiana *has made a laudable and properly guarded effort to determine the positive sequence in time of his titles; some two-thirds of the Clark Library items will be found in the* Lindesiana *catalogue (a note will direct attention to the correspondence in each case). Similarly, the occurrence of our titles in the British Museum's* Catalogue of Printed Books *is marked by the appropriate individual reference. By means of these annotations readers who so desire may explore the advisability of attempting to enforce severe chronological discipline upon the broadsides.*

There is, moreover, a positive advantage in leaving undisturbed the order that has come down to us, casual though it may appear. These ephemeral leaflets tumbled from the presses of many printers, at haphazard and apparently without the supervision of a Master Propagandist. The impact upon the public was therefore not an ordered, a regimented impact; it was, however heterogeneous, a collectively powerful impact. Our broadsides, in their somewhat improvised volunteer array, represent adequately the cohesion of many individual wills into one national will and purpose.

The Clark Library collection is presented here in its entirety and in its original arrangement. Each broadside is printed in full, with original footnotes and printer's advertisements. All notes supplied by the editors will be found bracketed at the end of each Number or grouped in appended sections of the book.

Our thanks are due to Miss Helen E. Livingston, Research Assistant in History, for the complete typescript, the reading of proof, and substantial assistance in the preparation of notes and identifications.

Mrs. Marian A. Waring, Reference Librarian at the Clark Library, has been helpful in various ways. Miss Cora Sanders, Curator of the Clark Library, has from the beginning of the enterprise made numerous valuable contributions in detail and in the larger aspects of the task.

To André Lobanov-Rostovsky, Professor of History, the editors would express their indebtedness for stimulating discussions of national psychologies and morales.

F.J.K.

S.B.H.

Contents.

Introduction.

THE MYSTERIOUS character of English public opinion, in its freedom of discussion and in its unity of agreement in a crisis, has puzzled scholars and observers for generations. There is the maximum of liberty, and yet, by an indescribable common consent, a complete unity such as no other nation has ever attained meets the challenge of an abdication, or a general strike, or an invasion.

Once a decision, which the day before was in solution, is made, the die is cast. The Church adds its voice, the Bank of England and other great corporations, many with world-wide contacts, support the agreement, but most amazing of all is the resolution and spontaneous response of all common folk. This national gift of agreement by open debate is the major English contribution to human liberty.[1]

These broadsides of the Clark Library collection throw an interesting light on this mobilization of public opinion. In the grave hours of 1803, sermons, tracts, newspaper and magazine articles, debates in Parliament, caricatures, all came in a flood directing and intensifying the national determination. Issued by hundreds and appearing throughout the twenty-two years of conflict, the broadside was an important weapon in solidifying English strength. The Clark Library offering gives a choice sampling on a variety of subjects by a goodly number of pamphleteers and writers from various callings. Some are military commentators, others are religious leaders, some are satirists. The masterly phrases, as in quips like "Fear God and level low" (No. 38), have reached to this day. One wag of the time hoped that the repeated "literary" annihilation of Napoleon in the broadsides would soon be fol-

---

[1] For an analysis of this insular heritage and the migration of part but not all of it to America see Robert R. Palmer, "Ideas That Did Not Migrate from America to Europe," and Frank J. Klingberg, "Ideas That Did Not Migrate from England to America," in the *Pennsylvania Magazine of History and Biography*, LXIII (October, 1939), 369–379, 380–389.

lowed by a similar military consequence. Here is rich fare, meat for every man, and distilled wisdom on how to get unity at home and action abroad. Great freedom of expression abounds; there is no regimentation such as Napoleon set up in his official organ, the *Moniteur*.[2]

At the opening of the nineteenth century the fires of the French Revolution were still burning. George Peabody Gooch has given an evaluation of its historical significance:

> The French Revolution is the most important event in the life of modern Europe. Herder compared it to the Reformation and the rise of Christianity; and it deserves to be ranked with those two great movements in history, because, like them, it destroyed the landmarks of the world in which generations of men had passed their lives, because it was a movement towards a completer humanity, and because it too was a religion, with its doctrines, its apostles, and its martyrs. It brought on the stage of human affairs forces which have moulded the actions of men ever since, and have taken a place among the formative influences of civilization. As Christianity taught that man was a spiritual being, and the Reformation proclaimed that no barrier should stand between the soul and God, so the Revolution asserted the equality of men, and declared each one of them, regardless of birth, colour, or religion, to be possessed of inalienable rights.[3]

The terrors of the Revolution, its expansive powers, and the aggressions of Napoleon alarmed Britons and, in 1803, filled, by voluntary methods, the forces for national defense. It might even be said that the century-long conviction of invincibility had to be punctured. The broadsides balance on this point of danger and invincibility. Unity on the home front made victory inevitable and, in time, sealed Napoleon's doom. The barrier reef of British resistance to an invasion of revolutionary ideas was comparable to the resistance of the British Navy and Army to the forces of Napoleon.

Although many men and events are introduced, in both the prose and the verse, there are four or five main themes

---

[2] These broadsides are presented without elaborate attempts to sift historical evidence, or to point out the exact facts in the various Napoleonic controversies which have been weighed by historians for a century.

[3] *The French Revolution* (London and New York, 1920), p. 7. Quoted by permission of the Macmillan Company, publishers.

upon which the broadsides focus. The repetition of subjects makes it unnecessary, or even impossible, to attempt to group the sheets in any special order. Reading them as a sheaf gives a fresh sense of a gathering storm and of man's grasp upon event through reason and emotion. These handbills appeared without any logical plan, and were read quickly, one by one, from day to day, by the public. They were intended to arouse all classes, all professions, all crafts, women as well as men. By skill in adaptation to different groups all components of the body politic were reached and unity of purpose and action attained.

Of the four or five pivotal attacks on the Napoleonic regime, perhaps the most effective indictment was that Napoleon and the French menaced all Christian faiths. This attack was particularly telling because, while the Frenchman was talking of the "rights of man," the Englishman for a generation or two had stressed the importance of religion in the creation of a just world. The leaders of the Evangelical Revival had committed themselves not only to reform at home but also to the Christianization of the world. No contrast could have been sharper than this gulf in ideology between England and France. The authors of broadsides who emphasized this chasm had a wider audience, present or potential, than England alone. Roman Catholic Europe had suffered body blows from the French Revolution. The lands of the clergy had been confiscated, a constitutional church independent of the Papacy had been established in France, a Goddess of Reason had been set up, Sunday abolished, a tenth day of rest introduced, and the names of the months changed. Napoleon's Concordat with the Pope, of July, 1801, was a compromise solution, quickly discarded in spirit, and ultimately ending with the imprisonment of the Pope.

A second conflict of ideology and practice, in addition to that of religion, lay in the fact that England in 1803 was a land of great men and meager institutions, whereas France under Napoleon was regimented in all aspects of life. The levy *en masse* of men into the Napoleonic armies, the centralization of government, the control of economic life and of the press, and terrorization by the police, all taken together, gave to the Napoleonic regime features of totalitarianism offensive to the whole English way of life. England had a minimum of organization and a minimum of government. Self-government in England meant inner self-control of the individual, without police supervision. The idea of a minister of police, a powerful functionary in the Continental states, has always been so repugnant to Englishmen that they have never had such an official. The broadsides recount endlessly that the homes of England, from cot to castle, are the householders' and cannot be entered by arbitrary action. Both peer and peasant are protected by law from arbitrary arrest and arbitrary imprisonment. Thus the recurrent phrases hark back to the common law, the bills of rights, the free press, the home, the altar, and the private property of the citizen. In brief, to Britons no freedom could come from across the Channel, but only enslavement. The French Revolution made France a democratic society, and Napoleon created for that society a centralized administration. These two processes not only divorced the French social order from that of Britain more completely, but also made the old Continental enemy more powerful and far more menacing.

Closely associated with religious and political freedom under law was a third heritage, economic freedom in all crafts and callings and property rights. Here the shoe fits rather closely, and the broadsides are particularly interesting in all that demonstrates the Englishman's stake in his country. As to land ownership, for example, two contemporary revolutions were afoot, running in opposite directions. The enclosure movement was still in progress in England and Scotland, creating land monopoly.[4] In Ireland, alien land ownership was the chief economic basis of Irish grievance.

---

[4] For a brief survey of English efforts to solve the social problems of intensified capitalistic farming, and the abuses of the industrial revolution, see Frank J. Klingberg, "The Evolution of the Humanitarian Spirit in Eighteenth Century England," in the *Pennsylvania*

In France, however, the lands not only of the clergy but also of the nobility had been confiscated and parceled out in the form of peasant farms, in which process tens of thousands of the twenty-five million Frenchmen had been killed or driven abroad. French propaganda, therefore, suggested that the slaughter of a mere "hundred rich men" (No. 42) would clean house in England. Indeed, the extreme concentration of land and capital in England was represented as being so great that the revolution would be "humane" and only a few men would need to be liquidated for a just distribution of the wealth of the country, which had been accomplished in France not only by legislative enactment but also by terror and civil war. The reader will note in every broadside the strategy of reply—recitation of the benefits under which all Englishmen lived, even the poorest. The joys of England are presented in terms by no means wholly economic, but always in such a way as to enhance the priceless intangibles inherent in English life, as compared with the "enslavement" of the French system. It is also made plain that English life was a seamless web—that leaders at the top could not be decapitated in the French style without damage to the livelihood of all men.

Fourthly, the economic fabric of life in England had one feature so distinctive that it must be especially stressed if we are to understand why the French Revolutionary and Napoleonic regimes did not spread to England. The middle class in England, as Thomas Jefferson pointed out, was the chief creative element of society.[5] We know now that this class was in a satisfied, not a revolutionary, mood, in contrast with that of France. There the Third Estate had taken

---

Magazine of History and Biography, LXVI (July, 1942), 260–278. The dislocations of a changing society from 1760 to 1832 are set forth in a series of volumes by J. L. and Barbara Hammond. The volume on *The Town Labourer* (London, 1925) is the most penetrating of the group and is important for the opening years of the nineteenth century.

[5] Jefferson, comparing the conditions of Great Britain and the United States in a letter to Thomas Cooper written from Monticello September 10, 1814, said of the British middle class, "the industry & manual dexterity of their journeymen & day laborers, and the science of their master-workmen keep them in the foremost ranks of competition with those of other nations." See *Jefferson Papers* (Library of Congress), Vol. 202-35958.

the lead in the Revolution and had supplied many of the leaders and administrators, as well as a score of the marshals of Napoleon's army. In England, the middle class of property owners, including of course the professional classes— lawyers, journalists, doctors, the clergy, and inventors,—saw boundless opportunities growing out of the industrial revolution, the agricultural revolution, and the revolutionary increase of population. The growth of the British Empire in India and of the colonies of settlement in open lands, such as Canada and Australia, and even the rapid development of the United States, were phenomena unmatched in earlier Anglo-Saxon expansion. This increase of manufactures and trade meant work for everybody at home or abroad and indicated higher standards of living, either current or soon to come. Confidence in this economic future is implicit in all the broadsides as well as in the specific statements of the merchants, bankers, and traders (No. 33). The fine phrase, "liberty grows out of an old and secure government; a new government must support itself with the bayonet" (No. 7), is a statement applicable to security in trade and business, and was, of course, so understood at the time.

And fifthly, the strategy of laying the whole case before the people was to fall back on the strength of history, on hereditary spirit, and on national pride in the three great defense services of the country, the Navy, the Army, and, no less strong, the entrenched social solidarity of the people. The national loyalties are distilled in a memorable way in these broadsheets, breathing as they do of all that is England. Knowledge of the nation's past history, daring, and resourcefulness had not been lost, and so there was no fatal gap in memory or in folk tradition. The authors of the broadsides had only, in their several ways, to draw upon the people's knowledge of their past, of their stand at Crécy in 1346, or again at Agincourt in 1415, and upon many other historic battlefields. The writers look backward to Richard the Lion-Hearted, or rejoice over Nelson's recent destruction of the

French fleet in the Battle of the Nile in 1798 and of the Danish fleet at Copenhagen in March, 1801. Written quite early in the period between May, 1803, and the decisive Battle of Trafalgar in October, 1805, all are a call to home defense.

The voice of history chants the country's continuity and the valor of the people in safeguarding the British Isles. From Roman times throughout the centuries, exploits of arms, heroic deeds, and other memorable events in the nation's past, at home and abroad, on the Continent and at sea, crowd men's minds. The great victories of the Fleet, the tradition of invincibility at sea, form a constant theme. But the necessity of the hour that England must now be defended by land forces as well as by ships is particularly stressed. Any "bridge" of invasion is to be manned by land defenders, and, as in the days of Marlborough a century earlier, an attack from across the Channel is to be reversed and the battle carried to the Continent. The Fleet must not be the sole defense. Each man on the home front will, therefore, take up his own musket or "a Pitch-fork, or a Hedge-stake if you cannot procure a Musket" (No. 1).

In order to understand the broadsides the reader needs to remind himself of the progress of the struggle between England and France in this last phase of the second Hundred Years' War between the two countries (1689–1815). A word must be said not only about the Navy, but also about the Army, which, of the two fighting services, at this time caused the greater anxiety, now that the serious mutinies in the Fleet of the year 1797 had been settled. Carlyle, when he said, "What walls you build, depend upon the state of the outer sea," uttered the truth graphically that Britain's first line of defense was always her fleet. The Navy had shown such invincibility in its power to defend the British Isles, and the Empire as well, that it had pinioned European armies to the Continent and kept the sea lanes open. Malta, Sicily, and many of the smaller islands such as Heligoland, although, like Britain herself, close to the Continent, could not at this time be reached in force by hostile land armies.

The "invasion" of England has a long history. Throughout the eighteenth century, as well as in earlier times, plans of invasion were a set problem for the French naval and military authorities. Among the many plans, that of 1759 "was more menacing than that of Napoleon,"[6] in that the southern and eastern coasts of England and also Scotland were to be attacked concurrently by the French, the Russians, and the Swedes. The English, by garrisoning the Isle of Wight and by attacking French shipping in its ports, destroyed the plan at its source. Only during the American Revolution did the English navy fail in its appointed task of blockading the French fleets at Brest and Toulon and thus immobilizing a large part of French naval power. During the French Revolutionary and Napoleonic decades, French fleets were blockaded in these home ports. Two of these fleets escaped from Toulon and were forthwith hunted down and destroyed by Nelson in the Battle of the Nile (1798) and at Trafalgar (1805).

England itself has not been invaded in force in modern times; and such was the sense of nationalism from Shakespeare's day that she could safely accept foreign rulers like William III and George I. It is to be remembered that Scotland and Ireland have their own separate histories and that for centuries Scotland was in virtual alliance with France against England. The Scottish invasions of England in 1715 and 1745 are reminders of this hostility. But the Act of Union between England and Scotland, of 1707, gradually united the two countries and consolidated their strength for war and peace. The happy attainment of English-Scottish friendship was not duplicated with respect to Ireland, which was in a position of sullen dependency for several centuries. Owned by alien landlords, compelled to support the established Anglican Church, controlled by a police under a severe penal code, and garrisoned by an army of occupation, Ireland might

[6] *Cambridge History of the British Empire* (New York and Cambridge, England, 1929), I, 481.

in each crisis welcome the foreign invader as a means of gaining her independence.

The defeat of the Spanish Armada in 1588 secured the independence of England. The wars two centuries later (1793–1815) form another well-known crisis in the long series of attempts to make Britain a satellite island of some Continental power. The Spanish Armada, with soldiers aboard, and doggedly pursued, sailed up the English Channel and through the Strait of Dover. Neither the admirals of the French Revolution nor those of Napoleon were able to bring into the Channel itself so menacing a force. Napoleon's army, although within sight of England, missed the fortuitous combination of available ships of the line, at the right moment, with the right naval leader. Napoleon's plans changed endlessly, shifting from month to month. He had on the Channel at various times an army of about two hundred thousand men, the finest in Europe, ready to strike.

But it must be noted that Napoleon's invasion plans, from the rupture of the Peace of Amiens in May, 1803, to the withdrawal of his army from the coast in August, 1805, faced the difficulty of two-front conditions. He did not control the seas and he had not destroyed the armies of Austria, Russia, and Prussia. Until December, 1803, he planned to cross the Channel with his invasion flotilla without naval control of these treacherous waters. From December, 1803, to August, 1804, he feverishly prepared for at least a temporary naval domination of the Channel by elaborate maneuvers to confuse and scatter the British admirals. The death of his ablest admiral, Latouche-Tréville, in August, necessitated the shelving of this scheme until the next year. Then, in alliance with Spain, he worked out the combinations of French and Spanish squadrons which sent Villeneuve and Nelson, in spectacular sea campaigns, from Toulon to the West Indies, and back to Europe, ending in Nelson's triumph at Trafalgar in October, 1805.[7]

---

[7] *Cambridge History of the British Empire*, II, 78–82, 94–102. Pages 36 to 128 are a survey of the whole period, 1793–1915. The footnotes give references to the work of French, Ger-

The financial, maritime, and naval strength of Britain was so overwhelming that paper schemes of conquest could not be carried out. William Pitt put the matter briefly: "We have a revenue equal to all Europe, a navy superior to all Europe, and to make us quite gentlemen, a debt as large as that of all Europe."[8] Throughout the years 1793–1815 the English had an advantage of two to one in naval strength. Even with all the shipyards of the Continent in Napoleon's control, the British outbuilt the French two to one. The fighting skill of British personnel from admiral to individual tar was an additional decisive factor in British strength. The English admirals were schooled to close with the enemy and annihilate him, regardless of risks and losses; the French, on the other hand, to fight defensively and to save their ships. French strategy and tactics in the Boulogne invasion plans, as stated above, sought to disperse the English naval units and gain control of the Channel while Napoleon crossed over. He was convinced that only the conquest of the island base from which ships came would give him a lasting victory.[9]

The British Fleet had a heavy, threefold responsibility: to protect the coasts of Britain, to convoy merchantmen, sometimes five hundred in a convoy, and to defend the vast Empire overseas. In the course of these duties, the Fleet carried out complicated maneuvers, perhaps in half a dozen areas, the units joining, separating, crossing the Atlantic, passing into the Mediterranean, into the Baltic, bottling the Spaniards up at Corunna and at Cadiz, the French at Toulon and Brest

---

man, and American, as well as British scholars, including the volumes of Desbrière. Harold C. Deutsch has a brief treatment of the "invasion" and Napoleon's Continental problems in "Napoleonic Policy and the Project of a Descent upon England," *Journal of Modern History*, II (December, 1930), 541–568. See also J. Holland Rose, *Life of Napoleon I* (London, 1902), I, 445–468, for a discussion of the Boulogne Flotilla, with sketches of Napoleon's invasion ideas, deceptions, and plans.

[8] Paul Frischauer, *England's Years of Danger* (New York, 1938), p. 124.

[9] British maritime strength is summarized in Geoffrey Bruun, *Europe and the French Imperium, 1799–1814* (New York, 1938), pp. 86–88. He states that, before 1789, 2,000 French ships were active in European and colonial trade; ten years later, the French flag had disappeared from the high seas. In contrast, in 1800 the British merchant marine consisted of 18,000 ships, with 1,500,000 tonnage. Ships and tonnage showed an annual increase. Marine insurance rates fell from 25 per cent in the 1790's to 12 per cent in 1806 and 6 per cent in 1810. When the French navy was not blockaded during the American Revolution, the insurance rates had been 50 per cent.

and in Martinique, and destroying the Danish ships at Copenhagen. An earlier rare error in timing was the cause of the failure to relieve Cornwallis and his army at Yorktown.

The operations of the Fleet might be offensive campaigns, or defensive movements in which the ships fell back upon the home ports after a series of hit-and-run fights. Two hostile fleets might sail to meet and fight each other, or to miss each other deliberately, or to seize enemy possessions or booty in distant areas. The British Empire had become an overseas Empire, Gibraltar being the only Continental possession. Any one engagement or voyage needs to be described with all the exact facts of position, weather and wind, kinds of vessels and forces, and types of leaders. Circumstances beyond human control belonged preëminently to the day of sail. An enemy fleet might escape the blockade and disappear for weeks or months, reach the West Indies, or the eastern Mediterranean, or roam at large, before it could be detected. In Nelson, England had the ablest naval captain of all time to pit against the Emperor, and this conflict is often called a duel between Napoleon and Nelson.

Three traditional French plans for defeating England were all used by Napoleon. First in time was the invasion of Egypt and Syria to arouse the Mohammedan world and shatter British influence from Tangier to Calcutta. The third in sequence was to exclude the "nation of shopkeepers," in Bonaparte's frequent phrase, by imposing a Continental blockade to force economic disorganization and collapse upon industrial Britain. The needs of Continental powers were so great that trade continued by means of smuggling and also through the many ports of entry not under Napoleon's control. He himself ordered shoes for his soldiers in Britain, and he had no objection to England's supplying Wellington's army in Spain, his theory presuming that the financial drain might bankrupt his enemy. The Rothschilds in various cities of Europe were in good part responsible for Britain's elaborate and successful schemes of finance.

The second plan, sharply to the fore during the time of the broadsides presented in this volume, was that of direct invasion of the Isles. The threat alone immobilized portions of the British Fleet, forced the raising of large land bodies, and in general made it possible to press on with adventures under Plans One and Three. Fatal to Napoleon's plans, however, was the vulnerability of his land frontiers, as has been noted above. To the eastward, three great hostile powers, Austria, Prussia, and Russia, represented mass human resources and interests opposed to the Napoleonic regime. In the final treaties of peace in 1814 and 1815, it was these powers, with Britain, that made the terms.

The size and character of British armies were determined by this basic fact of sea power. Moreover, from Cromwell's time a standing army had been unpopular and regarded as a menace to the liberty of England, and, in the words of F. W. Maitland, "had become hateful to the classes which were to become the ruling classes."[10] Armies, according to law, had to be raised, as Henry Hallam says, "for better preserving the balance of power in Europe," and also for expanding and maintaining the colonial empire. An Army enlarged during wartime was instantly reduced to small size when peace came, in sharp contrast to the standing armies of France. The British Mutiny Act, upon which the discipline and maintenance of the Army depended, had to be passed anew each year. This procedure made the use of the Army as an instrument of regimentation at home, against the liberties of England, an impossibility.

The severity of this crisis at the opening of the nineteenth century was such that exceptional measures were taken to increase the size of the Army by levies on the parishes and by calls to the volunteers to train in their spare time. Between May, 1803, and October, 1805, the English coasts were fortified with batteries and towers, small vessels were stationed to attack an invasion flotilla, the Army and militia were

[10] *Encyclopaedia of the Social Sciences*, II, 214.

increased to a hundred and eighty thousand, and four hundred thousand volunteers were raised. Any French force effecting a landing would probably have been bottled up in England by the Fleet. It may be said that after the year 1700 no British admiral regarded the effective invasion of the island of Britain as feasible without naval domination of the English Channel. These British land forces, before 1803, had been scattered all over the Empire in such a way that they could not effectively attack France herself. Fighting in the two major centers of empire, India and the West Indies, resulted in major successes in India, under Sir Arthur Wellesley, later the Duke of Wellington. In the West Indies, however, there had been disasters, not in loss of territory, but in the destruction of the flower of the British Army. Forty thousand men were lost and thousands more were incapacitated. The Spanish and French islands were taken, but disease killed the conquerors and few were left for garrison use.

These appalling losses led to the reorganization of the Army. For the defense of the West Indies, Negro troops were recruited, and British soldiers were henceforth reserved for European campaigns. Several of the broadsides contain criticisms and specific suggestions for improvement, which, in time, fashioned the British Army into the hardest and most respected fighting force in Europe. It was the first army ever to be provisioned from a home base, as was done during the Spanish campaign under Wellington. Its well-fed soldiers did not need to live on the country, as the armies of Napoleon often did. Ingenious British methods of recruiting and training made for morale and skill. A battalion at home absorbed recruits, sent them to a companion battalion abroad, and thus kept up full fighting strength. Experiments in tactics made for mobility, and for devices in meeting attack by the French marshals.[11]

[11] J. W. Fortescue, *British Statesmen of the Great War, 1793–1814* (Oxford, 1911). This short volume gives the West Indian losses (pp. 104, 130–131); the relation of the militia to the regular army (p. 133); the rebuilding of the new army (pp. 146–149); and an estimate of the seriousness of the invasion threat (p. 179).

The broadsides are, of course, closely related to the contemporary events. The Peace of Amiens, from March 28, 1802, to May 18, 1803, introduced an unsettled period of fourteen months, following nine years of war. When, in 1799, Napoleon rose to military and political dictatorship over France and her satellite states and quickly forced all Britain's Continental allies to sue for peace, Britain stood alone without an ally on the Continent. The results so far had followed the usual pattern of wars between Great Britain and a strong Continental power in its first stage: the French had won on land, and the British on the sea lanes of the world.

The Peace of Amiens was based on the tacit assumption by both sides that a sea power and a land power could maintain satisfactory working relationships. Both parties soon discovered that neither was willing to give up its rights within the area of the other. Britain did not wish to surrender to Napoleon her historic principle of the balance of power on the Continent. He, on the other hand, wished to acquire more Continental territory or to add to his colonial possessions in Australia, Newfoundland, the West Indies, to control Malta and Egypt, and to form an alliance with the Mahrattas in India. Britain, under these circumstances, kept Malta (left by the Treaty to the Knights of St. John) and allied herself with Russia and Austria. Although British trade with the Continent and the safety of her empire were the major economic interests at stake, the rupture of the Peace of Amiens came with the contention over the continued British occupation of Malta, the details of which need not be set forth here. Malta was the current symbol of control of the Mediterranean, a sea which England had dominated since the days of Cromwell in the middle of the seventeenth century.

The terrors of what would happen in England if the tyrant should come over are pictured in the bloodcurdling terms of what was declared to have happened on the Continent, in Syria, and in Africa. The riches of the English country are described in the people's terms, as are the threats of the pros-

pective plunderers, "famished Wolves, Cruel as Death, and
Hungry as the Grave, panting for an Opportunity . . . to
come into our Sheep-Fold" (No. 48). And carefully to be
noted is the fact that the call to resistance is not limited to
the "men of oak" in England, but is addressed to the whole
world.

Alone for some months before the Peace of Amiens (March,
1802), England was again alone for the two years and four
months after the rupture of the uneasy Peace. When the war
was renewed, in May, 1803, the French Revolutionary ideological forces, "liberty, equality, and fraternity," and military might of the only united people in Western Europe had
temporarily triumphed. There were, in fact, in Europe twenty-
five million Frenchmen, a population two and one-half times
as large as the population of the Island of Great Britain;
twenty-five million disunited and disorganized Germans; and
about thirty-six million Russians scattered over vast areas.
These figures make an extraordinary contrast with the relative populations of 1944, which total forty million Frenchmen, eighty million Germans, and one hundred and eighty
million Russians. In the Island of Great Britain today there
are not ten and one-half million, as in 1801, but forty-six
million. In 1801 there were an estimated five and a quarter
million in Ireland, with a ratio of one person in Ireland to
two on the Island of Britain. Today for one in Ireland there
are between ten and eleven in Britain.[12]

The references to Ireland must be read with knowledge of
the terror of that day that a French invasion of Ireland, with
its comparatively large population, one million larger than
the four and a quarter million in 1944, would spell the doom
of England. Small French bodies of troops had landed in
Ireland during the French Revolutionary period, and the
argument still rages whether, if Hoche's expedition, in 1796,

---

[12] For a summary of Irish conditions, see William Forbes Adams, *Ireland and Irish
Emigration to the New World from 1815 to the Famine* (New Haven, 1932), pp. 1–67. The
population estimates are given on pp. 3–5. For information on Europe's population, see
the *Encyclopaedia of the Social Sciences* (New York, 1934), XII, 243–245.

had landed, or if Humbert could have had not one thousand but ten thousand men in 1798, England would have been defeated. The threat of disaster from Ireland was real to English minds. It was remembered that French troops were present in force at the Battle of the Boyne, in 1690. Large numbers of Irishmen fought in the French armies during the whole period of the second Hundred Years' War (1689–1815). In fact, French soldiers repeatedly landed in Ireland, but not in numbers large enough to be victorious. Napoleon believed that a small invasion of Ireland, by thirty to forty thousand men, would accomplish his ends even if the invasion of England itself were beaten off.[13]

The hope repeatedly mentioned in the broadsides was that robust English nationalism would be able to recruit Continental nationalisms with which to fight French nationalism. The appeals to the peoples of Europe to regain their liberties had a most specific objective: to turn against the French dominance not only Spanish nationalism, but also German, Italian, Russian, Swedish, and Polish. This English plan could be carried out in the end only through the acceptance of the stable gains of the French Revolution, liberty, equality, and fraternity, in whole or in part, by the peoples of Western Europe. The social advantages of the French Revolution could not be denied. Napoleon's invasion of Spain, in 1808, marks the point at which nationalistic fervor began to overpower the slogans of the French Revolutionary crusade, a process which came to an end when all the nationalities of Europe, including the French, abandoned Napoleon to his fate.

To sum up, England and Ireland were immune from the Revolutionary attack on religion. Evangelicalism, or Pietism, had, as indicated above, deeply penetrated all ranks of Eng-

[13] Napoleon's own statement is quoted in J. Holland Rose, *The Life of Napoleon I*, I, 453: "Whether I have 30,000 or 40,000 men in Ireland or whether I am both in England and Ireland, the war is ours." For an earlier, less optimistic statement by Napoelon see *ibid.*, pp. 160–161, in which he wrote that, without naval supremacy, "we must really give up the expedition against England, be satisfied with keeping up the pretence of it, and concentrate all our attention and resources on the Rhine . . . or else undertake an Eastern expedition.'

lish society, including the Anglican Church, and the dissenting groups had become adjusted to Anglicanism by a process of practical religious toleration. The triumph of Evangelicalism in England, as reflected in the sheets, was a potent rallying cry. The French destruction of the Roman Catholic Church, the slaughter and driving out of thousands of French Roman Catholic priests—about four thousand to England alone—horrified English public opinion and intensified religion as a national force. The Age of Reason in France thus coincided with the Age of Pietism in England. The broadside from the leading lay representative of Evangelicalism, William Wilberforce (No. 53), in this series, is worth special attention. He does not rely on human forces alone, but clearly calls on God, and on the people to keep up their Christian defenses. Wilberforce had, throughout the early phases of the French Revolutionary War, questioned England's participation, and urged that financing the counterrevolutionaries and interposing in internal affairs would merely consolidate French nationalism and increase the fighting strength of the enemy. Against Napoleon, however, Englishmen were united.

In Ireland this same destruction of the French Roman Catholic Church had crippled Irish nationalism because the Roman Church there felt severely the blow to the French Catholic clergy. In fine, neither Irish Roman Catholic, Anglo-Irish Episcopalian, nor Scotch-Irish Presbyterian was in a mood to support the French Revolution on religious grounds. Thus religious hostility against the revolutionaries went a long way toward neutralizing the bitter enmity felt against the English by the Roman Catholics and Presbyterians in Ireland on other grounds.

The field of religion is an obvious coign of vantage from which to view the ideological forces in conflict. A totalitarian state cannot tolerate independent organizations or differing mass philosophies. In uprooting religion, such a state sacrifices other, intertwined heritages of culture, art, and literature. Then, too, it is extraordinarily true that freedom of worship is indivisible from freedom of speech, freedom of assembly, and freedom of the press.

In summary, too, how marked is the impression of the strength of history in the broadsides! To measure it, one needs only to consider how and in what terms, without the basic reference to the historical past, could this campaign, whether through force of arms or through propaganda, have been conducted? Would not permanent regimentation have been the only alternative? British foreign policy is fixed but intricate. George Macaulay Trevelyan, in memorable words, gives the over-all strategy of defense:

Modern England has four times fought with success a great war to prevent the conquest of Europe by a single Power: the Spain of Philip and the Inquisition, the France of the Grand Monarch and the Jesuits, the France of the Jacobins and Napoleon, and the German military monarch of our own day [1914] have each in turn been foiled. On each of these four occasions England had a double end in view,—the Balance of Power in Europe and the security of her own mercantile and colonial future beyond the ocean. And on each occasion European and maritime considerations alike required that England should prevent the Netherlands and the Rhine Delta from falling into the hands of the greatest military and naval State of the continent. It was no accidental coincidence, but danger to our shores and to our naval control of the Channel, that made the Netherlands the chief scene of English military interference on the continent, under Elizabeth, under William and Anne, and under George V. And for the same reason the wars conducted in the name of George III against Revolutionary France began with the defeat of our troops in the Netherlands in 1793-4, and ended with their victory in the same sector at Waterloo. . . .

The Napoleonic Wars stand half-way between the Marlborough wars and the Great War of our own day, in time, in size and in character. . . . The geography and strategy . . . of the naval and military operations which quelled Napoleon resemble those which quelled Louis XIV. Again, in the days of Pitt and Castlereagh, as in the days of William and Marlborough, the two props of the alliance against France were British sea-power and British subsidies, applied along all the coasts and in half the Treasuries of Europe. . . . Again a British General of genius, commanding a small but excellent British army, played a decisive part among the larger military establishments of the continent. Again British troops were landed in the Netherlands and in Spain, in Mediterranean islands and on

American coasts. And again, in 1815 as in 1713, the war ended for England with the establishment in the Netherlands of a Power from which she had nothing to fear, and by great additions to her colonial Empire and her maritime prestige.[14]

Now, in a fifth war to prevent the conquest of Europe, the immemorial discipline and courage of the British people are unbroken. Throughout the twenty years of the gigantic Napoleonic struggle, military, naval, and political changes were frequent, often disastrous or puzzling, yet public opinion kept an even keel. The home victory of unity was as overwhelming as the final triumph on the field of Waterloo.

The Clark Library broadsides show that English nationalism was so firmly established that the unity of the people was instinctive. A sense of danger was conveyed not to one, but to all. What other people had such inner powers of instantly facing in the same direction, or that voluntary self-discipline in supporting both home and Empire demands? The broadsides enable the reader, as if through a microscope, to see this phenomenon of English character and tradition.

The broadside as a vehicle of expression has indeed a conspicuous place in English tradition. Since the invention of printing it has served official and informal purposes of many kinds. Caxton, not surprisingly, appears as the first English printer to employ the useful medium. During the fifteenth century the single printed sheet carried, almost exclusively, ecclesiastical bulls and other pronouncements. In later periods it has assumed rapidly broadening range and variety. An examination of the lists prepared for the Society of Antiquaries and those for Lord Crawford's collection in the *Bibliotheca Lindesiana* will indicate something of the widening scope which in the course of time came to embrace a multitude of appeals to literate interest.

In the sixteenth and seventeenth centuries, while journalism was still in its tentative stages, the broadsheets had a most important function in the purveying of news, of propa-

---

[14] *History of England* (New York, 1926), pp. 570–571. Quoted by permission of Longmans, Green and Company, publishers.

ganda, of entertainment. In the eighteenth century, as the
periodical press reached increasing importance, the broadside
stubbornly held its ground in the service not only of hack
writers but of poets of name, who often entrusted first editions of briefer works to the fragile carriage of the folio sheet.
Thousands of the leaves have perished in the course of the
centuries; but thousands remain, thanks to the zeal of collectors such as Selden, Pepys, Pearson, Roxburghe, Luttrell,
and others of a like antiquarian stripe. Into the nineteenth
century, printers and collectors have kept pace. The British
Museum, besides a wealth of material from other periods, has
several larger collections of Napoleonic squibs.[15] The *Bibliotheca Lindesiana* contains another extensive group. To these
gatherings the Clark Library holdings form a respectable
counterpart.

The *Gentleman's Magazine*, in its review of new publications for September, 1803, notices a reprint of an ode by
Akenside "To the Country Gentlemen of England," accompanied by preface and notes to fit the poem to the current
occasion. The reviewer quotes from the notes as follows:
"The eagerness with which certain short publications, calculated for the lower orders of the people, have lately been
bought up, proves that military thoughts are rising in that
quarter. 30,000 copies of one of these publications, called
'John Bull,' have been sold within a few weeks; the very
beggars come to the shops for them."[16] No doubt the "short
publications" are to be identified with our broadsides. The
reprinting of Akenside's ode is clearly intended to provide a
patriotic appeal to the gentry in appropriately elevated com-
plement to the handbills so hungrily consumed by the "lower
orders." As a matter of fact, through numerous agencies the

---

[15] British Museum, *Catalogue of Printed Books*, *s.v.* "Napoleon I" (col. 257): "Loyal and
patriotic handbills, songs, addresses, *etc.* on the threatened invasion of Great Britain by
Buonaparte.... 140 pieces, including two portraits of Napoleon; fol. [London, 1803]."

[16] *Gentleman's Magazine*, Vol. LXXIII, Pt. 2, p. 842. Akenside's ode was first published
in 1758, upon the threat of an invasion at that time. See *Monthly Review* for August, 1803,
p. 442. This periodical, particularly the numbers for the second half of the year, contains
many longer and shorter notices of new publications, sermons, plays, poems, political and
military disquisitions, bearing upon the subject of the invasion.

tocsin was rung to such effect as to reach the ear of the well-bred and the home-bred alike. Before giving some illustrative examples of alarms directed especially to the high-born, we may appraise these broadsides for qualities that might be supposed to recommend them particularly to the lower orders.

A survey of the broader mechanisms of expression used by the writers will assist in the estimate. Much the larger proportion of the pieces here presented employs prose rather than verse. Such a proportion in itself suggests adaptation to a broad public but not necessarily to a lowly public. Within the range of prose presentation certain types of writing, formal and informal, emerge as the evident models for the broadside author, all circumscribed by the demands of brevity. Simple in form and antecedents is the advertisement of the man-tiger Napoleon, on view for a trifling consideration at Mr. Bull's menagerie (No. 69). Quite as cheering to the vulgar would be the quasi-legal posting of a reward of £20,000 for the apprehension of the Corsican master criminal (No. 65). Higher in the scale of genteel composition comes the epitaph, written, not in a country churchyard, but underneath a gibbet over a dunghill, to chronicle the wished demise of a mighty conqueror (No. 31).

The epistolary form occurs in attractive examples, such as the practical advice on military conduct coming as it were from a sage veteran (No. 3), and John Bull's familiar letter counseling his countrymen on appropriate heroisms at home (No. 50). Numerous addresses, like Sheridan's to the people (No. 16) and that of the soldier Irishman to his fellow Irishmen resident in England (No. 43), carry us in the direction of the oratorical eloquence suggested by the old Whig's non-partisan harangue (No. 13) and Wilberforce's lay sermon (No. 53). The official proclamation appears in an example given by Britannia herself (No. 8). Historical writing in a genuine form appears in excerpts from Sir Robert Wilson's *History of the British Expedition to Egypt* (No. 4); and the biographical sketch in a distorted account of Napoleon's life (No. 12). Such are the characteristic representatives of established types of prose discourse.

Several of the broadsides make use of dramatic elements. There is a sham playbill drawing attention to the approaching appearance of the buffoon Bonaparte in a farce entitled *The Invasion of England* (No. 17). The ghost of Shakespeare mounts the stage to speak stirring lines from *King John* in the character of a true Englishman (No. 32). The dramatist Massinger provides a bellicose passage from his play, *The Bondman* (No. 14). George Colman writes a patriotic epilogue for a new play (No. 19). Of a pseudo-dramatic character is the discussion between the artisan members of the Antigallican Club meeting at the sign of the British Lion (No. 56). The dialogue form, so frequently used in earlier periods for the most varied purposes of instruction and persuasion, comes into service in several broadsheets, such as the dialogue between the British tar and the brave soldier (No. 28); in others, John Bull and Bonaparte confront each other in verbal duels (No. 22, No. 25). Like the prose pieces in general, the dramatic vehicles are popular but not specifically designed for ruder readers.

Some of the dialogues are versified, as the one between Bonaparte and Talleyrand (No. 70). Other verse models are employed to good effect. Rhymed couplets by Nicholas Rowe, printed as a broadside just a century before, are reprinted for the new day of danger (No. 29). In the same cultivated medium, a millionaire exhorts the people of Great Britain (No. 37). Stanzaic verse, intended to be sung, makes up the larger part of the metrical group. Here we find John Mayne's patriotic address to English, Scots, and Irishmen (No. 51), and a number of anonymous songs set to popular tunes. For the songs, as for the broadsides altogether, the rhetorical patterns indicate the intention of reaching not merely rustics and artisans, but a wider range of the rural and urban population.

As much may be said with regard to the tone and temper of the utterances in their collective mass. The voices that come to us are not those of stoic philosophers debating relative values, or of fishwives and apprentices chanting their native billingsgate. The uttermost extremes may hardly be said to meet here. To be sure, there is a considerable range of expression, from the suave earnestness of Wilberforce and the measured eloquence of Sheridan to the lachrymose narrative of the Hanoverian blacksmith. "The Ploughman's Song" in simple language recites the dangers that confront the house and home of the poor; Jacob Bosanquet's phalanx of merchants and bankers in a diction more city-bred pledge their services to the cause not of Lombard Street alone, but of the entire nation. In sum, as the matter of the broadsides is marked by an unblinking perception of fact, so the rhetoric, if at times somewhat larded with robustious phrase, is direct and savory, well fitted to catch the assent of the common man without distressing the sensibilities of his more refined countrymen; it is, for practical—indeed, most practical—purposes, John Bull speaking.

The broadsides do not lose in importance, but rather gain effective relief, through a comparison with some of the more prominent among the other means of rousing public opinion. In the first rank of the allied instrumentalities of persuasion would come the work of the graphic artists. The cartoons of James Gillray, Isaac Cruikshank, and their named or anonymous fellow draftsmen drew crowds of buyers to the print shops. No false delicacy obscures the plain intent of their caricatures: to make Napoleon and his mamelukes, despite whatever panoplies of savagery, appear puny and to make the British tar, brandishing his oaken cudgel, appear the more heroic and formidable. It was not a day for subtleties, but for robust pictorial declamation which the many could not fail to understand and applaud. Caricature and broadsheet letterpress together provide a harmonious ensemble of popular appeal.

Perhaps no more comprehensive view of the confederated incitements to patriotism is available than that afforded by the newspapers and magazines of the threatening year. Several of the broadsides cite *The British Neptune* as a source. Others (as will appear from notes to individual numbers) were either first printed or afterward reprinted in various periodical publications; in fact, the printers of the handbills frequently requested insertion of their loyal papers in regular journals. A close scrutiny of a single volume of the *Gentleman's Magazine*[17] for 1803 will afford an illustrative conspectus of coadjutant factors in the common enterprise; here we find ourselves socially abovestairs, among the polite and well-read. Let us look at the collected numbers of the magazine from July to December. In the volume for the preceding half year the rumblings of the approaching storm are clearly audible; in the first half of the year 1804 the gales are relatively spent. The second half of the year 1803, the period represented in the main by our broadsides, marks a conspicuous concentration in the pages of the magazine upon the absorbing theme of the threatened invasion.

Every section betrays the grand preoccupation. The monthly reports of the proceedings of Parliament give readers an echo of stirring debates on the defense of the realm. Extracts from the *London Gazette* tell of battles on sea and land. Abstracts of Foreign Occurrences bring horrifying tidings of the burning in effigy of Mr. Addington at Paris[18] and the foreboding information that the usurper is compelling the Dutch to provide two hundred and fifty flat-bottomed boats to assist in freighting the invaders.[19] By way of reassurance the number for October presents an elaborate account of the "sublime spectacle of a Patriot Monarch" reviewing hundreds of

---

[17] An examination of the *European Magazine*, among the various periodicals of the day, would yield a comparable view of public concern over the imminence of invasion. In it, as in the *Gentleman's Magazine*, the latter half of 1803 is the period of critical interest. It is notable that the publisher of the *European Magazine*, James Asperne, has left his imprint upon a number of the broadsides. *Cobbett's Annual Register* for 1803, for the reader of the broadsides, is a most important repository of official information, as it seems to have been for the makers of the broadsides a ready source of material.

[18] *Gentleman's Magazine*, Vol. LXXII, Pt. 2 (August, 1803), p. 773.

[19] *Ibid.*, p. 775.

metropolitan Volunteers in Hyde Park.[20] These citizen soldiers and their comrades elsewhere will not set forth unfledged and unwarned if they heed Colonel Hope's Instructions to the First Regiment of Edinburgh Volunteers, cautionary on the most practical matters of military equipment and conduct, from the provision of flannel nightcaps to the proper use of musketry against an enemy attempting to land from boats.[21] The Church sends the defenders to their duties with its blessing and spiritual counsel.[22] On the eve of departure they may attend a theatrical revival of *King Henry the Fifth* or see other plays with such titles as *The Surrender of Calais*, or *The English Fleet in 1342*.[23]

Meanwhile, for those who sit at home, the poetry columns of the *Gentleman's Magazine* for the whole half year contain hardly a line that does not breathe its martial fervor. One of these may perhaps have a special interest as a sort of versified criticism of the broadsides as a group, inasmuch as the poet offers his ten lines by way of appropriate substitute for the "long handbills, rousing the public" which have recently been dispersed;[24] we may believe that the public did not altogether share his view of the efficacy of his iron rations of inspiration.

Altogether, the poetry in the magazine, in spite of its genuine zest, does not reach a high quality; nor are the poets among the best-known versifiers of the period.[25] We must look elsewhere. Yet even the famous romantic poets, much as they were influenced by the entire sequence of Revolutionary and Napoleonic events and ideas, do not appear to have risen notably to this particular occasion. The one conspicuous exception is Wordsworth, who has several sonnets written

---

[20] *Ibid.*, pp. 974 ff.

[21] *Ibid.*, pp. 1068–1070.

[22] *Ibid.* See review notices of various sermons preached especially for volunteers or other military groups; e.g., p. 1158.

[23] See the plays listed in the Theatrical Register of the magazine for the months under survey; cf. Genest's lists of productions for 1803.

[24] *Gentleman's Magazine*, Vol. LXXII, Pt. 2, p. 764.

[25] Two poems by the laureate, Pye, dealing with the theme of the invasion, appear in the magazine for 1804, one in January (p. 60), another in April (p. 348).

with an eye to the crisis. Among these is the one "To the Men of Kent," composed in October, 1803:

> Vanguard of Liberty, ye men of Kent,
> Ye children of a soil that doth advance
> Her haughty brow against the coast of France,
> Now is the time to prove your hardiment!
> To France be words of invitation sent!
> They from their fields can see the countenance
> Of your fierce war, may ken the glittering lance,
> And hear you shouting forth your brave intent.
> Left single, in bold parley, ye, of yore,
> Did from the Norman win a gallant wreath;
> Confirmed the charters that were yours before;—
> No parleying now. In Britain is one breath;
> We all are with you now from shore to shore;—
> Ye men of Kent, 'tis victory or death!

These are the lines of a man who, a year before, had contended that the poet should speak the language of men and that poetry has its origin from emotion recollected in tranquillity. Is it too much to say that Wordsworth in this sonnet thinks the thoughts and speaks the language, heightened though it be, of the broadside authors, that his verses are the tranquilized expression of the more unschooled emotions of the men who wrote and who read "John Bull's Invitation to Bonaparte" and "Britons, to Arms"?

It is hardly necessary to enter upon an elaborate demonstration of the present timeliness of these broadsides of 1803. Readers may find satisfaction in drawing for themselves such parallels as their own ingenuity and sympathies may suggest. One example may be singled out here by way of illustration. In the piece entitled "Union and Watchfulness" (No. 34) the enemy is presented as the unjust and dishonorable champion of a "glorious new order of things." Britain has for some time had and, as report speaks firmly, still has under effective military preparation an appropriate reaction to a widely heralded New Order premised upon the castigation of the unregenerate islanders whose fathers invited Napoleon to come across the Channel and get it. To borrow the language of one of the broadsides, the Ghost of Barlow still stalks through the towns and fields, the shafts of the Finsbury Archers are winged as never before, the pikes, bills, and calivers of the retainers of the Duke of Shoreditch make a formidable front.

It may be agreed that these broadsides have in them something unmistakably durable. In their grasp on the continuities of English history, their reliance on the stable elements in British character, they served the needs of their own day. Change their idiom a little, change their compass bearings a little more, and they will serve rather well the needs of today and still have in store a provision for tomorrow.

THE BROADSIDES

Publicola's Postscript to the People of England.

N.B.—I am apprehensive, my Countrymen, that some of your friends who have lately addressed you, have been too complaisant and over-inclined to flatter you: I am of opinion that plain truth is not only most honourable, but, at such a moment as the present, most politic. I do not deny that your breasts glow with as much patriotism, national spirit, and valour as ever led the successful armies of your illustrious forefathers to victory and triumph over your inveterate enemy, France; but I shall not descend to pamper your vanity, by admitting that these sentiments are sufficiently roused or excited to meet the dangers by which your independence and very existence are threatened. It is not by shouting out, DOWN WITH THE TYRANT—CONFUSION TO BUONAPARTE, that you will spread dismay throughout his ranks, or save your native land from subjugation; *it is by acting, not talking, that these things are to be done.*—Had the heroes of former times kept these fine feelings, this love of their country, pent up within themselves, we should never have heard of an EDWARD or a HENRY; the GLORIES OF CRESSY, POICTIERS, OR AGINCOURT would never have bloomed; nor should we at this moment have possessed the powers of questioning even the right of that ROBBER BUONAPARTE *to divide the spoils of this country among his* BANDITTI OF FREE-BOOTERS. What is the benefit of the miser's gold, either to himself or to his fellow-creatures, whilst locked up in his chest? He would be as well without it: the chest might as well be empty. By general circulation, it might diffuse comfort and happiness around; by being hoarded, it baffles the use and purpose for which it was ordained. Even so, my COUNTRYMEN, is this high pride, this feeling, this spirit of the

British character. Confine it to your own breasts, and it is useless, nay mischievous. ROUSE IT; let it burst forth and extend itself, and EUROPE united against us would find us impregnable!

I have heard some grumbling about Taxes. I am inclined, however, for the credit of my country, to believe that this is by no means general. Such, however, as are weak and unpatriotic enough to begrudge their mite toward the general stock should be informed of one circumstance, which perhaps they are either unacquainted with, or have not duly considered: They are called upon by Government, in the present crisis, to assist the common cause, by laying down ONE SHILLING IN TWENTY; that is, ONE TWENTIETH PART OF THEIR INCOME, *for the purpose of remunerating those* BRAVE SAILORS AND SOLDIERS WHO KEEP THE ENEMY AT BAY TILL WE ARE ABLE TO RECEIVE HIM AS WE OUGHT TO DO. Should BUONAPARTE make good his landing, and establish himself in the country, he would do here, what he has done every where else, HE WOULD LEVY CONTRIBUTIONS AT THE POINT OF THE BAYONET; *he would hear of no appeal to Commissioners for deductions or exemptions:* out of every TWENTY SHILLINGS which you might then possess, you would be very fortunate if you were permitted to retain ONE; that is, ONE TWENTIETH PART OF YOUR OWN POUND! If therefore you cry out now that the times are hard, and weep over the departure of One shilling from your pockets, what will be your doleful lamentation when the NINETEEN ARE WRENCHED FROM YOU BY THE SOLDIERS OF BUONAPARTE, and when nothing is to be procured by the solitary One you have left? for the bread of Britain must then support Frenchmen, and the HALF-STARVED FOLLOWERS OF THE CORSICAN TRAITOR *batten on English Porter and the Staff of Life. These are truths which you must be told.* You have not been used to warfare upon your native land, and therefore conceive it impossible to take place. Our brothers in arms have gallantly fought the enemy abroad, to avert such horrors from our homes; and you conceive that if you applaud and approve their conduct, and light up a few farthing candles, when they have stormed an enemy's strong hold, or sunk an enemy's fleet, that you have done your duty as true patriots and as good citizens: but woe to England's greatness, if, because *we have gained a good name, we should now go to sleep!* The Enemy approaches your shores, threatens your all, and vows to make this blessed land of Peace and Freedom the theatre of war, massacre, and blood!

How, you will ask, are we to avert such horrors? Have we no stay, no obstacle to oppose to this threatened Inundation? You have! and when BUONAPARTE calculated the chances to be an Hundred to One against him, he took into the account the national character for high Spirit, Vigor, and Energy; LET THIS ACCOUNT BE MADE UP, AND THE CHANCES ARE NINE HUNDRED AND NINETY-NINE TO ONE AGAINST HIM! I will tell you how this perdition, these horrors are to be averted—by feeling the full extent of your danger; by not despising the idea of the Enemy making good his landing; by not discrediting the possibility of his success, because he has never yet succeeded, or the probability of his not attempting it because he has only threatened it before; by recollecting that the high reputation for Greatness, Richness, Valor, Liberty, and Independence, which we are ever ready to bring forth as our Pride and Boast, were gained and established by the Blood of Thousands and Millions of your brave Ancestors, and not by supineness and indolence, or by waiting in their beds for the Enemy to undraw their curtains; by comparing our present state with the present state of every or any country in Europe, and thus confirming the value of those blessings which we have to lose. Thus you will pave the way to proper feelings, and a just estimate of your stake; Your minds will be prepared for your Salvation, for your Glory. To give these due effect, your actions must correspond with them. You must pay your Contributions cheerfully, AND PART WITH A SHARE TO SECURE THE WHOLE! You must, as I before advised, enrol yourselves in your different Parishes throughout the County—you must train yourselves to wield a Pitchfork, or a Hedge-stake if you cannot procure a Musket; practice the old English cudgel-play and quarter-staff; ASSEMBLE TOGETHER, AND LEARN TO MARCH, TO WHEEL, TO FORM COMPANIES, AND, IN SHORT, TO BECOME HALF SOLDIERS—THEN British Spirit and British Valour will supply the OTHER HALF, and manifest themselves in a most formidable manner to the imperious, the ambitious, and POWERFUL FOE.

Such an Army of Freemen would indeed dismay Buonaparte and his host of Freebooters—SUCH A SPIRIT WOULD CONSUME THE HOPES OF FRANCE, AND BLAST THE LAURELS OF THEIR HERO AND THEIR TYRANT!

Without it, we may be prostrate at the feet of both.

BRITONS, BE PREPARED!

If you suppose that Buonaparte will not attempt Invasion, you are deceived!   PUBLICOLA.

London, July 18, 1803.

Printed for J. Ginger, No. 169, Piccadilly; by D. N. Shury, Berwick Street, Soho.

From the many Frauds that have been practised on account of the very under price at which PUBLICOLA'S *Addresses have been sold, the Publisher has found it necessary to raise the Price to* ONE SHILLING *per Dozen for distribution.*

[Clark Library, No. 1. Single sheet printed on one side, in two columns. 17 × 21. *Bibliotheca Lindesiana,* No. 1527. British Museum, *Catalogue of Printed Books, s.v.* "Publicola."]

TO THE

Inhabitants of the British Isles.

Fellow-subjects,

OUR Country is threatened with destruction, which Heaven forbid! By the manes of our Edwards and our Henrys; by those of the great Elizabeth, a Princess not inferior to any monarch that ever swayed the British sceptre; by those of your gallant ancestors, who often bled and died for their country, I call upon you, one and all, to stand forward in her defence. It is no ordinary contest we are engaged in; it is for existence as a nation and free people; for that existence under which life is alone valuable, and which a brave man ought to fight for, and die, to hand down unimpaired to his posterity. We are to contend with an enemy of no mean abilities. Risen from obscurity to power and rank, he governs France, of which he is not a native, and over which he is an usurper, by military despotism. Those countries which he has taken under his protection and friendship by his armies, he plunders. Princes and States, once independent, and now affectedly so called, tremble at his mandates; and Europe, paralyzed, only waits a short period for her final destruction.

Happily at that spot*, where our illustrious Richard Cœur-de-Lion fought and conquered, the Corsican was checked in his career by a hero not less gallant, attended by a handful of brave seamen and soldiers. From Egypt his troops were conquered and expelled by British valour; and these United Isles now only stand barriers to his further ambition, and, as such, objects of his deepest resentment. Think you, ye illustrious Peers and Senators, many of you holding titles acquired by your brave ancestors, that your rank and honours will afford

---

* Acre, or Ptolomais. Hume says, "The English army arrived in time to partake in the glory of the siege; that Richard, animated with more precipitate courage than Philip, drew to himself the general attention, and acquired a great and splendid reputation." At this place Sir Sidney Smith added lustre to the British name.

you protection? No: the higher that rank, the danger will be greater, for the enemy has not forgot the language of Brissot and his associates. Ye wealthy Commoners and Citizens, will your wealth exempt you? I answer, No: that very wealth, and the luxuries you enjoy as attendant thereon, will be the greater temptation to rapine and plunder. Ye Merchants, Manufacturers, and Agriculturists, by whose ingenuity and industry, under a free government, commerce has been extended, and the arts and manufactures carried to the highest pitch of perfection, bear in your memory that it is only in free governments that these flourish, and that you and they are the objects of the Corsican's hatred, and, as such, will, if in his power, experience his vengeance. Independent of the loss of rank and wealth, there is one other and more important consideration, which should operate equally from the noble Peer to the humble Peasant. Your wives and daughters! think what will be their fate, if, unprotected, they become victims to a brutal enemy.

Rise then, my fellow-subjects, as brave men; shake off your apathy, rally round your *good Sovereign*—the *amor patriæ* beats not higher than in his *Royal breast*. Let an association be instantly drawn up in language energetic and plain: it is no time for political quibbles on forms of government—ours is established, and has stood the *test of ages*. Let it be an association to protect our RELIGION, our KING, and our COUNTRY —let this association be signed by every Freeman, from the Peer to the Peasant. Accompanied with this, let subscriptions be opened immediately, to be applied to the pressing exigencies of the times. The exalted Peer, and the not less generous, wealthy Commoner, the Merchant, Manufacturer, and Agriculturist, will contribute freely; the middling orders will not be deficient. Refuse no man's offer, for we are told in Holy Writ, that the widow's mite was found as acceptable as the rich man's offering. Apply this subscription to raise and support the yeoman, the mechanic, and labourer, while they are fighting the battles and serving in their country's cause.

They are the men for hardy soldiers—*they feel as Britons*, inspired and encouraged by the higher orders, with support for their wives and children—*they will act as such*. Do this, do it promptly, and we have nothing to fear. Fear! did I say?— The soul of a United Briton towers above it. These measures will shew to the Corsican Usurper, and the slaves of his ambition (for I will not debase a nation so much as to call them French citizens), more than ten thousand speeches, what men, brave and free, are capable to perform, when called upon to defend their country. It will *electrify* Europe; and Great Britain, as she oft has been the refuge of the distressed, will be a chosen spot from whence vengeance, under the protection of Heaven, will be hurled against the Usurper. We may then hope that the British Isles, still worthy of it, will pre-eminently merit the character drawn by the immortal Shakespeare†; and that France, freed from Corsican tyranny and military despotism, under a mild government, with one of her ILLUSTRIOUS, though EXILED PRINCES at her head, will return to peace with her neighbours, and to order, tranquillity, and happiness within herself.   PHILO-BRITANNIARUM.

---

† This royal throne of Kings, this sceptred
      Isle,
This earth of majesty, this seat of Mars,
This other Eden, demi-Paradise;
This fortress, built by Nature for herself,
Against infection, and the hand of war;
This happy breed of men, this little world;
This precious stone set in the silver sea,
Which serves it in the office of a wall,
Or as a moat defensive to a house,
Against the envy of less happier lands;

This blessed spot, this earth, this realm, this
      England,
This nurse, this teeming womb of royal
      Kings
Fear'd for their breed, and famous by their
      birth;
Renowned for their deeds as far from home,
For Christian service and true chivalry,
As is the sepulchre in stubborn Jewry,
Of the world's ransom, blessed Mary's Son.
                              —*Richard II*.

To the Bard's description, may we add the pious wish of the good Father Paul, *Esto perpetua*.

Printed for JOHN STOCKDALE, 181, Piccadilly. Price 6d. a dozen, or 1d. each.

Just published, the Second Edition, Price only 2s. 6d. illustrated with a coloured Chart of Great Britain and Ireland, with the whole Line of opposite Coast, from the North to the Mediterranean Sea; on which every Descent is correctly delineated—A Sketch of every Attempt to invade the British Islands, from the Landing of William the Conqueror, to the present Time.   S. Gosnell, Printer, Little Queen Street, Holborn.

[C. L., No. 2. Single sheet printed on one side, in two columns. 10½ × 17¾. *Bibl. Lind.*, No. 1519.]

A Letter to the Volunteers.

GENTLEMEN,

IN the present great and momentous contest—a contest undertaken on no common, no trivial motives, but on which depend our dearest rights as men and Britons, it is our duty, as it is our interest, to strain every nerve in defence of our native land.

Actuated by no vain desire of appearing in print, prompted by no hope of gain, but glowing with an ardent and patriotic wish to render a service to my country, I step forward to address you. This is all the apology I can or I hope need make for taking up the pen. Thank God! the liberty of the press, that glorious privilege of Englishmen, which our enemy would have destroyed,* enables the most obscure individual to lay his opinions and remarks before his countrymen.

Gentlemen, the voluntary offer of your services last war† evinced your loyalty. That was then sufficient; but now the danger has increased, so must your exertions. We then had powerful allies—we now stand alone. Never did the situation of affairs more imperiously demand wisdom, activity, and courage. Let us not deceive ourselves, and so fall into a fatal security. France possesses numerous armies and great resources. We must gather all our strength to oppose her. You, Gentlemen, constitute a part of our strength, therefore it behoves you to act with judgment. It is no child's play, but a business of serious moment. Let us not, through cowardice or prejudice, shut our eyes to the danger: the brave and wise man views it with calmness, and prepares to meet it with fortitude and discretion.

The enemy is daring, and, being at peace with the rest of

---

* Vide Tallyrand's letter to Lord Hawkesbury, demanding the suppression of certain pamphlets.

† I address you as the Gentlemen who volunteered last war, it being probable most of those will join the corps now forming.

the world, will be able to turn his whole force against us. He has declared, and doubtless will use every endeavour to effect a landing. We are certain our brave tars will give a good account of him whenever they can meet with him; but we cannot command the elements. We may blockade every harbour of importance, and our navy ride triumphant in the Channel: but how long can we ensure this situation? A storm arises, our fleets are driven from their coasts, dispersed, and obliged to return to port to repair; and the vigilance of months is rendered useless in an hour. The enemy puts to sea, and before a sufficient force is again collected, he will have landed; for the same wind which detains our fleets in our harbours, will bring theirs over. The possibility of the fact was demonstrated last war at Bantry Bay. The attempt is dangerous, and it is to be hoped will never be achieved; but as it is a favourite project of the enemy, and the probability of success has in some measure been proved, it ought to excite our most serious attention. Let us proportion our exertions to the extent of the dangers, and magnitude of the object at stake, which is no less than our existence as a free and independent nation.

If ever a foreign force gains footing on British ground, we must rely on our internal strength. You, Gentlemen, will compose a numerous, I wish we may be enabled to say, a formidable body. You cannot be the latter without discipline: it is to be hoped you will profit by the experience, and avoid the errors of your first associations. You now have an opportunity of wiping off the disgrace you have suffered—disgrace I must call it, though the term sounds harsh. Several Members of the House of Commons have treated you with unreserved contempt;‡ and all, however qualified with panegyrics on your loyalty, agree in opinion, that very little reliance is to be placed on you for the defence of the country. With these

‡ A Right Honourable Gentleman, Mr. Windham, in the Committee, on a motion for leave to bring in a bill for raising an additional force for the defence of the country, said, "The Volunteers answered very well for the purpose of police officers."—A volunteer corps lately formed, countenances this Gentleman's opinion, by the declaration of the nature of their service; which is, to preserve peace and good order in the metropolis; in other words, to act as constables.

Gentlemen the people in general, excepting the Volunteers, I believe coincide. This opinion is too justly founded on the experience of the last war. It is observed, that dress, parade, and ostentation occupied more of your time and attention than discipline: that pride, and a desire of evading the duties of other citizens, actuated you more than patriotism. Your conduct, Gentlemen, gave but too much ground for these heavy charges. I shall note another error: the system of extravagance you adopted produced the most baneful effects; it created in the breasts of the poorer class, by this means excluded, the greatest envy and hatred. Thus when the exigencies of the times required unanimity and cordial co-operation from every description of persons, you rapidly, but I would believe unintentionally, sowed divisions between yourselves and fellow-citizens.

Gentlemen, be wise, act like patriots, act like Britons; banish all puerile, all useless parade, and endeavour to become good soldiers: so you will justify the Government which has accepted your services, promote your own glory, and be of essential advantage to your country. It will not be sufficient that you are able to overawe an unarmed rabble, desirous of revenging their calamities on a set of detestable monopolizers. No; if you are called into the field, it will be to act against an enemy, whom nothing but invincible courage, excellent discipline, and consummate ability can withstand.

Flatter not yourselves with the wretched falsehoods and absurdities daily teeming from certain newspaper and other presses. The men who passed the bridge at Lodi, who traversed the deserts of Egypt, and who conquered at Marengo, commanded by a Moreau, a Massena, and a Buonaparte, are formidable foes to the bravest people of the world. We hear the ignorant and conceited of all ranks exclaim, in the height of bravado, "Why, let 'em come." These noisy, impotent boasters shew the weakness of their understandings, by the contempt with which they speak of the enemy. Should every body join in their opinion, a security fatal to the happiness and glory of Englishmen would ensue.

Before the famous battle of Agincourt, that proud day for England, the French had in imagination divided the spoils of the English camp; but their security proved their ruin, for the little though gallant band of Britons that day triumphed over the mighty army of France, and took her monarch prisoner.

When Harold, rejecting the sage advice of his officers, resolved, with haughty confidence, to give battle to the Norman Duke, he paid the forfeit of his rashness with his life and crown. He who despises his enemy ensures his own defeat.

Far be it from me to utter the language of despondence. No; I would pluck from your minds the poisonous weed, security, and plant in its place vigilance and resolution.

Nothing but the grossest ignorance, or the blindest prejudice, can disguise the danger to which we are exposed. Let not the whims and extravagancies of an enthusiastic nation divert our attention from this grand point; nor the wildness of their plans lead us into an opinion that they will not attempt what they threaten. If we prepare for the worst, we cannot be in the wrong. It is to be feared, that, in preparing for the worst, we shall only be preparing for what will happen; for there is every reason to suppose they are seriously fixed on the invasion of this country. Whenever they do attempt it, their best troops will doubtless be employed— troops who are inured to all the hardships of war, and have learnt discipline in the field; commanded by officers, whose knowledge has been matured by the experience of several of the most active campaigns which history records. What were thought the best soldiers in the world have in vain combated against them. Is there a man so infatuated or vainglorious as to imagine, that men without discipline, and officers with scarce an atom of military knowledge, can successfully oppose such forces? Who, Gentlemen, that witnessed (I speak of the last war) your tardy and ill-performed evolutions, and your commanders waiting, like actors not studied in their parts, the word of a prompter, who was generally some subordinate officer of the regulars—who, I say, Gentlemen, that witnessed these things, would anticipate aught but ruin and disgrace in the event of your being called out to act against a well-disciplined army?§ My friends, do not consider yourselves as idle pageants, strutting in regimentals, to gratify a paltry vanity. No; at a moment's notice you may be called to take an active part in the defence of your country. You have voluntarily promised to defend her; and if you neglect to render yourselves capable of performing that promise, you betray her.

You may immortalize yourselves, or your names may be transmitted to posterity, marked with indelible infamy.

Gentlemen, I repeat, for it cannot be too often insisted on, you must be earnest in your endeavours. Choose for your officers men of sound judgment, and who have leisure time to devote to study.‖ This is not the period to pay court to pride. Wealthy citizens must be content to take their stand in the ranks, unless they have abilities for more arduous stations. I am far from wishing you to exclude the rich from the more honourable situations; nor have I the least intention of making invidious distinctions: but I would guard you against the powerful influence of birth and riches, when the urgency of the case calls for a clear and unbiassed judgment to direct your choice. If we observe the method of the election of officers last war, and which has been again adopted by several associations, we shall find it the most absurd that folly could devise. It is true, they are elected by ballot: but how is this ballot conducted? In the most shameful manner. The principal and most busy men in the parish are nominated candidates by their friends: these men are unknown, most probably, to three fourths of the corps; consequently, as

§ These observations do not apply with equal force to every corps. Some had certainly attained a higher state of discipline than others; and also some officers I could mention, who knew enough of the military art, to merit praise for their application to study. It might make me suspected of invidious partiality, or I would gladly name the Gentlemen I conceive deserve to be excepted from censure.

‖ We are assured, that General Moreau, at the end of three months, understood the tactics of a regiment better than many old officers. This demonstrates what may be done by men of judgment, with assiduous application. The parliamentary officers during the usurpation, and the French revolution, produced many examples of this kind.

there is no opportunity of discovering the abilities of the candidates, interest is alone consulted. Thus the choice often falls on those who have no merit to entitle them to such distinction.

To remedy this evil, and give the members a knowledge of the talents of the candidates, I propose that they should be examined by some distinguished officers of the regulars before the whole corps: and, to obviate the unpleasantness of voting against particular interests and connexions, that every voter should write on a card "Yes," or "No," and put it into a box, which should be examined after all the members had voted. These propositions are so just and reasonable, that they need no argument to enforce them.

By many, discipline is thought of little utility. They say, the native courage of Englishmen, fighting in defence of their country, would be irresistible; and advise a rising *en masse* to oppose the enemy. What can be more wild, more inconsiderate, than such discourse? What would an undisciplined multitude avail against veterans? We would crush them with numbers. Would you throw oil on a flame to extinguish it? Numbers would but increase the confusion, and ensure more fatal ruin. Discipline can alone oppose discipline. Listen not to those who tell you, courage can surmount every thing—they deceive you. If they are mad enough to believe it themselves, they are to be pitied; if they are wicked enough to promulgate the opinion to lure you to destruction, they are to be detested. You may fall unrevenged on the enemies bayonets; but unless your valour is aided by skill and judgment, you cannot hope to conquer.

I believe there are people who will say, I over-rate the courage and abilities of the enemy; for that old and deep-rooted antipathy against the French, which, a few years past, seemed to be dying away, notwithstanding all the arts of the then Ministry to keep it alive, has again revived. It is not to my purpose to inquire, whether it is honourable to the national character: it might be useful at present, were it not attended with the most ineffable contempt. With these people, every man who points out the danger of our situation, is a friend to Buonaparté, a traitor, a coward, and, in fact, every thing that is bad. Notwithstanding their abuse, I will declare, that, whatever may be the French character in other respects, their conduct during the last war, was sufficient to convince any reasonable man, that they possess military talents in a very eminent degree. These talents we must emulate: indeed, I would strongly recommend it to you, to consider yourselves as performing your evolutions in the face of the enemy. Thus would every faculty be roused, every motion would be performed with rapidity; scarcely would the command be uttered, before it would be executed.¶

I must observe, that the time which is usually passed in drilling men's bodies into certain shapes or forms, not at all necessary, and acquiring a precise formality in the manual exercise, might be much more beneficially employed in perfecting yourselves in the tactics. If you can go through the manual exercise with ease, and (which is the principal thing) load your pieces with celerity, you will do very well in that respect; it is not necessary you should perform it with all the neatness enforced by a drill serjeant of the Guards. The emergencies of the state render it almost criminal to employ

¶ The field-days and reviews of the regulars merit attention; choice is made of a piece of ground as even as a bowling-green; not a tree, a brook, or a hedge, to interrupt the manœuvres. This may serve as an expedient to conceal the ignorance of the commander; for when these difficulties are avoided, any serjeant would most probably perform the usual routine of duty, as well as the colonel: but if the reviewing officer has the requisite skill for his post, he is effectually prevented from displaying it, and from giving his men a useful lesson.—In addition to this, the soldiers want the grand stimulus to activity and energy—rivalship. The consequence of which is, that an evolution, which might be performed in five minutes, generally requires ten; and the soldier is unaccustomed to quickness of motion, which is frequently of more importance in battle, than courage itself.

To remedy these evils, undoubtedly of great magnitude, I submit the following plan for consideration: Make choice of a piece of ground for the field of exercise, containing both level and rugged places. This will use the soldier to act in all situations, and accustom the commanding officer to seize the most advantageous positions with a *coup d'œil*. The cavalry should always, if possible, act with the infantry, that they might understand the mutual assistance each is of to the other. We have yet only conquered the smallest portion of the difficulty. The principal thing is to inspire the officers and men with a spirit of emulation. No method, it appears to me, would ensure this end so effectually, as that of opposing one regiment to another on field-days. In this case every man, from the commander to the private, would interest himself in the honour of his regiment; for it would be esteemed as disgraceful to be outmanœuvred at a review, as to lose a battle. I am convinced, these mock encounters would be of essential service, both to the officers and men. It is not to be understood that a settled order of engagement should be previously agreed on.

These observations will also apply to the volunteers.

a moment, but to the greatest advantage. And I believe, it
will be acknowledged by every military man, that soldiers
who could perform the evolutions with expedition and exactness, would be infinitely preferable to others, adepts at the
manual exercise, but bunglers at manœuvres. If, however,
some things in the drill are useless, there is also a part, by
you, Gentlemen, much neglected, though of the utmost importance. To march well, seems the least of your aim: in this
point, every corps which I have seen was miserably defec-
tive! it is the foundation of discipline. To march with the
proper step, and in perfect time, should be the soldier's first
care. Unless he is *au fait* in this, we cannot hope to see the
close-compacted column, or the line advancing with firm and
equal step, presenting a well-knit and commanding front. A
steady and exact method of marching, gained the Prussians,
under the great Frederic, all their victories and celebrity.
Evolutions are not so complex, but a moderate capacity may
acquire a knowledge of them; the difficulty consists in performing them with others: practise the march with zeal, and
the difficulty will vanish.

The remarks which occur to me on this subject are, that
your steps are too confined; that they are unequal in length
and time; sometimes long, sometimes short; sometimes slow,
sometimes quick. This unavoidably throws every thing into
confusion; it is necessary to observe, that short steps are not
adapted for a soldier. He should be firm on his feet; whereas,
short steps give him a habit of lounging.

The advantages of long steps are several: in the first place,
by taking a longer stride than is usual in walking, the feelings
or sensations (if I may use the expression) are so struck by it,
that a great exactness may be acquired. Secondly, in proportion as the steps decrease in number, so much is the difficulty
lessened. And lastly, the rapidity of motion is increased; for
a man can take one long step in much less time than two
short ones. I would advise you to fix stones in your drill
ground at certain distances, as was practised in the Bird-cage

Walk; and to accustom yourselves to practise the march, to the beat of a drum only, taking a step at each stroke; and to habituate yourselves to count one for each stroke: thus; one, two, three, four, for the first four beats, and repeating them. By these means, I presume, you would soon be able to march in excellent order.

The whole of the observations on discipline are supported by the opinions of the most celebrated writers on the military art. It would have been endless labour to quote the authors; I have compressed their thoughts into as few words as possible, hoping that truth will make its own way.

Gentlemen, I hear that numbers join the associations under an idea, they will not be sent out of London. If such is the promise of Government, doubtless it will be kept to the last moment that circumstances will admit. I say, to the last moment that circumstances will admit; because there may be a time, when Government will be obliged to request you to go beyond the terms of your agreement, and which you will not be able to refuse. Suppose the enemy lands on an unthought-of part of the coast in a great body, and there is not a sufficient number of troops to oppose them: in this case, those who are nearest the scene of action must be called on. It might fall to your lot, Gentlemen. For these emergencies I would have you prepare. No human foresight can predict the events which may take place; therefore, as I have said before, let us suppose the worst that can happen, and be ready to meet it.

Gentlemen, I cannot take leave of you, till I have pointed out a more honourable, a more gratifying, and a more useful method of appropriating your money, than in dress. Let those who have money to spare, subscribe to a fund for the relief of the families of those who fall, and are in need of assistance. The pleasures of vanity are evanescent, but the consciousness of having felt for, and relieved, the distress of a fellow-creature, would be a heart-soothing reflection to the last moment of existence.

Gentlemen, the foregoing observations (though hastily thrown together) are, I hope, worthy your notice. If they can call your minds to a serious consideration of the engagement you have entered into, and urge you to a zealous endeavour to perfect yourselves in discipline, I shall be amply rewarded for my labours. But whether attention or neglect awaits them, I shall still enjoy the satisfaction of having fulfilled the duty which every man owes his country.

May you, Gentlemen, by your conduct, convince the world, that Englishmen possess both the courage and wisdom to protect their country and liberty from the power of France, or any power whatever! Farewell.

Printed for JOHN STOCKDALE, 181, Piccadilly—Price 1*d*. each, or 6*d*. a Dozen;
Of whom may be had the following
LOYAL ADDRESSES,
Particularly recommended for Distribution throughout GREAT BRITAIN *and* IRELAND.

1. Invasion.—Scene of a Play. ⎫ With characteristic Prints.
2. ————.—Scene 2d of a Play. ⎭
3. Corporal Trim on the Invasion.
4. John Bull to Brother Patrick in Ireland.
5. Declaration of the City—with Bosanquet's Speech.
6. Rise in Defence of your Country.
7. Letter to the Volunteers.
8. To the Inhabitants of the British Isles.
9. To the United Kingdom.
       The above Price 1*d*. each, 6*d*. the Dozen, or 4*s*. per Hundred.
                              Also
10. Abridgement of the Postscript to the Third Edition of Hunter's Vindication, Price 6*d*. or 4*s*. per Dozen.
11. Speech of R. B. Sheridan, Esq. Price 6*d*.
12. A few Facts to shew the Ambition of France, Price 6*d*.
13. Substance of Mr. Pitt's celebrated Speech, Price 6*d*.
14. The Speech of Earl Moira, Price 6*d*.
15. Vindication of the Cause of Great Britain.—By W. HUNTER, Esq. Price 2*s*.
16. Candid Appeal to Public Confidence.—By T. M. MOORE, Esq. Price 1*s*.
17. Vindication of Europe, by GENTZ, 2*s*. 6*d*.
18. A Sketch of all the Invasions of the British Isles, from the Landing of William the Conqueror to the present Time—with a coloured Chart, on which every Attempt is delineated.—Second Edition, Price 2*s*. 6*d*.
19. Reflections on the present Crisis of Public Affairs.—By CHARLES TWEEDIE, Esq. Price 2*s*.

20. Germanic Empire reduced into Departments, Price 2s. 6d.
21. Bonaparté's Correspondence during the Negotiation for Peace, Price 2s. 6d.
22. Correspondence between the Governments of Great Britain and France, subsequent to the Treaty of Amiens, Price 2s. 6d.
23. Do. Part II. Price 1s.
24. Woodfall's Parliamentary Register for 1803—No. 1 to 35, Price 1s. each.
25. The Importance of Egypt and Malta.—By Colonel MARK WOOD, M. P. in 4to. with a Map, Price 5s. in boards.

S. GOSNELL, Printer, Little Queen Street, Holborn.

[C. L., No. 3. Single sheet printed on both sides, in two columns. 10½ × 18. *Bibl. Lind.*, No. 1500. Brit. Mus. *Catalogue, s.v.* "Letter."]

THE TENDER MERCIES OF BONAPARTE IN EGYPT!

Britons, Beware.

SIR ROBERT WILSON, in his "History of the British Expedition to Egypt," gives the following narrative of the cruelties committed by order of GENERAL BONAPARTE, now First Consul of France.

"The Turks justified themselves for the massacre of the French by the massacre at Jaffa. As this act, and the poisoning of the sick, have never been credited, because of such enormities being so incredibly atrocious, a digression to authenticate them may not be deemed intrusively tedious; and, had not the influence of power interfered, the act of accusation would have been preferred in a more solemn manner, and the damning proofs produced by penitent agents of these murders; but neither menaces, recompence, nor promises, can altogether stifle the cries of outraged humanity, and the day for retribution of justice is only delayed. Bonaparte having carried the town of Jaffa by assault, many of the garrison were put to the sword, but the greater part flying into the mosque, and imploring mercy from their pursuers, were granted their lives; and let it be well remembered, that an exasperated army in the moment of revenge, when the laws of war justified the rage, yet heard the voice of pity, received its impression, and proudly refused to be any longer the executioners of an unresisting enemy. Soldiers of the Italian army, this is a laurel wreath worthy of your fame, a trophy of which the subsequent treason of an individual shall not deprive you! Bonaparte, who had expressed much resentment at the compassion manifested by his troops, and determined to relieve himself from the maintenance and care of 3800 prisoners,* ordered them to be marched to a rising ground near Jaffa, where a division of French infantry formed against them. When the Turks had entered into their fatal alignment, and the manifold preparations were completed, the signal gun fired. Vollies of musquetry and grape instantly played against them; and Bonaparte, who had been regarding the scene through a telescope, when he saw the smoke ascending, could not restrain his joy, but broke out into exclamations of approval. Indeed, he had just reason to dread the refusal of his troops thus to dishonour themselves. Kleber had remonstrated in the most strenuous manner; and the officer of the etât-major who commanded, (for the general to whom the division belonged was absent,) even refused to execute the order without a written instruction; but Bonaparte was too cautious, and sent Berthier to enforce obedience. When the Turks had all fallen, the French troops humanely endeavoured to put a period to the sufferings of the wounded; but some time elapsed before the bayonet could finish what the fire had not destroyed, and probably many languished days in agony.

---

*"Bonaparte had in person inspected, previously, the whole body, amounting to near 5000 men, with the object of saving those who belonged to the towns he was preparing to attack. The age and noble physiognomy of a veteran Janissary attracted his observation, and he asked him sharply, 'Old man, what did you do here?' The Janissary, undaunted, replied, 'I must answer that question by asking you the same; your answer will be, that you came to serve your sultan; so did I mine.' The intrepid frankness of the reply excited universal interest in his favour. Bonaparte even smiled. 'He is saved,' whispered some of the aids-du-camp. 'You know not Bonaparte,' observed one who had served under him in Italy; 'that smile, I speak from experience, does not proceed from the sentiment of benevolence; remember what I say.' The opinion was too true: the Janissary was left in the ranks, doomed to death, and suffered."

Several French officers, by whom partly these details are fur-
nished, declared this was a scene, the retrospect of which
tormented their recollection; and that they could not reflect
on it without horror, accustomed as they had been to sights
of cruelty. These were the prisoners whom Assalini, in his
very able work on the plague, alludes to, when he says, that
for three days the Turks shewed no symptoms of that disease,
and it was their putrifying remains which produced the pesti-
lential malady which he describes as afterwards making such
ravages in the French army. Their bones still lie in heaps, and
are shewn to every traveller who arrives; nor can they be
confounded with those who perished in the assault, since this
field of butchery lies a mile from the town. Such a fact should
not, however, be alledged without some proof or leading circumstance, stronger than assertion, being produced to support it; but there would be a want of generosity in naming
individuals, and branding them to the latest posterity, for
obeying a command, when their submission became an act
of necessity, since the whole army did not mutiny against
the execution: therefore, to establish farther the authenticity
of the relation, this can only be mentioned, that it was
Bonn's division which fired; and thus every one is afforded
the opportunity of satisfying themselves respecting the truth,
by enquiring of officers serving in the different brigades composing this division.

"The next circumstance is of a nature which requires, indeed, the most particular details to establish; since the idea
can scarce be entertained, that the commander of an army
should order his own countrymen (or, if not immediately
such, those amongst whom he had been naturalized) to be
deprived of existence when in a state which required the
kindest consideration. But the annals of France record the
frightful crimes of Robespierre, a Carriere; and historical
truth must now recite one equal to any which has blackened
its page. Bonaparte, finding that his hospitals at Jaffa were
crowded with sick, sent for a physician, whose name should

be inscribed in letters of gold, but which, from weighty reasons, cannot be here inserted: on his arrival, he entered into a
long conversation with him respecting the danger of contagion, concluding at last with the remark, that something
must be done to remedy the evil, and that the destruction of
the sick in the hospital was the only measure which could be
adopted. The physician, alarmed at the proposal, bold in the
confidence of virtue and the cause of humanity, remonstrated
vehemently, representing the cruelty as well as the atrocity
of such a murder; but, finding that Bonaparte persevered
and menaced, he indignantly left the tent with this memorable observation: 'Neither my principles, nor the character
of my profession, will allow me to become a human butcher;
and, General, if such qualities are necessary to form a great
man, I thank my God that I do not possess them.' Bonaparte
was not to be diverted from his object by moral considerations.
He persevered, and found an apothecary, who, dreading the
weight of power, (but who has since made an atonement to
his mind by unequivocally confessing the fact,) consented to
become his agent, and to administer poison to the sick.
Opium at night was administered in gratifying food; the
wretched, unsuspecting victims banqueted; and in a few
hours 580 soldiers, who had suffered so much for their country, perished thus miserably by the order of its idol. Is there a
Frenchman whose blood does not chill with horror at the
recital of such a fact? Surely, the manes of these murdered,
unoffending people must be now hovering round the seat of
government and . . . If a doubt should still exist as to the
veracity of this statement, let the members of the institute
at Cairo be asked what passed in their sitting after the return
of Bonaparte from Syria; they will relate that the same virtuous physician, who refused to become the destroyer of
those committed to his protection, accused Bonaparte of high
treason, in the full assembly, against the honour of France,
her children, and humanity; that he entered into the full
details of the poisoning of the sick, and the massacre of the

garrison; aggravating these crimes by charging Bonaparte with strangling previously at Rosetta, a number of French and Copts, who were ill of the plague; thus proving, that this disposal of his sick was a premeditated plan, which he wished to introduce into general practice. In vain Bonaparte attempted to justify himself. The members sat petrified with terror, and almost doubted whether the scene passing before their eyes was not illusion. Assuredly, all these proceedings will not be found in the minutes of the Institute!—No! Bonaparte's policy foresaw the danger, and power produced the erasure: but let no man, calculating on the force of circumstances which may prevent such an avowal as is solicited, presume on this to deny the whole; there are records which remain, and which in due season will be produced. In the interim, this representation will be sufficient to stimulate enquiry; and, Frenchmen, your honour is indeed interested in the examination."

GENERAL ANDREOSSI, in the late Official Correspondence, terms the above "a most atrocious and disgusting calumny." In consequence, Sir Robert has since written the following Letter to the Editors of the Public Newspapers, which we consider as conclusive on the subject.

To THE EDITOR, &c.

"SIR,

"In the official correspondence lately published, there appear some remarks, which the French Ambassador was instructed to make on my History of the Expedition to Egypt, and of which I feel called upon to take notice; not in personal controversy with General Andreossy, for, conscious of the superior virtue of my cause, I find myself neither aggrieved nor irritated by the language he has used; but that the public may not attribute my silence to a desire of evading further discussion, and thus the shallow mode of contradiction adopted by the Chief Consul acquire an unmerited consideration.

"The Ambassador observes, 'That a Colonel in the English army has published a work in England, filled with the most atrocious and disgusting calumnies against the French army and its General. The lies it contains have been contradicted by the reception which Colonel Sebastiani experienced. The publicity of his report was at once a refutation and reparation, which the French army had a right to expect.'

"But surely a new signification must have been attached in France to the word calumny, when such a term is applied to my account of the conduct of the French troops in Egypt, and the consequent disposition of the inhabitants towards them!

"Independent, however, of the proofs to be adduced in corroboration of my statement, Europe may justly appreciate the probable truth of what I have written, when she recollects the unparalleled sufferings endured by the unoffending countries into which, during the last war, a French army penetrated; and she will at least hesitate to believe that the same armies should voluntarily ameliorate their conduct in a country more remote, where the atrocities they might commit would be less liable to publicity, and that this extraordinary change should be in favour of a people, whose principles and resistance might have excited the resentment of more generous invaders.

"I will not enter into an unnecessary detail of the numerous facts which I could urge; but I appeal to the honour of every British officer employed in Egypt, whether those observations are not sacredly true, which describe the French as being hateful to the inhabitants of that country, which represent them as having merited that hatred from the ruin and devastation with which their progress through it has been marked; and I am ready, if there be one who refuses to sanction this relation, to resign for ever every pretension to honourable reputation, and submit, without farther struggle, to that odium which should attach to calumny, and a wilful perversion of truth.

"But, Sir, I feel confident there is no individual, who will not amply confirm all that I have written on this subject; and perhaps Europe has a right to condemn me for not having

made the accusations still stronger, when I can produce
general orders of the French army, for the destruction of villages and their inhabitants; when I can prove, that above
20,000 of the natives perished by the swords of the French
soldiery; and that every act of violence was committed, and
particularly in Upper Egypt, which could outrage humanity,
and disgrace the character of civilised nations. When writing
a history of the campaign, was it possible not to express indignation against the authors of such calamities? Would it
have been natural not to have felt the animation of that virtuous pride, which a reflection on the different conduct of the
British soldiery must inspire in the breast of every Briton? I
have asserted that a British soldier could traverse alone
through any part of Egypt, or even penetrate into the Desert,
secure from injury or insult. I have described the natives as
considering the British their benefactors and protectors, so-
liciting opportunities to manifest their gratitude, and esteem-
ing their uniform as sacred as the turban of Mahometanism;
and I may venture to predict, that hereafter the French
traveller will be compelled to conceal the name of his nation,
and owe his security to the assumption of the British character.

"But, Sir, does the effect of Colonel Sebastiani's report
justify the Chief Consul's conclusion, that it is 'a complete
refutation of what I have advanced,' even if we attach to
that report implicit belief in its candour and veracity? Is it
possible that the Chief Consul can suppose the world will
trace respect for the French name in the circumstance which
occurred to Colonel Sebastiani at Cairo, and which rendered
it necessary for him to demand protection from the Vizir? or
would he imagine that the apologue of d'Gezzar Pacha was
not intelligible even previous to the instructions being published which M. Talleyrand sent to the French *commercial
agents?*

"That illustrious senator, to whose virtues and stupendous
talents England owes so much of her prosperity, has de-

clared, that this report of Colonel Sebastiani in no case con-
tradicts my statement; and I should consider that high
opinion as amply sufficient to remove any impression which
the French Ambassador's note might otherwise have made,
did I not think it a duty to press some observations on that
part of the paragraph which alludes to the direct accusation
against General Bonaparte, that the public may know I was
fully aware of the important responsibility which I had
voluntarily undertaken, and in which much national honour
was involved. I would wish the world seriously to examine,
whether the accuser or accused have shrunk from the investigation, and then hold him as guilty who has withdrawn from
the tribunal of enquiry.

"I avowed that I was his public accuser; I stood prepared
to support the charges. The courts of my country were open
to that mode of trial, which, as an innocent man, he could
alone have required, but of which he did not dare to avail
himself. It was no anonymous libeller against whom he was
to have filed his answer, but against one (and without any
indecent vanity I may say it) whose rank and character
would have justified his most serious attention.

"The charges were too awful to be treated with neglect,
and we know that they have not been read with indifference.
Nor is it possible that the First Consul can imagine the fame
of General Bonaparte is less sullied, because a few snuff-
boxes bearing his portrait were received by some abject or
avaricious individuals with expressions of esteem. Or can he
hope, that the contemptible, but not less unworthy insinuation, directed against the gallant and estimable British
General, will divert mankind from a reflection on the crimes
with which he stands arraigned?

"Fortunately for Europe, she is daily becoming more inti-
mately acquainted with the character of this hitherto miscon-
ceived man; and I confess that I feel considerable gratification
when I indulge the thought that I have contributed to its
development.

"Success may, for inscrutable purposes, continue to attend him; abject senates may decree him a throne, or the Pantheon; but history shall render injured humanity justice, and an indignant posterity inscribe on his cenotaph—

> "Ille venena Colchia
> Et quicquid usquam concipitur nefas,
> Tractavit.

"I am, Sir yours,
ROBERT WILSON, K.M.T.
Lieutenant-Colonel."

London: Printed for J. ASPERNE, at the Bible, Crown, and Constitution, No. 32, Cornhill, by T. MAIDEN, Sherbourn-Lane.

[Price 2d. or 1s. 6d. per Dozen]   [July 24, 1803?]

[C. L., No. 4. Single sheet printed on one side, in two columns. 18 × 21. *Bibl. Lind.*, No. 1529.]

The British Flag Maintained.

AND shall we then renounce the Flag?
Hear this ye British Sailors,
 While of the stuff remains a rag,
 'Tis you shall teach the French to brag,
The Devil take the *Failers*.

Still may the Flag undaunted sail,
Though some in Britain haply rail,
 And talk of cowing Reason;
 The Gallant sight shall make France Pale,
Who doubts—I say 'tis Treason.

The Song shall be "my Sons Strike Home,"
Dash with French Blood the proud sea-foam,
   Resurging from the Billows;
From France to Egypt let them roam,
   We'll make the waves their pillows.

See* Britain's Cymon born to brave
All that contend by land or wave,
   Who quell'd† "this Fortune's Minion";
And Nelson from Aboukir's grave
   A Phenix with fresh pinion.

Unfurl the Flag its fullest length,
There Britain owns her heart-springs strength
   Expanding with its motion:
While from‡ "the giddy *Top-masts* height,"
'Tis Vict'ry waves her pinions bright:
   Be yours, She cries, the Ocean.

O! Freedom, best of blessings known,
In Britain still erect thy Throne,
   The seas and rocks surrounding.
O Happy Isle thou standst alone,
   Her foes and thine confounding.

---

* Sir Sydney Smith
† Shakespeare
‡ Shakespeare

Printed for J. HATCHARD, *190 Piccadilly.*

Price *Threepence* per Dozen.   J. Hales, Old Boswell Court.

[C. L., No. 5. Single sheet printed on one side, in one column. 6 × 11.]

Britons! to Arms!!!

BRITONS, TO ARMS!—of Apathy beware,
And let your Country be your dearest Care;
Protect your Altars! guard your Monarch's Throne,
The Cause of GEORGE and Freedom is your own!
What! shall that ENGLAND want her Sons' Support,
Whose Heroes fought at CRESSY*—AGINCOURT†?
And when great MARLB'ROUGH‡ led the English Van,
In France, o'er Frenchmen, triumph'd to a Man!
By ALFRED's great, and ever-honour'd Name!
By EDWARD's Prowess, and by HENRY's Fame!
By all the gen'rous Blood for Freedom shed,
And by the Ashes of the Patriot Dead!
By the bright Glory Britons lately won
On EGYPT's Plains, beneath the burning Sun,
BRITONS, TO ARMS! defend your Country's Cause,
Fight for your KING! your LIBERTIES! and LAWS!
Be France defied, her slavish Yoke abhor'd,
And place your Safety only on your SWORD.
The Gallic DESPOT, sworn your mortal Foe,
Now aims his last—but his most deadly blow;
With England's Plunder tempts his hungry Slaves,
And dares to brave you on your native Waves!
If Britain's Rights be worth a Briton's Care,
To shield them from the Son of Rapine—swear!
Then to Invasion be Defiance given,

* In the Year 1346, Edward Prince of Wales (commonly called the Black Prince), son of our King Edward III. gained the famous Battle of Cressy, in which Thirty Thousand of the French were killed upon the Field.

† In the Year 1415, Henry V. King of England invaded France, and gained the memorable Battle of Agincourt, when Ten Thousand of the French were slain, and Fourteen Thousand were taken Prisoners. The Prisoners were more in Number than the victorious English Army!

‡ In Queen Anne's Reign, A. D. 1706, the great Duke of Marlborough gained the renowned Battle of Blenheim. Twelve Thousand French were slain, and Thirteen Thousand taken Prisoners, together with the French General, Marshall Tallard.

Your Cause is just, approv'd by Earth, and Heaven!
Should adverse Winds our gallant Fleet restrain,
To sweep his "bawbling" Vessels from the Main;
And Fate permit him on our Shores t'advance,
The TYRANT never shall return to FRANCE;
Fortune herself shall be no more his Friend,
And *here* the History of his Crimes shall end—
His slaughter'd Legions shall manure our Shore,
AND ENGLAND NEVER KNOW INVASION MORE.

July 14, 1803.   W. T. F-G.

NICHOLS and SON, Printers, Red Lion Passage, Fleet Street.

[C. L., No. 6. Single sheet printed on one side, in two columns. 13 × 15. Brit. Mus. *Catalogue,* *s.v.* "Britons."]

Buonaparte's Confession of the Massacre of Jaffa.

EUROPE might, with great reason, rely on the assertions of Mr. MORIER*, Sir ROBERT WILSON, and Dr. WITTMAN, respecting the MASSACRE of JAFFA. The minute particulars, the undaunted frankness, and the solemn challenge of contradiction, which Sir ROBERT has given to the world, claim the highest respect, not for his veracity, for that is not to be doubted, but for the responsibility he evidently feels himself liable to in bringing forward the charge; the extreme temperateness of Dr. Wittman's language, and the tenor of his expressions, manifest his veneration for truth, and repug-

---

* Mr. Morier was secretary to Lord Elgin, whom Buonaparte, for that reason, with peculiar malignity, detains in France, notwithstanding the unfortunate state of his health.

nance to hasty reports; but after all, is it not of the highest importance to consult Buonaparte himself, who so well knows whether, and in what degree, the story be true?

Certainly it is; and yet Buonaparte's evidence has never been called for! Is it wholly forgotten that he himself, with that cold indifference so visible in every thing he writes, and so characteristic of CRUELTY, in its most emphatic sense; he himself, distinctly and unreservedly, was the first to publish the fact?

Buonaparte did first publish it; he published it in all its essential features; our countrymen have only collected the minute circumstances. We refer to his official letter, dated *Head Quarters, Jaffa,* 23 Ventose, 7th Year (14th March, 1799.)

Buonaparte's account helps us to correct, in some less essential points, the accounts of the English writers; while the latter help us to expand and illustrate his.

We regret that the length of his letter will not allow us to insert it entire; but we shall extract all that relates to *Jaffa,* and refer for its authenticity to the *Moniteur* and other publications of the day, and to *Pieces Officielles de l'Armee d'Egypte, printed at Paris, in the year* 8 (1801), *premier partie,* p. 146.

"SIEGE OF JAFFA (YAFA)

"Kleber's division at first invested Jaffa, and afterwards threw itself on the river Hhayha, to cover the siege. Bon's division invested the right front of the town, and Lasne's division the left.

"The enemy opened forty pieces of cannon from all points of the walls, from which he poured upon us a vigorous and continued fire.

"On the 16th *Ventose,* (*8th March*) two batteries of approach, a battery in breach, and one of the mortars were ready to play. The garrison, a multitude of men, variously clothed, and of all colours (Maugrabins, Albanians, Curds, Natolians, Caramanians, Damascenes, Allepins, and blacks of Tekrur), made a *sortie,* and attacked the battery in breach. They were strongly repulsed, and sent back more quickly than they wished. My Aide-de-Camp, Duroc, an officer in whom I have the greatest confidence, particularly distinguished himself.

"At day-break on the 17th, I caused the commandant to be summoned. He cut off my messenger's head, and gave me no reply. At seven, the fire began. At one, I conceived the breach practicable. General Lasne prepared for the assault. Netherwood, adjunct of the Adjutant Generals, with ten carbiniers, mounted the first, and was followed by three companies of grenadiers of the 13th, and of the 69th demi-brigade, commanded by adjutant-general Rambaud, for whom I request the rank of Brigadier General. At five o'clock, we were masters of the town, which, during twenty-four hours, was given up to all the horrors of war, which never appeared to me so hideous. Four thousand of Djezzar's troops, among whom were eight hundred cannoneers, were put to the sword; part of the inhabitants were massacred.

"In the course of the following days, several vessels came from Saint-Jean-d'Acre, with food and ammunition. They were taken in the port. They were greatly astonished at seeing the town in our power. The opinion had been that it would have detained us six months.

"A'bd-ûllah, Djezzar's General, had the address to conceal himself among the Egyptians, from among whom he came and threw himself at my feet.—I have sent home more than five hundred persons of Damascus and Aleppo, as well as from four to five hundred Egyptians. I have pardoned the Mamelukes and Cashers whom I took at el-Arish; I have pardoned O'mar Makrâm, Sheik of Cairo; I have been merciful with the Egyptians, as well as with the people of Jaffa, but severe with the garrison, which was taken with arms in its hands.

"We have taken at Jaffa fifty pieces of cannon, of which thirty are field pieces, after the European model; ammunition; more than four hundred thousand rations of biscuit, two thousand quintals of rice, and some magazines of soap."

Buonaparte, then, did, beyond a doubt, put FOUR THOUSAND of Djezzar's troops, composing the garrison, to death.

The only questions are, WHEN and HOW were they put to death?

As to the manner, HOW, Mr. Morier, Sir Robert Wilson, and Dr. Wittman, have described it.

As to the time WHEN, Berthier described the garrison as fighting to the last, and falling in the assault; but is this consistent with Buonaparte's own words (*severe envers la garnison, qui s'est laisse prendre les armes a la main*), as above translated? Does the term *severe*, and its opposition to *merci-*

ful, apply to the killed in battle? Do not Buonaparte's words shew a total absence of inclination to conceal that he put them to death *after* he had them in his power; and that he did this by way of punishment for their not having laid down their arms!

Punish soldiers for not having laid down their arms!!! When did a civilized warrior do this? When was ever a general, among those whom we call (and God grant we always may call) illustrious, backward to applaud the brave resistance of his enemy?

Punish soldiers for not laying down their arms!!!—Buonaparte is a stranger to all that has rendered soldiering- [sic.] honourable, to all that has placed it among the most dignified of human pursuits! His enemy's soldiers he regards as malefactors!!!

BRITONS! This is a consideration that comes home to you. Were Buonaparte as covered with virtues as he is with vices, were he as glorious as he is infamous, were he the best, were he better than the best of men, his subjugation of your country must be a calamity which you would resist as long as you had an arm to lift against it. His situation forces him to be despotic; liberty grows out of an old and secure government; a new government must support itself with the bayonet; if your government were shaken, your liberty would be gone: all this is in the nature of things. Whether or not Buonaparte, therefore, is to subjugate your country, is out of the question. You do not think of it for a moment. You swear that while you live he shall not. But the consideration is, with what a Barbarian you have to fight!!! His word is nothing. He has no emotions. He is not a man, but a monster. Read over again the above letter—see with what indifference he tells of bloodshed! Nothing moves him.

With what a Barbarian you have to fight! You cannot accept quarter; he will hang you for having attempted to oppose him! You cannot surrender at his approach; he will hang you for having threatened to oppose him; he will hang you because he has not prisons in which to keep you, or poison you, because he wants the bread you would eat! You cannot listen to his promises, you cannot trust in his word. Enquire concerning him in every way, and you will find, at every step, that contempt for truth, an utter disregard of what he says, a deception upon principle, are the resources to which he uniformly flies.

With what a Barbarian you have to fight! You must remember this. You must break yourselves, as it respects him, of the habit of trusting in the word of a soldier: his uniform, indeed, is the uniform of a soldier, but his weapons are the weapons of an assassin. You must believe him, only when you have deprived him of the power to lie. You must lay down your arms, only when you can no longer hold them.

Printed by C. Rickaby, Peterborough-court, Fleet-street. Sold by Mr. Asperne, Cornhill; Mr. Hatchard, Bookseller to her Majesty, 190, and Mr. Ginger, 169, Piccadilly; and Mr. Booth, 14 Duke-street, Portland-place.—Price Two-pence, or One Shilling and Six-pence per Dozen, or Twelve Shillings per Hundred.

Shortly will be published, from Designs by Mr. ROBERT KERR PORTER, four Coloured Prints, illustrative of the atrocious actions of BUONAPARTE.

[C. L., No. 7. Single sheet printed on one side, in two columns. 17½ × 23. *Bibl. Lind.,* No. 1478.]

Proclamation,

Made to every Man in the United Kingdom of *Great Britain and Ireland,* this First Day of August, in the Year of our Lord One Thousand Eight Hundred and Three, and in the Forty-fourth Year of the Reign of our especially dear Son KING GEORGE THE THIRD.

WHEREAS by the Blessing of God, the Patriotism, Courage and Industry of Englishmen, the natural Advantages of our Situation, the Excellence of our Constitution, and the Wise Administration of our Government, we are a Glory to ourselves, the Seat of Freedom, the Empire of Happiness and Wealth, the *Mistress of the Seas:*—And whereas at the Head of the Corrupt and Despotic Government of the Neighbouring Realm of France, there is an USURPER, a *Corsican* by birth, and called by the Name of NAPOLEONE BUONAPARTE, who having subjugated to the most Abject Slavery the whole of the vast Empire over which he *unjustly* reigns, and on the Continent of *Europe*, as well as in *Asia, Egypt* and *Syria*, and divers other places, spread MURDER, RAPINE, SLAVERY and DEATH, *in Cruel and horrible Wantonness;* and not having the Fear of God before his Eyes, but being thereto moved by the instigation of the *Devil*, and filled with Envy, Malice, and Hatred to Us for the aforesaid Blessings We enjoy, as well as at our Magnanimous Resolution to resent effectually his Outrages and Insults, hath presumptuously threatened, and doth actually intend to attempt an INVASION OF OUR LAND, and for which said Diabolical Purpose he hath been, and at present is collecting a vast Armed Force, whose Orders are to *Murder all our Inhabitants bearing Arms in our Defence, violate the Wives and Daughters of our People, and plunder our Cities;* and all this to reduce this Happy and Independent Empire to a mere Province under his Vile Dominion: We have therefore thought fit to address this Proclamation unto you, calling upon you as you would express your Love to us, and your wish to transmit to Posterity your Country as you received it from the hands of your Forefathers, and to preserve yourselves and yours from the aforesaid Barbarous and Sanguinary Measures, that you, with one heart, immediately give effect to the Wise and Salutary Proceedings of our Government, thereby exhibiting to those who would destroy You, AN ARMED HOST OF BRITISH FREEMEN, READY TO DIE IN OUR DEFENCE—And altho' in Reliance on God, we know the Blood and utter Discomfiture of the Enemy will be the price of his Temerity, yet it is your Duty so to arouse and prepare yourselves, and so vigorously and unanimously to join in the Common Cause, that you may be able not only to inflict an

Awful Punishment on the Legions of Murderers who may assail you, but by a Grand and Dreadful Direction of your Vengeance, strike Deadly Terror and Confusion into the Hearts of all your Enemies:—And as our brave SEAMEN, should they meet them, will save you on Land, great part of the trouble, if not the whole, yet as in the nature of things our Fleets may miss them, have no other reliance for your safety than what arises from TRUST IN PROVIDENCE, CONFIDENCE, UNANIMITY, AND VIGOUR AMONG YOURSELVES.

Given at our Metropolis of London.

BRITANNIA!

London: Printed for J. ASPERNE, Successor to Mr. SEWELL, at the Bible, Crown, and Constitution, No. 32, Cornhill, by J. and E. HODSON.

[Price 1 d. each, or 6 s. the 100]

WHERE MAY BE ALSO HAD,

A Collection of all the Loyal Papers that have been and will be Published.

[C. L., No. 8. Single sheet printed on one side, in one column. 7½ × 12¼. *Bibl. Lind.*, No. 1538.]

[SIX SONGS]

Britons' Defiance of France.

Tune —"Can of Grog."

I.

MAD with the plunder of the world,
　　France like a fury raves,
And shakes her blood-stain'd lance to fight
　　The masters of the waves.
Firm as the rocks that skirt our coast,
　　At all her threats we smile,
And swear upon our unsheath'd swords
　　That free shall be our isle.
　　　　And swear, &c.

2.

A bastard Briton he must be,
    His heart contain no oak,
Whose base-born mind could tamely bend
    To bear the Gallic yoke.
No! let her pale-faced standard fly
    Where Freedom ne'er was known;
And tho' all Europe bend the knee,
    Let England stand alone.
        And tho' all, &c.

3.

And should these *Sons of Plunder* come
    To Albion's rocky shore,
Their frantic troops shall see a sight
    They never saw before:
A Nation, generous and great,
    In one determin'd band,
Prepar'd to crush them at a blow,
    And save their native land.
        Prepar'd to crush, &c.

4.

Oh! call to mind the gallant deeds
    Your noble Sires have done,
And may the Spirit of the Sires
    Descend upon the Son!
Then Britons of the good old breed
    Affrighted France shall see,
And find, when Englishmen unite,
    Old England must be free.
        And find, &c.

R.B.

One Halfpenny each, or 50 for 1s. 6d. or 2s. 6d. per Hundred for distribution. Printed for J. Ginger, 169, Piccadilly; where a variety of Patriotic Hand-Bills and Songs may be had.
Wheeler, Printer, 57, Wardour Street, Soho.

Britons Unconquerable!

A NEW SONG.

1.

AFRAID of the French! and afraid of Invasion!
Afraid of the men whom on ev'ry occasion
We've beat since our EDWARD gain'd so much renown,
By bringing the King of these Frenchmen to town.

2.

Yes, afraid of the French we will be when the moon
Shines as clear and as bright as the sun does at noon;
When the stars in their places no longer will stay,
But turn into marbles, and boys with them play:

3.

When the sea becomes dry, and when men may walk over
From Dover to Calais, from Calais to Dover;
When hogs leave off grunting, and lawyers agree
To plead for their clients without any fee:

4.

When the brave British Tar from a Frenchman shall run,
And haul down his flag without firing a gun;
When England's sweet lasses shall cease to have charms,
And no pleasure be tasted within their dear arms:

5.

When BRITONS no more shall be Lords of the Waves,
And Frenchmen love freedom, and cease to be slaves;
When the *Pois'ner* of *Jaffa* in mildness shall sway,
And the dictates of Justice and Mercy obey:

6.

When all these things happen, then England shall fear,
And tremble with dread when these Frenchmen are near;
Till then, as of old, we will beat them wherever
We meet them—OLD ENGLAND AND FREEDOM FOR EVER!

One Halfpenny each, or 50 for 1s. 6d. or 2s. 6d. per Hundred
for distribution.
Printed for J. GINGER, 169, Piccadilly; where a variety of Patriotic
Hand-Bills and Songs may be had.
WHEELER, Printer, 57, Wardour Street, Soho.

JOHN BULL'S

Invitation to Bonaparte.

A NEW SONG —Tune, "A Cobler there was."

1.

THE Chief Consul declares that to England he'll come,
Tho' there's some won't believe it, and think it a hum;
But should it prove true, and he brings his Monsieurs,
Some of them may go back without head or ears.
    Derry down, down, &c.

2.

In flat bottom boats they swear to come over,
And, if nothing prevents, to land safe at Dover;
But we have a few TARS, in our CASTLES of OAK,
That will shew these fine Frenchmen that *fighting's no joke.*
    Derry down, down, &c.

3.

But if BRITONS unite, 'tis in vain to contend,
And it matters but little how many they send;
For the more they send over, the more will be slain,
And the more we kill off, the less will remain.
    Derry down, down, &c.

4.

Let them come when they will we're ready to meet 'em,
With powder and shot in great plenty to greet 'em;
We have Millions of Warriors who never will fly,
For our Warriors are BRITONS, who'll conquer or die.
    Derry down, down, &c.

5.

For our KING and our COUNTRY, RELIGION and LAWS
Like lions we'll fight, for just is our cause;
In our GOD is our trust, he has long been our friend,
Our Foes he will scatter, and VICTORY send.
    Derry down, down, &c.

A. Volunteer.

One Halfpenny each, or 50 for 1s. 6d. or 2s. 6d. per Hundred
for distribution.

Printed for J. GINGER, 169, Piccadilly; where a variety of Patriotic
Hand-Bills and Songs may be had.

WHEELER, Printer, 57, Wardour Street, Soho.

Bonaparte Answered;

or,

The Briton's War Song

I.

"Bow, Britons! bow the haughty head;
   "Bend, Britons! bend the stubborn knee;
"Own your ancient virtue dead,
   "And know not that ye once were free.
      "Think not, as your fathers thought,
      "Speak no more, as Britons ought;
      "Act no more the Briton's part
      "With valiant hand and honest heart;
      "What indignation bids you feel,
      "Dare not, dare not to reveal;
"Tho' Justice sharpen, dare not grasp the lance,
"Nor single-handed tempt the might of France.

2.

"Me Holland, Italy obey;
   "Her breast with many a war-wound gor'd,
"And, crush'd beneath my iron sway,
   "Me Helvetia owns her Lord,
      "Boast not then your Fleets, that sweep
      "The eastern and the western deep;
      "Boast not then your sea-wash'd land,
      "Rampart-girt by Nature's hand;
      "Fleets and billows stay not me—
      "Then bow the head and bend the knee.
"Britons, no more your rival ranks advance,
"Nor single-handed dare to cope with France."

3.

Yes! as our Albion's root-bound oak
　　Stoops to the tempest, we will bow!
Yes! we will bend as the tall rock
　　Mocking the wave that chafes below!
　　　　Now by the sable Prince embrued
　　　　Once and again in Gallic blood;
　　　　By the laurels, that intwine,
　　　　HARRY, thy helm; and MARLB'ROUGH, thine;
　　　　By our Chiefs on Nilus' tide,
　　　　Him who triumph'd, him who died;
　　　　By him whom Acon's turrets raise
　　　　To lion-hearted RICHARD's praise;
Yes! we will still our rival ranks advance,
And single-handed brave the might of France.

4.

Come then, come thou Consul-King!
　　Launch thy navies, arm thine host,
And, beneath night's fav'ring wing,
　　Thy banners plant on England's coast.
　　　　Come! but hope not to return:
　　　　Here other thoughts thou soon shalt learn;
　　　　Shalt feel, that Britons still may claim
　　　　The honours of the British name;
　　　　Can fearless still maintain their stand
　　　　On British as on Syrian land;
Still rise superior to the Sons of Chance,
Still single-handed crush the pride of France.

———————

One Halfpenny each, or 50 for 1s. 6d. or 2s. 6d. per Hundred
for distribution.
Printed for J. GINGER, 169, Piccadilly; where a variety of Patriotic
Hand-Bills and Songs may be had.
WHEELER, Printer, 57, Wardour Street, Soho.

Britons Strike Home!

A NEW SONG.

I.

SHOULD Frenchmen e'er pollute Britannia's strand,
Or press with hostile hoof this sacred land;
The daring deed should every Briton arm,
To save his native land from dire alarm;
Her free-born Sons should instant take the field,
The Altar and the Throne at once to shield.
  Britons, strike home! Avenge your Country's cause,
  Protect your KING, your LIBERTIES, and LAWS!

2.

Repel the Foe, that desperate, dares invade
The land protected by great SYDNEY's shade;
And in the cause for which your HAMDEN bled,
Should ev'ry Briton's blood be freely shed;
A cause no less than Liberty and Life,
The poor Man's home, his Children, and his Wife.
  Britons strike home, &c.

3.

The base Usurper comes—his troops advance,
And line, with threat'ning front, the shores of France;
Already has the Despot given the word;
Already has he drawn his blood-stain'd sword;
While JAFFA's plains attest th'Assasin's skill,
Poison and blood—the dagger and the pill.
  Britons strike home, &c.

4.

No common war we wage—our *native land*
Is menac'd by a murderous, ruthless band;
The Throne and Altar by their Chief o'erturn'd,
And at his feet one half the prostrate world!
"Plunder, and Rape, and Death's" the hostile cry,
"Fire to your towns—to Britons slavery!"
     Britons strike home, &c.

5.

Come, Bonaparte, come! we are prepar'd;
No British heart a foreign foe e'er fear'd.
What! tho' an abject world in arms should rise,
In ENGLAND's cause a Briton death defies:
If to herself she prove but firm and true,
Gaul, and her frantic Chief she'll make to rue.
     Britons strike home, &c.

6.

Plung'd in the deep her navy we'll confound,
Or with French blood manure our British ground;
Drive backward to the sea the Gallic slaves,
And whelm their host, like Pharaoh's, in the waves;
Restore lost Peace and Plenty to our isle,
And make the land again with gladness smile.
     Britons strike home, &c.

One Halfpenny each, or 50 for 1s. 6d. or 2s. 6d. per Hundred
for distribution.

Printed for J. GINGER, 169, Piccadilly; where a variety of Patriotic
Hand-Bills and Songs may be had.

WHEELER, Printer, 57, Wardour Street, Soho.

Invasion.

A NEW SONG.

[1.]

BRITONS! cease your long forbearing,
Let insults fire your gen'rous blood;
Arouse, arouse! to martial daring,
And deeds of noble hardihood.

2.

Proud *Frenchmen* brave us—quick assemble,
Join BRITANNIA's patriot band;
Make these boasting Frenchmen tremble,
If they dare invade our land.

3.

FREEDOM ever held her station
On this happy favour'd Isle;
FREEDOM calls ye; rouse, brave Nation!
Cease the works of Peace awhile.

4.

Shall *Frenchmen* threaten our enslaving?
Shall slaves in BRITAIN e'er be found?
Shall Gallic banners, proudly waving,
E'er be fix'd on British ground?

5.

Now I mark your hearts' quick motion;
Yes, let them come, I hear you cry;
Yes, let them pass our subject ocean;
Yes, let them come, they come to die.

6.

Come, *Bonaparte*, tyrant savage!
　Thy armies marshal on our coast;
Awhile thy slaves our fields may ravage,
　But ruin soon shall whelm thy host.

7.

Gallant comrades! think of CRESSY,
　And ABOUKIR's well-fought field;
Departed heroes' shades will bless ye,
　Whilst the avenging sword you wield.

8.

Quick, ye gen'rous youths assemble,
　Join BRITANNIA's patriot band,
Make these boasting Frenchmen tremble,
　If they dare invade our land.

H.P.

Greenwich.

———————

One Halfpenny each, or 50 for 1s. 6d. or 2s. 6d. per Hundred,
for distribution.

Printed for J. GINGER, 169, Piccadilly; where a variety of Patriotic
Hand-Bills and Songs may be had.

WHEELER, Printer, Wardour Street, Soho.

[C. L., No. 9. Single sheet printed in three columns, two songs to a column, head to head, six songs altogether. 17 × 21. Brit. Mus. *Catalogue, s.v.* "Britons" and "Napoleon I."]

Old England to Her Daughters.

ADDRESS TO THE FEMALES OF GREAT BRITAIN.

Countrywomen!

WHEN ev'ry Class of *Men* are called upon for the purpose of repelling this Invasion, 'tis surely Time that *you* should be reminded of those great Duties which, well or ill perform'd, must in such Moments produce Consequences sudden as serious; and *may* save or overturn the State of Britain. The Days are past when one Moiety of Mankind affected to treat the other Moiety with a peculiarity of Manner, expressing half Admiration and half Contempt. Ev'ry Statue now stands without its Pedestal, so that its true Size can no longer be mistaken. Women no longer have a Right to complain of a confined or sterile Education, or to throw off their Faults upon their Fathers. Nobody now hinders them from being wise or strong, learned or courageous; nor does any one I see pretend to like them better for being weak, ignorant, or pusillanimous. You are therefore here solemnly call'd upon, to act rationally and steadily, and to maintain that Place among reasonable Beings, we have so often heard you urge a Claim to; and for this Purpose I first address you

Ladies!

Meaning all Wives, Daughters, Mothers, Nieces, Sisters, and Intimates of Land and Sea Officers, Clergymen, and Members of either House of Parliament, and of rich Citizens, and Servants of the King's Household: and I do hereby prohibit all Screamings, Faintings, &c. when our Enemies appear, as out of Time and Place. Leave *them* to the Novels and the Novel Writers; and as you value Happiness or

Honour, cling not around your Parents, Husbands, Lovers: holding their Hands and weakening their Exertions, when every Exertion is no more than necessary. Let me then hear no Lady say, "I am frighted out of my Wits." She must keep *in* her *Wits*, and not be frighted; but lend her best Ability to help us:

> Nor run with raving Cries to fill the City,
> But rather whilst your Brothers, Fathers, Friends,
> Pour Storms of Fury on our fierce Invaders,
> Do you implore kind Heav'n to shield your country,
> With silent Earnestness and calm Devotion.

Remember the Halsewell Indiaman! 'Twas lost; merely because the Ladies came on Deck, clung around the Captain, fainted in his Arms; hindr'd his giving necessary Orders, and, as he said himself, *wholly unman'd him. Now* behave better! or if you *will* fear, fear to perplex the Men with silly Questions, and an ill-timed Softness. Fear to confound *them*, whose true Valour can alone protect *you* from everlasting Shame and Sorrow; and by your Readiness to co-operate with their Endeavours, give good Example to inferior

Women,

Who being many of them busy Shop-keepers and active Huswives in the Town or Country, know well enough the value of a Sober and well regulated Conduct; such must be diligent to take Thought for their own Property, and to preserve it from the Hands of Robbers—they must be Honest too, and faithful if entrusted with ought belonging to a weaker Neighbour. It will be *their* Care to keep their Doors locked as *much*, and suffer their Servants to go out as *little* as possible, remembering—'tis for *them* that life is hazarded, and Money set at nought for *their Defence*.

Labouring Women!

May get in the Harvest, and feed the Horses tho' they cannot clean them. *All* may be useful to the wounded Soldiers;

all may employ Needles to work for *them*. Pictures of Lady
Harriet Ackland in an open Boat fired on by Enemies, hangs
up in many Houses of the Continent, and written under

The brave English Lady!

She went to war beyond Sea with her Husband—*You* have
but to keep *Home*, and save that Home by Prudence.

Had not the Women of old Times betrayed their Country
to Ferdinand Cortez, the Spaniards had never got Possession
of America, where they soon broil'd the King upon a Grid-
iron, and made the rich Nobility all Slaves; tying the Peasants together by Hundreds and burning them in Heaps. Had
not the LADIES of Italy three Years ago, encouraged the
French, when first they broke in upon *their* beautiful Country—Genoa, Venice, Milan, had still been free. Let *me* hope
better from *my* noble Girls: it is on British Virtue, British
Courage, that all the World at present has its Eyes fix'd.
Shew them the Difference between *our* Females and those
that inhabited less happy Nations——You have been gay
and airy long enough, "Let us divert the Wenches," "Let us
amuse the Ladies," has been the Cry now for these Fifty
Years, I think—as tho' the Ladies, like Leviathan, came only
into the World to take Pastime. But if you ever wish to see
good Days again, be serious *now;* cease to be frivolous, study
to be circumspect—Oh! these mad Marauders, starving
Frenchmen, must die and perish in a foreign Land, if totally
deprived of *your* Assistance. Lost and perplex'd, unknowing
of the Country, Roads, and Distances—unskilled in Language to enquire their Way—if every Woman will be but
true, and shew no Favour to a Foreigner, none will be left in
Three Weeks after Landing. Let the Sight of them be hateful
to you and not terrifying. Consider them as Rats or Frogs—a
Plague, but not a Danger—for I am confident that if the
Women act with becoming Spirit and true Caution, never
betraying by a Look or Gesture where any Treasure is con-
cealed, but suffering Death rather than divulge a National

Secret—Infinite Good may be done, and Mischief inconceivable prevented. This I the rather require at your Hands, my dear and lovely COUNTRYWOMEN, because my brave Sons have already done such Wonders, that You alone are able upon this Emergence to increase my Glory, or add one Laurel to the Wreath which *You* must keep from fading upon the Brows of

Poor Old England.

London: Printed for R. FAULDER, *New Bond Street.*
Price 1d. or 9d. per Dozen.　　　　　　　　　　[J. BRETTELL, Printer.

[C. L., No. 11. Single sheet printed on one side, in two columns. 11 × 17½. *Bibl. Lind.,* No. 1506.]

[Napoleon's Life.]

A Full, True and Particular Account of the Birth, Parentage, Education, Life, Character, and Behaviour, and Notorious Conduct of NAPOLEONE BUONAPARTE, the CORSICAN MONSTER, *alias* the POISONER, who is shortly expected to arrive in England, where he means to massacre, assassinate, burn, sink, and destroy. With a short Description of the various Murders, Poisonings, and Assassinations committed by him and his Gang in Foreign Parts.

NAPOLEONE BUONAPARTE was born not only of very poor, but of very notorious Parents in the Island of Corsica,* who not having wherewithal to educate their Children, having a large Family, very little Business, and no Credit, were obliged to subsist Part of the Year upon Chestnuts and other Fruits, the common Produce of that Island.

---

* Buonaparte's Great Grandfather, kept a Wine House for Factors (like our Gin-shops) and being convicted of Murder and Robbery, he died a Galley Slave at Genoa in 1724; his Wife was likewise an Accomplice, and she died in the House of Correction at Genoa in 1734—His Grandfather was a Butcher of Ajaccio, and his Grand-mother Daughter of a Journeyman Tanner at Bastia.—His Father was a low petty-fogging Lawyer, who served and betrayed his Country by turns, during the Civil Wars. After France conquered Corsica, he was a Spy to the French Governors, and his Mother their Trull—*What is bred in the Bone will not come out of the Flesh.*

When Little Bony was Twelve Years of Age, he by great good Luck got into a Charity School; shortly after he was recommended to, and brought up at, one of the French King's Free Schools, at Autun, from whence he was removed to Brienne, and from thence to Paris. In return for the King's Kindness towards him in bringing him up, he being of a very vile Disposition, and given to ungodly Company, most traiterously joined and assisted Robespierre in murdering his good Benefactor. After which he gave himself up entirely to him, and received a stated salary for murdering 1500 Gentlemen, Merchants, and Tradesmen, at the Town of Toulon, just after Lord Hood left that Place, and of all Days in the Year, on Christmas Day, 1793: he had them brought into the open Streets, and fired Grape Shot upon them from the Cannon's Mouth; he was so diabolically cruel, that he desired those who survived to get up and go home, which they no sooner did, than he gave Orders to have them stabbed and cut to Pieces, with Pikes, Swords, and Bayonets, in which he assisted himself. Some Time after, on the Execution of his Master, Robespierre, he was committed to the Jail at Nice, for Murder, from whence he was released by one of his Associates, named Barras, who having got into Power, engaged him to murder the People of Paris (who began to be tired of the Revolution) telling him, he would make him a General, and give him beside his cast-off Mistress, one *Sukey Badharness*, if he succeeded; which he did so effectually, that on the 4th of October, 1794, he slaughtered 6000 of the Citizens of Paris, firing Grape Shot in the principal Streets. All the Shops of Paris were shut for 8 Days after. After this Exploit he was made General of the Army of Italy, where he burnt several Towns to Ashes, first robbing the Inhabitants, and most dreadfully ill-using the poor defenceless Women, and all because they would not let his Gang have their Desires of them. At the Town of Lugo he cut to Pieces 1000 of the Inhabitants, and when they had even surrendered, he gave the Town to Pillage. He massacred the People of Pavia, because they would not suffer their Churches to be robbed of the Ornaments of Gold and Silver, and fine Pictures, which he afterwards took away, and sent to Paris. At Benasco he massacred 800 of the Inhabitants, and then burnt the Town to Ashes; first robbing every Body, nay, he was so cruel as to rob all the different Charities, and force the poor little Children belonging to them away. This he did in May, 1796. At Venice he stole a beautiful Diamond Necklace for his Woman *Sukey Badharness*, a Million of Money, several Ships of the Line, every Thing in the Arsenals, and all the naval Stores he could find, all the Pictures he could lay his Hands on, telling the Inhabitants he was their Friend, that he came to make them happy, and then he sold the Town to the best Bidder. In short, it would fill at least Ten Volumes of the *Book of Martyrs* to mention all the Robberies and Murders committed by him and his Gang in that unfortunate Country in the Years 1796 and 1797. On the 30th of May, 1798, he set off for Egypt, and the first place he landed at, the Town of Alexandria, he gave another Specimen of his Atrocity. He told the poor Egyptians that he came as their Friend, to relieve them from their Tyrants, and then ordered a general Massacre for Four Hours together. The poor unfortunate People flew to their mosques (the same as our Churches) but the Men, Women, old, young, Children at the Breast, all were murdered. This Monster said, after that, there was no Necessity for doing this, as "100 men could easily have taken the Town; but it was necessary," said he, "to strike Terror amongst them." This happened on the 14th Day of July, 1798. He then told the People, that he was a good Mahometan, that he had done all in his Power to destroy the Christian Religion. He had the Blasphemy to tell them that he did every Thing in the Name of the Almighty, and that he was the Envoy of God; that he had destroyed the People of Malta, because they were Christians. Some Time after he went to the Town of Jaffa, where, because they would not believe the impious and horrid rant he uttered to them, he committed, if possible, a more hellish Transaction than he had yet done; for he desired Four Thousand Eight Hundred of the Inhabitants which he called his Prisoners, to be brought upon a Hill at a little distance from the Town, and then ordered his savage Officers and Men to fire upon them with Grape Shot, and stab them with their Bayonets till they were all killed, whilst he surveyed them at a distance through a Spy Glass, laughing and smiling all the Time.—Many of these poor loyal Turkish People were between 60 and 70 Years of Age, and had served their Sovereign many Years.— In the very same Town he poisoned 580 of his own Soldiers with Opium, only because they were ill in Bed, and could not be of any farther Use to him.—He afterwards wanted to stab our gallant Countryman Sir Sidney Smith, for having with only a handful of British Sailors and a Thousand Turks threshed him and Ten Thousand of his Murderers for Sixty Days together, obliging them to run away from the Town of Acre, only Thirty-seven Miles from the holy City of Jerusalem (which he likewise wanted to destroy). Thanks be to God he failed, and that Heart of Oak lives to give him another good threshing. He was so mad that he failed in stabbing Sir Sydney Smith, that he set fire to all the fine Corn Fields just ready for Harvest, for many Miles together, and he has threatened to do the same in Old England, if John Bull is silly enough to let him—for since he has been so mauled he cannot bear the British Nation, as he says he could murder unmolested all Mankind if it were not for them. The name of Lord Nelson drives him mad, because he took his Ships from him.—After committing numberless other massacres, particularly at Demanhour, where he gave the town to pillage, the women to his soldiers for violation, and killing 1500 of the inhabitants, he was obliged to make his escape from Egypt, in the Middle of the Night, covered with Bloody Spots; he has never been able to wash himself Clean since that Time.—He afterwards went to Paris, banished his friend Barras, and by means of fresh Murders has got himself placed in his good King's situation, whom he helped to murder and is the most despotic, incestuous, bloody-minded Tyrant that ever disgraced Human Nature; and now quite forgets that he once lived upon chestnuts;—*set a Beggar on Horseback, and he will ride to the Devil.* He raves Night and Day against Old England, because he says, we are well off, and have plenty of Trade: he is of such an envious Nature that he cannot bear to see any Body happy. He says, we expose him and his Banditti to the whole World—that he will not let us talk about him—that we shall have no Liberty of the Press, and that our Parliament Men shall not even utter a Word concerning him, for as he is haunted to death by Night and by Day with a guilty Conscience, he cannot bear that any Body should speak about him. He wants our good Old King (God bless him!) to be his lackey, and the honest people of John Bull to be his slaves, and he threatens to murder us all, even our aged Fathers and Mothers, our Wives, and our blessed little Children, yea, even those sucking at the Breast—he says, he will assassinate us for his Amusement, as he did at many other Places, and that he will rob and plunder us from one end of the Country to the other: and to convince us that he will, he has already begun in Hanover, only because it is Part of the King's Dominions, to violate the poor Women, rob the People burn Villages and Towns, and murder the Inhabitants. Therefore let us get ready: let [us] stick by one another like a band of Brothers; let us be preparing for the very worst, for he cometh like a Thief in the Night, seeking whom he may devour.

Old England For Ever

Cox, Son, and Baylis, Printers, No. 75, Great Queen Street, Lincoln's-Inn Fields, London.—In order that *Bony's* Character may be known in every city, town, village, and remotest cottage in the United Dominions, Gentlemen, are requested to get copies printed in their respective places of residence, and have them well circulated, particular on market days; as *Bony* has already begun his diabolical Tricks in *Ireland*.

[C. L., No. 12. Single sheet printed on one side, in two columns. 7½ × 14½. *Bibl. Lind.*, No. 1494.]

My Friends and Countrymen,

AN OLD WHIG begs to address you at this Crisis, a Crisis unexampled in the History of these Kingdoms—not as a Partizan—not to stimulate you to Party Prejudices—but to awaken that bold, that intrepid, that stirring Spirit, which in earlier Times led on to daring Deeds—to Victory, and to Fame.

No man surely can hesitate. His Country calls upon him to cast aside every Prejudice, every Party Pique; and gladly, joyfully to co-operate Hand and Heart, with every Sinew strained, to maintain her Dignity and Independence; it cannot be possible for him to remain indolently supine when these are assailed.

Shall we, with whom the sacred Flame of Liberty, of real rational Liberty, has remained for Ages unextinguished; shall we crouch to a foreign Yoke; shall we bow the Neck to a Despot, submit ourselves to a Corsican Usurper?—Forbid it, Honour! Forbid it, Freedom! Forbid it, Valour!

The determination of the French to invade this Island is no longer problematic; and though our Fleets are numerous, our Seamen brave, our Army large and well disciplined, there still remains a great Space for the Exertions of Individuals. Every Man possessing Property ought freely to supply a Part to protect the Remainder. It behoves us to be liberal: Let us shew to the World that we can give our Fortunes to preserve our Rights.—Let the young Men—let us all arm; let us live a Nation—or die: And let us exhibit to the admiring World, the grand Spectacle of an armed, unanimous Nation, at once eager to protect our Coast or annoy our Foes; then we can safely bid Defiance to the proud and haughty Gaul, and teach him his Expectation of Assistance here will serve but to render his Defeat more certain, more perfect.

Let us look up, my Friends, to the higher Walks of Life. They beckon us by their Example to Unanimity. Let us not tarry for Compulsion.

Press on, my Friends, to the first Rank. Be ready with your Bayonet for the first hostile Foot upon your Shore. The Romans decreed a Civic Crown for the Man who saved his Comrade's Life. Arise, my Countrymen. *We* have a glorious Crown before us—a Crown of Honour. We shall save our Wives, our Sisters, and our Daughters from Shame: our Liberties, our Religion from Violation; and ourselves from Slaughter.

AN OLD WHIG.

Little Britain, July 27, 1803.

London: Printed by W. Flint, Old Bailey,

For F. and C. RIVINGTON, St. Paul's Church-Yard; and J. SPRAGG, No. 16, King-Street, Covent-Garden.

Price One Halfpenny; 2s. 6d. a Hundred; or One Guinea a Thousand.

[C. L., No. 13. Dated July 27, 1803. Single sheet printed on one side, in one column. 9 × 10¾. *Bibl. Lind.,* No. 1534. Brit. Mus. *Catalogue, s.v.* "Friends."]

Countrymen!

THE City of Syracuse (in Sicily) had maintained a successful Contest with the Carthaginians; lulled into Security, however, by an advantageous Peace, she had reduced her Fleets and Armies, and the Carthaginians, who still retained their Envy and Hatred of her, seized the Opportunity to renew the War, with the avowed Purpose of reducing her to absolute Slavery. The Neighbouring States looked on with the most stupid Indifference. One little POWER, however, CORINTH, saw the Danger, and sent a small Supply of Men, and, what

was of infinitely more Importance, her Favourite General
TIMOLEON, the ablest Commander of the Age. At his Arrival,
he found Syracuse in a State of torpor; the Inhabitants without Public Spirit, the Coasts without Troops; all sensible of,
and trembling at, the impending Danger, but none willing to
make the necessary Sacrifices to avert it. His first Care,
therefore, was to call a General Assembly of the People; here,
after upbraiding them sharply with their Avarice, Pride, and
Sloth, he proposed the Means of Safety and Defence. The
Scene which follows was written by our great Dramatic
Poet, MASSINGER: it is at once ELEGANT, NERVOUS, and
SUBLIME; and it would be to call in Question the good Sense,
no less than the Spirit and Patriotism of Englishmen, to suppose the forcible Arguments here used, will have less effect
upon THEM, than they had on the SYRACUSANS!

ARCHIDAMUS.*

You've made us see, Sir,
To our Shame, the Country's Sickness: Now from you,
As from a careful and a wise Physician,
We do expect the Cure.

TIMOLEON.†

Old fester'd Sores
Must be lanc'd to the quick and cauteriz'd:
Which, borne with Patience, after I'll apply
Soft Unguents: For the Maintenance of the War,
It is decreed all Monies in the Hands
Of private Men, shall instantly be brought
To th' public Treasury.

TIMAGORAS.‡

This bites sore.

---

* Prætor of Syracuse.   † The Corinthian General.   ‡ The Son of Archidamus.

CLEON.§

The Cure
Is worse than the Disease; I'll never yield to't:
What could the Enemy, although victorious,
Inflict more on us? All that my Youth hath toil'd for,
Purchas'd with Industry, and preserv'd with Care,
Forc'd from me in a Moment.

DIPHILUS.‖

This rough Course
Will never be allow'd of.

TIMOLEON.

O blind Men!
If you refuse the first Means that is offer'd
To give you Health, no Hope's left to recover
Your desp'rate Sickness. DO YOU PRIZE YOUR MUCK
ABOVE YOUR LIBERTIES: And rather choose
To be made Bondmen, than to part with that
To which already you are Slaves? Or can it
Be probable in your flattering Apprehensions,
You can capitulate with the Conqueror,
And keep that yours which they come to possess,
And, while you kneel in vain, will ravish from you?
—But take your own Ways; brood upon your Gold,
Sacrifice to your Idol, and preserve
The Prey intire, and merit the Report
Of careful Stewards: Yield a just Account
To your proud Masters, who with Whips of Iron
Will force you to give up what you conceal,
Or tear it from your Throats; adorn your Walls
With *Persian* Hangings wrought of Gold and Pearl;
Cover the Floors on which they are to tread,
With costly *Median* Silks; perfume the Rooms

---

§ An avaricious and indolent Senator.   ‖ A Senator.

With Cassia and Amber, where they are
To feast and revel; while, like servile Grooms
You wait upon their Trenchers; feed their Eyes
With massy Plate, until your cupboards crack
With the Weight that they sustain; set forth your Wives
And Daughters in as many vary'd Shapes
As there are Legions, to provoke their Lusts,
And let them be embrac'd before your Eyes,
The object may content you; and, to perfect
Their Entertainment, offer up your Sons,
And able Men for Slaves; while you that are
Unfit for Labour, are spurn'd out to starve,
Unpity'd, in some Desert, no Friend by,
Whose Sorrow may spare one compassionate Tear
In the Remembrance of what once you were.

TIMAGORAS.

Observe how old *Cleon* shakes,
As if in Picture he had shown him what
He was to suffer.

CLEORA.¶

If a Virgin,
Whose Speech was ever yet usher'd with Fear;
I' th' Presence of so many Reverend Men,
Struck dumb with Terror and Astonishment,
Presume to clothe her Thought in Vocal Sounds,
Let her find Pardon. First, to you, great Sir!
A bashful Maid's Thanks, and her zealous Prayers
Wing'd with pure Innocence bearing them to Heaven,
For all prosperity that the Gods can give
To one whose Piety must exact their Care;
Thus low I offer.

TIMOLEON.

'Tis a happy Omen.
Rise, blest one, and speak boldly.

¶ The Daughter of Archidamus.

CLEORA.

Then thus to you,
My noble Father, and these Lords, to whom
I next owe Duty; no respect forgotten
To you, my Brother, and these bold young Men
(Such I would have them) that are, or should be,
The City's Sword, and Target of Defence;
To all of you I speak; Think you all Treasure
Hid in the Bowels of the Earth, or shipwreck'd
In *Neptune's* watry Kingdom, can hold Weight,
When Liberty and Honour fill one Scale,
Triumphant Justice sitting on the Beam?
Or dare you but imagine that your Gold is
Too dear a Salary for such as hazard
Their Blood and Lives in your Defence? For me,
An ignorant Girl, bear Witness, HEAVEN! so far
I prize a Soldier, that, to give him Pay,
With such Devotion as our *Flamens* offer
Their Sacrifices at the holy Altar,
I do lay down these Jewels, will make sale
Of my superfluous Wardrobe, to supply
The meanest of their Wants.

TIMOLEON.

Brave masculine Spirit!

DIPHILUS.

We are shown, to our Shame, what we in Honour
Should have taught others.

ARCHIDAMUS.

Such a fair example
Must needs be follow'd.

TIMAGORAS.

Ever my dear Sister;
But now our Family's Glory.

TIMOLEON.

We have Money:
And Men must now be thought on.

ARCHIDAMUS.

We can press
Of Labourers in the Country (Men inur'd
To Cold and Heat) ten thousand.

DIPHILUS.

Or, if Need be,
Inrol our Slaves.

CLEORA.

How! Your Slaves?
O Stain of Honour!—Once more, Sir, your Pardon;
And to their Shames let me deliver what
I know in Justice you may speak.

TIMOLEON.

Most gladly:
I could not wish my Thoughts a better Organ
Than your Tongue to express them.

CLEORA.

Are you Men?
(For Age may qualify, tho' not excuse,
The Backwardness of these) able young Men?
Yet, now your Country's Liberty's at Stake,
Honour and glorious Triumph made a Garland
For such as dare deserve them; a rich Feast
Prepar'd by VICTORY, of immortal Viands,
Not for base Men, but such as with their Swords
Dare force Admittance, and will be her Guests;
And can you coldly suffer such Rewards
To be propos'd to Labourers and Slaves?
While you, that are born Noble, cry, WELL DONE!
Like idle Lookers on, till their proud Worth
Make them become your Masters?

TIMOLEON.

By my Hopes,
There's Fire and Spirit enough in this to make
Thersites valiant.

CLEORA.

Will you grant to them
The Privilege and Prerogative of great Minds,
Which you were born to? HONOUR WON IN WAR;
AND TO BE STIL'D PRESERVERS OF THEIR COUNTRY,
ARE TITLES FIT FOR FREE AND GENEROUS SPIRITS,
AND NOT FOR BONDMEN. Had I been born a Man,
And such ne'er dying Glories made the prize
To bold heroic Courage, by *Diana*,
I would not to my Brother, nay, my Father,
Be brib'd to part with the least Piece of Honour
I should gain in this Action.

TIMOLEON.

She's inspir'd,
Or in her speaks the Genius of your Country,
To fire your blood in her Defence: I am rapp'd
With the Imagination.—Noble Maid!
Timoleon is your Soldier, and will sweat
Drops of his best Blood, but he will bring home
Triumphant Conquest to you.

IT is needless to mention what followed this animating Debate. A Part of the Enemy was sunk at Sea, those that landed were immediately put to the Sword, and their Commander slain, fighting Hand to Hand, by one of the Speakers.

Printed for J. HATCHARD, 190 Piccadilly.

Price *One Shilling*, per Dozen.

[HALES, PRINTER, OLD BOSWELL COURT.

[C. L., No. 14. Single sheet printed on one side, dialogue in three columns, rest in one column. 18 × 21½.]

Song.

To the Tune of "HEARTS OF OAK, &c."

SHALL FRENCHMEN RULE O'ER US?—King EDWARD said,
           No!
And No! said King HARRY; and QUEEN BESS she said, No!
And No! said OLD ENGLAND;—and No! she says still.
They shall never rule US; let them try if they will.
     Hearts of Oak We are all, both our Ships and our Men,
         Then steady, Boys, steady,
           Let's always be ready;
     We have trimmed them before, let us trim them again.

2

SHALL FRENCHMEN RULE O'ER US?—King GEORGE he says
           No!
And No! say our LORDS, and our COMMONS they say No!
And No! say ALL BRITONS of every degree:—
They shall never rule Britons, UNITED AND FREE.
         Hearts of Oak, &c.

3

Shall Frenchmen rule us, the FREE SONS OF THE WAVES?
Shall England be ruled by a NATION OF SLAVES?
Shall the CORSICAN TYRANT, who bound on their chains,
Govern US in the room of OUR GOOD KING who reigns?
         Hearts of Oak, &c.

4

Though HE'D fain stop our Press, yet we'll publish his shame;
We'll proclaim to the World his detestable Fame:
How the Traitor RENOUNCED HIS REDEEMER, and then
How he MURDER'D HIS PRIS'NERS and POISON'D HIS MEN!
         Hearts of Oak, &c.

5

Then, DOWN WITH THE TYRANT! and DOWN WITH HIS ROD!
Let us stand by our FREEDOM, our KING, and our GOD!
Let us stand by our CHILDREN, our WIVES, and our HOMES!
Then WOE to the Tyrant WHENEVER HE COMES!

Hearts of Oak, &c.

Printed for J. HATCHARD, 190, Piccadilly, 3d. per dozen; or, 3s. 6d. per 100.

[Brettell, Printer.

[C. L., No. 15. Single sheet printed on one side, in one column. 8 × 12 ¾.]

Sheridan's Address
to the People.

Our King! our Country! And our God!

MY brave Associates—Partners of my Toil, my Feelings and my Fame!—can Words add Vigour to the VIRTUOUS ENERGIES which inspire your Hearts?—No—YOU have judged as I have, the *Foulness* of the *crafty Plea* by which these bold INVADERS would delude you—Your generous Spirit has compared, as mine has, the *Motives* which, in a War like this, can animate *their* Minds, and OURS.—THEY, by a strange Frenzy driven, fight for Power, for Plunder, and extended Rule—WE, for our Country, our Altars, and our Homes.—THEY follow an ADVENTURER, whom they fear—and obey a Power which they *hate*—WE serve a *Monarch* whom we love—a GOD whom we adore.—Whene'er they move in anger, *Desolation* tracks their Progress!—Where'er they pause in Amity, *Affliction* mourns their Friendship!—They boast, they come but to improve our State, enlarge our Thoughts, and free us from the Yoke of Error!—Yes—THEY will give enlightened Freedom to *our* Minds, who are themselves the *Slaves* of Passion, Avarice, and Pride.—They offer us their Protection—Yes, such Protection as *Vultures* give to Lambs—covering and devouring them!—They call on us to barter all of Good we have inherited and proved, for the desperate Chance of Something better which they *promise*.—Be our plain Answer this: The Throne WE honour is the PEOPLE'S CHOICE—the Laws we reverence are our brave Fathers' Legacy—the Faith we follow teaches us to live in Bonds of Charity with all Mankind, and die with Hope of Bliss beyond the Grave. Tell your *Invaders* this; and tell them too, we seek no Change; and, least of all, such Change as *they* would bring us.

R. B. SHERIDAN.

London: Printed for J. ASPERNE, Successor to MR. SEWELL, at the Bible, Crown, and Constitution, No. 32, Cornhill, by T. MAIDEN.
[Price 1d. or 6s. the 100.]

[C. L., No. 16. Single sheet printed on one side, in one column. 8 × 13. *Bibl. Lind.*, No. 1514.]

Theatre Royal, England.

IN REHEARSAL, AND MEANT TO BE SPEEDILY ATTEMPTED, A FARCE IN ONE ACT, CALLED

The Invasion of England.

Principal Buffo**, Mr BUONAPARTE
Being his FIRST (and most likely his Last) Appearance on this Stage.

ANTICIPATED CRITIQUE.

THE Structure of this Farce is very *loose*, and there is a *moral* and radical Defect in the Ground-Work. It boasts however considerable Novelty, for the Characters are ALL

MAD. It is probable that it will *not* be played in the COUNTRY, but will certainly never be *acted* in TOWN; where ever it may be represented, we will do it the Justice to say, it will be received with *Thunders* of—CANNON!!! but we will venture to affirm, will never equal the Success of

JOHN BULL.

It is however likely that the Piece may yet be put off on account of the INDISPOSITION of the PRINCIPAL PERFORMER, Mr. BUONAPARTE. We don't know exactly what this Gentleman's Merits may be on the Tragic Boards of France, but he will never succeed here; his Figure is very Diminutive, he Struts a great deal, seems to have no Conception of his *Character*, and treads the Stage very badly; notwithstanding which Defects, we think if he comes here, he will get an ENGAGEMENT, though it is probable that he will shortly after be reduced to the Situation of a SCENE-SHIFTER.

As for the Farce, we recommend it to be withdrawn, as it is the Opinion of all good Political Critics, that if played, it will certainly be

DAMN'D.
"Vivant Rex & Regina!"

London: Printed for J. ASPERNE, Successor to Mr. SEWELL, at the Bible, Crown, and Constitution, No. 32, Cornhill, by E. MACLEISH, 2, Bow-street, Covent-Garden

Price Two-pence; or 12s. the 100; *or 1s. 6d. per Dozen.*
Where may be also had, a Collection of all the Loyal Papers that have been published.

₊ Noblemen, Magistrates, and Gentlemen, would do well, by ordering a few Dozen of the above Tracts of their different Booksellers, and causing them to be stuck up in the respective Villages where they reside, that the Inhabitants may be convinced of the CRUELTY of the CORSICAN USURPER.

[C. L., No. 17. Single sheet printed on one side, in one column. 16½ × 23. *Bibl. Lind.*, No. 1516.]

Epilogue to the New Play

OF

The Maid of Bristol.

[Ed., by James Boaden]

Written by GEORGE COLMAN, *the Younger*.

(Being an Address to the Patriotism of the English.)

And Spoken by MR. ELLISTON, *in the Character of a British Sailor*.

IN times like these, the Sailor of our Play
Much more than common Sailors has to say;—
For Frenchmen, now, the British Tars provoke,
And doubly tough is every Heart of Oak;
Ready to die or conquer, at command,—
While all are Soldiers who are left on land.
Each English soul's on fire, to strike the blow
That curbs the French—and lays a TYRANT low.
Sweet wolf!—how lamb-like!—how, in his designs,
"The maiden modesty of Grimbald" shines!
Strifes he concludes twixt Nations who agree;
Freedom bestows on States already free;
Forcing redress on each contented town,
The loving Ruffian burns whole districts down;
Clasps the wide World, like Death, in his embrace;
Stalks Guardian Butcher of the human race
And, aping the fraternity of Cain,
Man is his brother,—only to be slain.

And must Religion's mantle be profan'd,
To cloak the crimes with which an Atheist's stain'd?
Yes:—the mock Saint, in holy motley dress'd,
Devotion's Public Ledger stands confess'd;—
Of every, and no Faith, beneath the sun;—
"Open to all, and influenc'd by none";
Ready he waits, to be, or not to be,
Rank Unbeliever, or staunch Devotee.

Now, Christians' deaths, in Christian zeal, he works,
Now worships Mahomet, to murder Turks;
Now tears the Creed, and gives Free-thinking scope,
Now dubb'd "Thrice Catholic," he strips a Pope.
A mongrel Mussulman, of Papal growth,
Mufti or Monk, now neither, or now both;
At Mosque, at Church, by turns, as craft thinks good,
Each day, in each,—and every day in blood!

God! must this Mushroom Despot of the hour
The spacious World encircle with his pow'r?
Stretching his baneful feet from pole to pole,
Stride Corsican Colossus of the whole?
Forbid it Heaven!—and forbid it Man!
Can Men forbid it?—Yes; *the English* can.
'Tis theirs, at length, to fight the World's great cause,
Defend their own, and rescue others' laws.

What Britons would not, were their hairs all lives,
Fight for their Charter, for their Babes and Wives;
And hurl a Tyrant from his upstart throne,
To guard their King securely on his own?

LONDON: Printed by Cox, Son, and Baylis, Great Queen Street,
For J. DEBRETT, Piccadilly.—(Price, 1d. or 9d. per Dozen.)

[C. L., No. 19. Single sheet printed on one side, in one column. 10 × 14. Brit. Mus. *Catalogue,*
s.v. "Boaden, James."]

Britons Triumph
OR
Bonapartes Knell.

1.

COME, with all thy slaves around thee,
BONAPARTE! haughty foe!
This little Island shall confound thee,
And lay thy giant projects low
Yet proud Chief before thy sailing
Bid thy State a long farewell
The shouts thy rash departure hailing
Cruel Tyrant, sound thy Knell.

2.

Lo! Holland to the dust is crumbled,
Her busy crowds are heard no more,
Spain's once aspiring pride is humbled,
The Swiss thy treach'rous aid deplore;
For freedom gone, they drooping languish
And silent pace each rocky dell
To Heaven they raise their hands in anguish
And pray for some avenging Tell.*

3.

Poor Italy! her honours blighted,
Her Roman virtue all forgot,
Bows beneath the yoke affrighted;
And Belgium shares her wretched lot.
France, too, enchain'd in base subjection,
Lies prostrate, trembling at thy Name,
Nor Marks what deeds, of dark complexion
Obscure and blacken all thy fame.

* Wᵐ Tell the Celebrated Swiss Patriot.

4.

Behold the hapless victims lying,
Stretch'd on Jaffa's† burning sand,
Behold them mangled, groaning, dying,
Then think 'twas done by thy command.
Yes, Yes, their shades for vengeance calling,
Shall hurl destruction on thy head,
And in the fight thy soul appalling,
Shall shake thy guilty frame with dread.

5.

And wouldst thou now, with wild ambition,
To this blest Isle thy Vessels steer.
What, wouldst thou seek thy own perdition.
The general cry of Britons hear;
Come, come, but, Chief, before thy sailing,
Bid thy state a long farewell;
The shouts thy rash departure hailing,
Cruel Tyrant sound thy Knell.

A. Hamilton Printer   221 Piccadilly.

[C. L., No. 20. Single sheet printed on one side, in one column. 7½ × 12. Brit. Mus. *Catalogue,*
s.v. "Napoleon I."]

Bonaparte's true Character,

And the Consequences which await England,

Should we, by our Supineness, suffer him to put his Threats of Invasion
into Execution.

HAVING enslaved the People, whom he undertook to free,
and plundered and subjugated all Orders of the Inhabitants,
rich and poor, of Holland, Switzerland, and Italy, under the

† 4000 Men penn'd together like Sheep (without Arms) and basely Slaughterd.

331376

solemn assurances of Fraternity and Friendship, he is now determined on the INVASION of this UNITED KINGDOM, and is making the most formidable preparations for that purpose.

And although Bonaparte himself is of opinion, the success of such an undertaking is highly improbable, and that he must sacrifice Army after Army, if he perseveres in the Attempt, yet the Threat having been denounced, nothing can sustain the Honour of our Country, but the most energetic and universal Exertion. It is not enough for our reputation, that his success should be improbable, it ought, by the numbers and gallantry of our Volunteers, under the blessing of Divine Providence, to be rendered impossible. By such a Conduct only can this Nation continue to enjoy tranquillity, have a disposable Force in the hands of Government for offensive Operations, and share the glory of avenging the wrongs of Europe, against the Destroyer of its Liberty, its Happiness, and its Honour.

We are invited, fellow-citizens, to come forward in defence of the happiest and wisest Constitution known to the world; in defence of a Sovereign, who, for a Period of more than forty Years, has shewn himself to be the Father of all those who have the happiness to live under the British Government. In defending objects thus sacred and dear, we deplore that our Country is called upon to encounter a People with whom England wishes to live in amity, but who, unhappily for themselves and the civilized world, have submitted to the degradation of being made subservient to the aggrandizement and ambition of one man—an obscure Corsican, who began his murderous career, with turning his Artillery upon the Citizens of Paris—who boasted in his Public Letter from Pavia, of having shot the whole Municipality—who put the helpless innocent and unoffending Inhabitants of Alexandria, Man, Woman, and Child, to the Sword, till Slaughter was tired of its Work—who, against all the Laws of War, put near 4000 Turks to Death, in cold Blood, after their Surrender—who destroyed his own Comrades by Poison, when lying sick and wounded in Hospitals, because they were unable to further the Plan of Pillage, which carried him to Jean d'Acre—who having thus stained the Profession of Arms, and solemnly and publicly renounced the religious Faith of Christendom and embraced Mahometanism, again pretended to embrace the Christian Religion—who, on his return to France, destroyed the Representative System—who, after seducing the Polish Legion into the Service of his pretended Republic, treacherously transferred it to St. Domingo, where it has perished to a Man, either by Disease or the Sword—and who, finally, as it were to fill the Measure of his arrogance, has dared to attack what is most dear and useful to civilized Society, the Freedom of the Press, and the Freedom of Speech, by proposing to restrict the British Press, and the Deliberations of the British Senate.—Such is the Tyrant we are called upon to oppose; and such is the Fate which awaits England, should we suffer him and his degraded Slaves to pollute our Soil.

Printed for J. WALLIS, No. 16, Ludgate Street, Price Two Pence, or 1s. 6d. per Dozen.
Printed by J. Crowder and E. Hemsted, Warwick Square.

[C. L., No. 21. Single sheet printed on one side, in one column. 17½ × 22½. *Bibl. Lind.*, No. 1480.]

Plain ANSWERS to plain QUESTIONS, in a Dialogue between

John Bull and Bonaparte,

Met *Half-Seas over* between DOVER and CALAIS.

John Bull. HOW do you do?
Bonaparte.—Pretty well; but hope to be better when I am in *London*.
John Bull.—When do you expect to get there?

Bonaparte.—About the end of September; or October at latest.

John Bull.—Why would not you remain at PEACE with us; which you know we were anxious to preserve?

Bonaparte.—Because I had set my heart on the recovery of EGYPT, which I had disgracefully quitted; and in recovering EGYPT, to pave the way for driving you out of INDIA, to the productions of which you owe so much of the Wealth, the Strength, and the Prosperity, which you enjoy.

John Bull.—But what did *Malta* signify?

Bonaparte.—I could not cleverly get to EGYPT without it.

John Bull.—Why are you such an Enemy to our LIBERTY OF THE PRESS?

Bonaparte.—That's a foolish Question, *John*. Why?—Because it exposes all my deep designs. Because it makes me odious amongst my own subjects, and in all Europe, by pointing out all the bloodshed, desolation and rapine by which I have obtained power, and by which I must preserve it. Because it recommends love, loyalty, and support to a King whom I mean to dethrone; and unanimity to a country, which I mean to conquer, to ravage, and to annihilate.

John Bull.—What RELIGION are you of?

Bonaparte.—None.—I was first a Deist; then a Papist in *Italy;* afterwards a Mahometan in *Egypt;* and am now an Atheist.

John Bull.—Why then did you restore the Catholic Religion in France?

Bonaparte.—Because it answered my purpose best.

John Bull.—Why have you suffered your Soldiers to burn so many Towns, shed so much innocent Blood, destroy Cottages as well as Palaces so indiscriminately, murder in cold blood Thousands of poor Men, and ravish Thousands of poor Women, in ITALY, in EGYPT, in SYRIA, and lately in HANOVER?

Bonaparte.—Foolish again, *John*.—I did not merely suffer it—I encouraged it.—My object has always been to strike terror. I don't mince matters. Witness the deliberate mas-sacre of four thousand Turks at *Jaffa*, who were my prisoners; and my poisoning several hundred of my own soldiers, who were of no use to me.

John Bull.—What do you mean to do if you come here?

Bonaparte.—I won't tell you. It would make your hair stand an end.

John Bull.—Arn't you a bit afraid of us?

Bonaparte.—To tell you the truth, I am. But I am not afraid to sacrifice 100,000 men in an attempt to invade you.

John Bull—As an honest man, what do you most depend upon for success?

Bonaparte.—On foggy weather—long nights—a want of discipline in your troops—a want of spirit and of union in your people.

John Bull—You had better let it alone, *Bony;*—if these are your only grounds for hope, you're a damn'd Fool if you attempt it.

Bonaparte.—To tell you the truth, *John*, I don't much like some of your late proceedings in Parliament. But I am de-termined on the attempt; so, look to it.

London: Printed for J. Hatchard, *No.* 190, *Piccadilly.*
Price 6d. per Dozen.

Printed by J. Brettell, 54, Great Windmill Street, Haymarket.

[C. L., No. 22. Single sheet printed on one side, dialogue in two columns, rest in one. 17½ × 21. *Bibl. Lind.*, No. 1510. Brit. Mus. *Catalogue, s.v.* "Bull (John)."]

Citizens of London!

YOUR generous spirited Forefathers more than Two hundred Years ago being threatened as we are now with a foreign Invasion, raised and armed Ten Thousand Two hundred and Seven Men, in the several Wards of this City, as appears in Detail by the annexed Schedule; besides which they voluntarily voted Government Sixteen of the largest Ships in the Thames, and Four Pinnaces or light Frigates, the Expense and Charges of which of every Kind were voluntarily defrayed, during the Whole Time they were in the Service of the Public, by the Citizens of London.

FELLOW CITIZENS!

Let us imitate the noble Example of such Ancestors.—We are ten Times more numerous!—Ten Times more Opulent!— May their sublime Spirit inspire us with a similar Ardour!— Then will the Citizens of London, alone, bring into the Field to oppose this flagitious Foe *Ten times Ten Thousand Men!*

Let us shew a bright Example to our Country.

Let us raise, arm, and maintain, during the Contest, *One hundred Thousand Men!*

[Broadside continues with table on facing page.]

SPANISH INVASION.

An Account of the Number of Troops raised and armed by the City of London, in the Year 1588, when the Spaniards threatened to invade England, as *Bonaparte* threatens to invade us now.—The Number of Men raised in each particular Ward, and the different Weapons with which they were armed are particularly distinguished.

Wards.	WEAPONS							Number of Men raised and armed in each Ward.
	Shot or Fire-Arms.	Corslets with Pikes.	Corslets with Bills.	Callivers.	Bows.	Pikes.	Bills.	
N⁰ 1 Farringdon, Within..	242	194	48	96	65	128	34	807
2 Bassishaw..........	36	30	7	15	65	20	4	177
3 Bread-Street........	116	92	24	47	31	15	61	386
4 Dowgate...........	116	84	24	46	62	16	36	384
5 Lime-Street........	29	24	6	12	8	16	4	99
6 Farringdon, Without.	398	318	18	159	106	212	53	1264
7 Aldgate...........	98	80	18	40	26	53	12	347
8 Billingsgate........	110	87	22	44	29	58	15	365
9 Aldersgate.........	69	56	14	27	18	10	38	232
10 Cornhill...........	57	36	21	22	16	31	8	191
11 Cheap............	108	86	21	44	28	58	13	358
12 Cordwainers.......	99	79	20	11	26	53	13	301
13 Coleman-Street.....	67	53	20	27	18	35	9	229
14 Broad-Street.......	112	89	23	45	30	60	14	373
15 Bridge, Within......	115	92	22	46	31	61	16	383
16 Castle-Baynard.....	165	132	32	66	44	88	24	551
17 Queen-Hithe........	121	96	25	48	33	64	17	404
18 Tower-Street........	133	107	26	53	36	71	18	444
19 Walbrook..........	87	67	17	35	24	47	11	290
20 Vintry............	109	88	21	44	29	58	15	364
21 Portsoken.........	73	59	13	30	20	38	10	243
22 Candlewick.........	64	51	13	26	18	35	8	215
23 Cripplegate........	278	222	55	111	74	148	37	925
24 Bishopsgate........	98	78	19	40	26	53	12	326
25 Langbourn.........	104	84	21	42	28	56	14	349
							Total	10,207

LONDON: Printed, for J. ASPERNE, Successor to Mr. SEWELL, at the Bible, Crown, and Constitution, No. 32, Cornhill, by C. and W. GALABIN, Ingram-Court, Fenchurch-Street.

[*Price Twopence, or Twelve Shillings per Hundred.*]

[C. L., No. 23. Single sheet printed on one side, in one column. 17½ × 21½.]

The Sailor to His Messmates.

"MY worthy Comrades, I have now served with you in
defence of Old England, upwards of twenty years, there are
many of you that have fought side by side with me, and
bravely conquered, for whenever England goes to war, it is
to recover the rights of nations, which are infringed upon by
Usurping Tyrants. The Fame of Englishmen is known in
every quarter of the world, beloved and feared on every
coast, our friendship is courted, our resentment dreaded. Has
not England sustained the balance of Europe? Has not she
given laws to the world? Who then would not be an Englishman—who would not fight for England?—And at a moment
too when her very existence is threatened by the insatiate
Monster, that tyrannic Corsican, who has made every Power
bow but England—Our brave Country which has checked
his arm—cut off the flower of his army, and humbled the
Usurper—He *intends* to put to sea with 300,000 troops, destined for the conquest of England, a few hours after, your
clemency will be called forth, to snatch from the waves those
poor wretches who, deluded by his promises, attempt to
invade us.—THEY FIGHT FOR RAPINE AND PLUNDER—WE
FIGHT FOR OUR COUNTRY, OUR WIVES, AND OUR CHILDREN!
Choose, then, whether you will wear the chains of Gallic
Slavery, or preserve those honours which our ancestors have
bequeathed to us, and devised in [en]tails to their heirs.
Whether shall we choose to have it said, that in the year
1803, England was attempted to be invaded with an immense force by the combined Armies and Fleets of France,
Holland, and Italy, that the brave English, atchieving mir-
acles, defeated, burnt, sunk, and took the whole fleet, and
did not leave a single vessel to bear the tidings back to
France.—Or would you rather have it said by posterity, 'till

the year 1803, the English arms were dreaded by the whole world, but in that very year they shamefully deserted their flag, and suffered a base Corsican, whom they had formerly driven before them, to take their Country for spoil, and in one day ruin the monuments of glory which their bravery had been raising for two thousand years!!—No, my lads, should the loud-braying Ass presume to enter the Lion's Den, in the hope of finding him asleep, his perfidy will be punished by being torn in pieces."

LONDON:

Printed for S. HIGHLEY, No. 24, Fleet-Street, price 1*d.* or 9*d.* per dozen; where may be had, in Octavo, price 1*s.* BONAPARTE, or THE FREE-BOOTER, a Drama, from which the above is extracted, and recommended by the Literary Journals, for August, 1803.

Glendinning, Printer, 25, Hatton Garden.

[C. L., No. 24. Single sheet printed on one side, in one column. 8¾ × 13½. *Bibl. Lind.,* No. 1546. Brit. Mus. *Catalogue, s.v.* "Sailor."]

A Second Dialogue between Buonaparte and John Bull.

SCENE.—*CALAIS.*

Buonaparte. HOW do you do, Monsier *Anglois?*

John. What's that to you?

Buon. Nay, John, don't be angry.

John. Angry! I am angry, and I will be angry.

Buon. But still, John, a little Civility to your Betters—

John. Betters! And pray who are my Betters!—Not such a Vil——

Buon. There! there! Now you are going to be rude again. I hate Rudeness. You look like a sensible Man; cannot you and I discuss this Matter coolly?

John. I have nothing to discuss with you:—Keep out of my Reach, I advise you.

Buon. One Moment, my dear Friend. You seen hurt at the Word BETTERS. For myself, indeed, I have no Vanity of any Kind; and yet, when you consider my Atchievements—

John. Name them!

Buon. The Battle of Lodi—

John. What! Where, with equal Ignorance and Barbarity, you sacrificed Six Thousand of your best Troops in forcing a Pass, which you might have taken, by crossing a few Furlongs above, without the Loss of a Man!

Buon. The Storming of Alexandria, then—

John. There, indeed, the Sacrifice was less.* But is it not a pitiful Vanity in you to boast of storming a Place without a Garrison, and open on every Side? And why do you suppress all Mention of the Massacre which took Place there, when your brutal Soldiery, BY YOUR ORDERS, entered the Mosques, which were filled with defenceless Citizens, and "FOR THE SPACE OF FOUR HOURS," in the Words of one of your own Officers, *"indiscriminately put to the Sword*, MEN, WOMEN, AND CHILDREN AT THE BREAST!"

Buon. You are always so warm. If you would but take Time for Reflection, you would perceive that this MASSACRE, (as you perversely call it,) was an Act of Mercy.

John. MERCY!

Buon. Yes, John, Mercy. It was calculated to strike Terror into the Enemy, and prevent the Necessity of recurring to such Measures in future.

John. But when the Example had operated, and FOUR THOUSAND Turks surrendered, you still had Recourse to the same Act of "MERCY," and SAVAGELY BUTCHERED THEM ALL, IN COLD BLOOD. Where was the "NECESSITY" of this?

Buon. I wish you would come a little nearer: I really do not hear you.

---

* "We lost 150 Men, all of whom we might have saved, by only summoning the Town." General Boyer's Dispatch.

John. I believe you:—but I will speak louder. It was MERCY, then, that induced you to POISON your own Soldiers!

Buon. Yes, it was; and so you will allow, when I have explained the Matter to you. But why POISON? Was it not ENDING THEIR DAYS BY A SOPORIFIC? I hate that unmannerly Way you Englishmen have of calling every Thing by its vulgar Name.

John. And I abhor still worse that deceitful Method you have of glossing over the greatest Enormities with specious Titles.—But come, let me have your Explanation.

Buon. What could I do? I had 580 Men in the Hospital. Of these, some had lost an Arm, or a Leg, and were totally unserviceable; others had been badly wounded, and would have required MORE TIME THAN I COULD SPARE to cure; and not a few were labouring under temporary Blindness. In this Situation, a Burden and a Disgrace to their Country, I ordered them to be judiciously dosed with Opium; and all but eleven went off as quietly as Lambs.—

John. Stop, Sir! Do you term those who suffer in fighting the Battles of their Country a Burden and a Disgrace to it? You have never been in England, and you never will come there, except as a Fugitive and a Prisoner; but if you could see our Hospitals of Chelsea and Greenwich you would find that we think very differently on the Subject. A Soldier or a Sailor, who has shed his Blood in the Service of his Country, and is requited with a comfortable Residence for Life, in the most magnificient Palaces in England, or perhaps in Europe, is to us an Object of heart-felt Pride and Pleasure.

Buon. I know nothing of this. You will grant, however, that MY METHOD OF PROVIDING FOR MY INVALIDS, is not so bad as you imagined.

John. It is, perhaps, not altogether so cruel as BURYING THEM ALIVE;† which was your constant Practice in

---

† Buonaparte was formally charged with throwing his wounded Soldiers into the Ditches, without Examination!!!—The Writer of this has seen the horrible Details which were brought forward, not long before the First Consul sailed for Egypt, and suppressed for that Time by the Director Barras.

Italy!—but sufficiently so, to stigmatize you for the most barbarous and bloody Villain that ever disgraced Humanity.

Buon. Since you are determined to keep no Measures, Sir, I can be as plain as you. I shall be in England soon, and if I once get upon you—

John. You will ride us to the Devil;—that I believe. I would not advise you, however, to make the Attempt: we are apt to kick and fling, and he must be a much better Horseman than you that could keep his Seat for a single Moment. You say, I am PLAIN, and I have given you a Proof of it. For the rest, I defy the Devil and all his Works. I HAVE A KING THAT I LOVE!—God bless him! I HAVE A COUNTRY THAT IS FREE!—God bless that, too! and I HAVE A WILL OF MY OWN, that will make me as strong as Forty *French Slaves.* To conclude, Citizen, you will never get to England.

Buon. I will try, however.

John. Do, and the sooner the better.

Buon. Yes, and I will try, too, to teach YOU good Manners.

John. And I will try to teach YOU the Difference between an Englishman and a Frenchman, of which you know nothing. You may ride THEM, if you please; they are Slaves by Nature, and will carry well:—but if you touch an Englishman, nay, if you do but look at an Englishman, and he does not like your Looks, he'll knock you down. You teach!—teach a Pudding's End! But I am talking when I should be in Action. Adieu! I am not much given to prophecy, but for once I'll venture:—Your Reign will be short; you will not die in your Bed; and the Devil, whom you faithfully serve, will have you as soon as the Breath is out of your Body. Once more, Citizen Consul, adieu! We shall never meet again in this World, nor—in the next.

Buon. Morblieu!—I fear it.

Exeunt, different Ways.

PRINTED FOR J. HATCHARD, No. 190, PICCADILLY. *Price Sixpence per Dozen.*   [HALES, PRINTER, OLD BOSWELL COURT, LONDON

[C. L., No. 25. Single sheet printed on one side, in two columns. 17½ × 21½. *Bibl. Lind.,* No. 1511. Brit. Mus. *Catalogue, s.v.* "Bull (John).")

ANOTHER CONFIRMATION OF THE TENDER MERCIES OF

Bonaparte in Egypt!

SELECTED BY HIS OLD FRIEND JOHN BULL

AS a Proof of the Veracity of SIR ROBERT WILSON's Account of the tremendously inhuman MURDERS perpetrated at JAFFA by Order of that most sanguinary Monster, and detestable Tyrant, BONAPARTE, Dr. WITTMAN, who was Physician to the British Military Mission which accompanied the Army of the Grand Vizier in its Route through Turkey, Syria, and Egypt, during the late Campaign in that Country, in his Narrative of his Travels, Page 128, thus speaks: "*Four Thousand* of the wretched Inhabitants who had sur- "rendered, and who had in vain implored the Mercy of their "Conquerors, were, together with a Part of the late Turkish "Garrison of El-Arish, (amounting, it has been said, to Five "or Six Hundred,) dragged out in *cold Blood*, Four Days after "the French had obtained Possession of Jaffa, to the Sand "Hills, about a League distant, in the Way to Gaza, and there "most inhumanly put to Death. I have seen the *Skeletons of* "*those unfortunate Victims*, which lie scattered over the Hills "a modern Golgotha, which remains a lasting Disgrace to a "Nation calling itself civilized. Indeed, I am sorry to add, "that the Charge of *Cruelty* against the *French General* "(BONAPARTE) does not rest here. It having been reported "that, previously to the Retreat of the French Army from "Syria, their Commander in Chief (BONAPARTE) had ordered "all the *French Sick at Jaffa to be Poisoned*, I was led to "make the Enquiry, to which every one who had visited the "spot would naturally be directed, respecting an Act of such "*singular*, and it *should seem*, *wanton Inhumanity*. It con- "cerns me to have to state, not only that *such a Circum-*

"*stance was positively asserted to have happened, but that, while*
"*in Egypt, an Individual was pointed out to us as having been*
"*the Executioner of these diabolical Commands.*"!!!

Englishmen, can you possibly read this Account without
Horror? Can you read it, and not wish for the most consummate Vengeance on the Head of the Wretch who caused it?
Not only in cold Blood to murder Four Thousand Five Hundred of his Captives, but to destroy, by Poison, his unfortunate Comrades—*his own Sick Soldiers!* Never was there an
Action committed in the World—so barbarous, so horribly
cruel. And it is this execrable Fiend who menaces your Shores
with Invasion, who has presumptuously ordered a general
Massacre of Britons, and the unlimited Pillage and Plunder
of your Metropolis, as a Reward to his recreant Army! That
he will attempt to invade you, *ought not* for one Moment to
be doubted—That he will fail in his Attempt *cannot* for one
Moment be disputed.—You have only with Heart and Hand
to rally round the Throne of your King, and the Constitution
of your Country, and, with the Blessing of God, which you
may most confidently expect on so excellent a Cause, the
proud, the insulting Foe, should he come, will, to his eternal
Dismay, prove that the Descendants of the Heroes of Cressy,
Agincourt, &c. (some of whom are the Heroes of Aboukir, of
Acre, and of Alexandria,) are animated with the same Soul,
possess the same Courage and unshaken Zeal for their Country, which glowed in the Breasts of their Forefathers.

32, *Cornhill*,   JOHN BULL.
July 25, 1803.   _____

London: Printed for J. ASPERNE, Successor to Mr. Sewell, at the Bible,
Crown, and Constitution, No. 32, Cornhill, by T. Maiden.
[Price 1d. or 6s. the 100]

[C. L., No. 26. Single sheet printed on one side, in one column. 8 × 13½. *Bibl. Lind.*, No. 1531.
Brit. Mus. *Catalogue, s.v.* "Bull (John) *pseud.*"]

Englishmen!

You have been unjustly charged with Supineness and Despondency. The Enemies of Government, and the Admirers of the

Corsican Tyrant,

have interpreted your silent Confidence, into despair and dismay. They allege against you, that although the Union, Courage, and patriotic Spirit, which you displayed in the late Contest, deterred the Enemy from the design of INVADING YOU, your present Inactivity bespeaks your Disapprobation of the War, and raises in the Mind of your INSOLENT AGGRESSOR the Hope of Success. Let not however a wellfounded Confidence in your Strength, Bravery, and Resources, be misconstrued into distrust by an artful Enemy, with whom Bravado and Clamour are held as the only Indications of Courage, and who observes Silence, only under the Influence of Terror and Oppression.

EXAMPLE is but wanting to embattle the Nation—SYSTEM only is required to call forth

Half a Million of
BRITONS

to avenge the Insults they have too long endured from a Love of PEACE, and to shew themselves the Avengers of their own RIGHTS, and of HUMANITY herself, so grievously outraged in every other Corner of the civilized World!

Your Counties and Shires

are now assembling for the Purpose of LOCAL DEFENCE, under a System, which will be found as formidable to the Enemy, as efficacious towards your Security and internal Peace.

Hasten then to demonstrate to your DARING INVADER, how high your National Spirit rises at the Insult, and that although his DISCOMFITURE and RUIN be certain in the Attempt, let your strenuous and unceasing Efforts in

General Armament

manifest to the Foe, a firm Appearance of the same manly Vigour in Defence of every Thing dear to ENGLISHMEN, which purchased with so much Blood, your envied LIBERTY and glorious CONSTITUTION, and which can emanate only from the Spirit of BRITONS!

The final overthrow of FRANCE will be the Reward of your Courage, and the certain Consequence of her Temerity and Madness. Hear the prophetic Words of General DUMOURIEZ, the Natural Enemy of England, and the most sanguine Officer who ever commanded the Armies of France:

"Should this Expedition however, be unsuccessful, which is very "possible; should the *Invincible British Fleet* gain a decisive Victory over "the French, Spanish, and Dutch Fleets, whether combined or separate; "should the English Nation, proud and energetic as the French, equally "animated by Patriotism and National Dislike, repulse the French Army "soon after it has landed; should they destroy it, force it to re-embark "with Loss, and cut off its Communication with the Sea; should they "weaken, harrass, or reduce it to Famine, and render this Great Expe- "dition abortive, which on a *large Scale* can only be attempted, and may "partially or altogether fail in the Execution, then FRANCE IS TOTALLY "RUINED; all her LAURELS ARE WITHERED; her Allies will ABANDON HER "AND TURN AGAINST HER; the other Powers of Europe will attack her on "every Side; she will have lost the Flower of her Warriors and the Repu- "tation of her Arms; she will be without Money, and internal Discord "will COMPLEAT HER DESTRUCTION.

"It is AT PARIS HER DISAPPOINTED AND INDIGNANT SOLDIERY, will seek "the *Rewards and* PLUNDER PROMISED THEM IN LONDON. The Generals "themselves will either be the first Victims of the *excusable fury of the* "*Troops*, or will partake of their Indignation, and their Revolt!"

Such, ENGLISHMEN, will be the Fruits of your Activity, your Steadiness, your UNION, and Valour.

Lose not therefore a Moment

in preparing the Means of atchieving so much Glory for your COUNTRY, of gaining so much Honour for YOURSELVES, and your proud POSTERITY!!!

TIMOLEON.

London: Printed by J. BRETTELL, for J. H. HATCHARD, No. 190, PICCADILLY.—Price 6d. per Dozen.

[C. L., No. 27. Single sheet printed on one side, in two columns. 17½ × 21½. *Bibl. Lind.*, No. 1491.]

A Dialogue

BETWEEN

A British TAR just landed at Portsmouth, and
A Brave SOLDIER lately returned from Egypt.

[*N.B. The Oaths usually interwoven, without either meaning or sense, in the discourse of the Valiant Defenders of their Country, are omitted; as at all times highly improper, and particularly when talking upon such a serious subject as the utter ruin of the whole Nation.*]

Soldier.—What, Jack, ashore again?

Sailor.—Ah, our noble Captain, just run in to warn you brave Landsmen what you have to expect.

Soldier.—What, some naval victory?—Is the French fleet out?

Sailor.—No, no Tom; I wish it was. We'd soon pour in a few broadsides, and sink every man of them that did not acknowledge our superiority. But no such luck, Tom; we have just been taking a peep into some of the French ports, and see such multitudes of vessels of all descriptions, and such quantities of troops all along the coast, that no doubt the Bloody Atheist is resolved to attempt the utter ruin of the British nation.

Soldier.—What then, Jack, is the report true, that there are 8000 vessels prepared to bring over the army of France into this country?

Sailor.—Aye, and more too, my Brave Egyptian Hero: There will be plenty of laurels both for Sailors and Soldiers too now.

Soldier.—Why, Jack, we on shore don't expect that you Sailors will leave us any chance of shewing that Britons fight even more fiercely if possible on their own native land than they have done in Egypt.

Sailor.—Fear not, Tom.—You will have opportunity enough of shewing yourselves; for tho' the British Navy rides triumphant on the Seas, yet adverse winds, or calms, or fogs and long dark nights may in all probability prevent our giving more than half of them their belly-full of shot and water; and even that is very doubtful;—for to confess the truth, tho' the enemy can never stand against the Navy of Britain when we chance to fall in with them, yet the probability of meeting on the wide ocean is very uncertain.

Soldier.—Why, Jack, there is great truth in that, and I fear we on shore are by no means ready to receive such an army of butchers; but if you tars will keep a good look out for a few weeks, whilst the British heart is roused to real exertion, we shall be ready for their reception, and I have no doubt shall be a match for the whole force that shall escape the vigilance of the Navy.

Sailor.—Well, remember, you on shore must prepare for the worst; for the enemy are so numerous, and are so determined to spare neither age, sex, or condition, that if they should escape us, the British shore will stream with blood; and 'ere you can conquer so large an army, thousands must fall a sacrifice to their country's cause.

Soldier.—God forbid that that butcher of the human race should possess an acre of British ground, upon which to shew his defiance of all the laws of God and Man, by ordering his miscreant bloodhounds to fire into the midst of thousands of

English prisoners, who may chance to fall into his hands, as he did the Turks at Jaffa; where I have myself seen on a spot of rising ground, heaps of bones, now whitened by time, which still prove the diabolical fact of his having in cool blood ordered the murder of all his prisoners. And Heaven grant that the British name may never be contaminated by a repetition of that vilest of all acts, committed by the order of BUONAPARTE himself, who poisoned 580 of his own wounded Soldiers to be relieved from the burden of supporting them.

Sailor.—What say you—are these stories really true?

Soldier.—Aye, as sure as I have been in Egypt; and many more villainous transactions of that desperate Atheist, such as no Briton can ever hear of without shuddering from head to foot. If our honest countrymen at home had seen the flood of blood shed on foreign land, they would not delay one moment to come forward in defence of their Country and their Religion, and to save their Wives and Children from falling into the hands of the determined extirpator of the British name.

Sailor. Aye, Tom, you who have seen the horrors of war against an Atheistical army, speak the true language of a British Soldier; and when our brave Captain has communicated to Government those preparations which are making for an immediate invasion of this country in various places at once, I have no fear but that all will prepare to drive back the numerous and fierce army of the Poisoner of his own Soldiers, to drink the last cup of brine under the cannon of the British Sailors, who, having destroyed all the vessels of the enemy, and cut off their retreat, will still cruize near shore to join in a general hallelujah to the God of Heaven, who, we trust, will ever defend the British Christian against the Atheistical Tyrant of Europe.

Cambridge, Printed; London, Re-printed for J. HATCHARD, *Piccadilly, by J. Hales, Old Boswell Court. Price* Sixpence *per Dozen.*

[C. L., No. 28. Single sheet printed on one side, in two columns. 10½ × 17½. *Bibl. Lind.*, No. 1487. Brit. Mus. *Catalogue, s.v.* "Dialogue."]

Britannia's Charge

TO THE

Sons of Freedom.

By Nicholas Rowe, Esq.

THE Tyrant for destruction eager burns,
Free passages and bloodless ways he scorns;
In fierce conflicting fields his arms delight,
He joys to be oppos'd, to prove his might;
Resistless through the widening breach to go,
To burst the gate, to lay the bulwark low,
To burn the villages, to waste the plains,
And massacre the poor laborious swains.
Abhorring Law, he chooses to offend,
And blushes to be thought his Country's friend,
* * * * * * * * * * *
Ye brave avengers of your Country's wrong,
Who to England and Liberty belong,
Whose hearts, your fathers' virtue truely warms,
Whose hands the sacred Senate order arms,
With cheerful ardour meet the coming fight,
ASSUR'D THE GODS WILL SMILE UPON THE RIGHT,
Behold the mournful view, Italia yields,
Her flaming villages, and her wasted fields;
See where the Gauls a dreadful deluge flow,
And scorn the boundaries of Alpine snow;
Already Gallia's sword is stain'd in blood,
Be that, ye Gods, to us an omen good,
That glory still be their peculiar care;
Let them begin, while we sustain the war,

Yet call it not a war to which we go,
We seek a malefactor, not a foe,
BRITANNIA'S INJURED MAJESTY DEMANDS
THE PUNISHMENT OF TRAITORS AT OUR HANDS,
If this be war, then war was wag'd of old,
By curst Cethegus, Catiline the bold,
By ev'ry villain's hand, who durst conspire,
In murder, robbery, or midnight fire.

LONDON:
Printed, for S. HIGHLEY, No. 24, Fleet-Street, price 1*d*. or 9*d*. per dozen; where may be had, BONAPARTE, or THE FREE-BOOTER, a patriotic Drama, price 1*s*. and other patriotic publications.

Glendinning, Printer, 25 Hatton Garden.

[C. L., No. 29. Single sheet printed on one side, in one column. 8½ × 13½. Brit. Mus. *Catalogue,* *s.v.* "Rowe, Nicholas."]

Victorious Englishmen.

MR. ASPERNE,

If you like the inclosed, print it; if not burn it, and charge the postage to the first Enemy of England that comes into your Shop.

EDWARD ENGLISH.

England, Aug. 8, 1803.
The Constitutional Bookseller, 32, Cornhill.

FRIENDS and Countrymen, sons of Mars, the terror and dread of surrounding nations; an opportunity now presents itself, wherein you may shew, that in TWO THOUSAND YEARS, you have not degenerated.—A proud, imperious, Corsican Bastard, threatens to annihilate you. He has menaced Europe with destruction, and reduced the Dutch, the Italians, the Swiss, &c. to vassalage; his proud project is UNIVERSAL

EMPIRE, and were it not for England, he would gain it: but Britain, the Guardian Angel of Europe, has checked his usurping hand, and said to the wide wasting Monster, "Hither shalt thou go, and no further."—It is for this that he means to attack us with an army of 200,000 men. They know that the British have humbled their pride, and stript off their laurels, and for this they will fight us. Shall we calmly see a usurping Tyrant lead us to the Guillotine? Shall *Buonaparte* reduce the English to the obedience of *his will?* Shall the domineering commands of a base Invader be imposed upon us? Shall his will be *our Laws?* Heaven forbid!—Where is the man, that in such a moment, will refuse to fight. If such a vile wretch can be found, let him be accounted infamous,— if there is a man who prefers slavery under Buonaparte, to liberty under our King, let him be shunned as a Basilisk; such a man be assured is a rebel, and only waits the moment when he may be able to deliver you up to the enemy.

What are 200,000 men? England can produce *three millions*, able and willing to bear arms! Why then should we regard his menaces? Nay, it is certain, that with 30,000, we can conquer their whole army. Have you forgot the plains of CRESSY, AGINCOURT, or MINDEN? If you have, your enemies have not. No, no; they will never forget them.

Of their army, my brave heroes, there are enough to be killed, wounded, and made prisoners,—but none to run away.—No, they will not run away. Buonaparte's invincibles will not run away, because we will prevent them. England shall be their graves.—Think for a moment that you have only to encounter 200,000 men, whose hearts fail within them; who fight because they are compelled, and wish rather to be English prisoners of war, than French soldiers. Arm, therefore, ye worthy heroes; arm, though you will not be wanted; arm, that you may convince your friends of your loyalty; arm, that you may show yourselves worthy of what you have already performed. Let Freedom be the standard of Liberty, the counter-sign amongst an army of Patriots, an army of heroes, and, which is the same, an army of Britons! What Englishman is there who would not be proud of being enrolled in the annals of posterity, as the Saviour of his Country. The babes of posterity shall lisp with pleasure, MY GRANDFATHER BEAT THE FRENCH; MY UNCLE HELPED TO DRIVE THEM AWAY.

What father is there who does not feel elated at the idea of his name being venerated by posterity? Can he bear the idea, that, while children are lisping the praises of their grandsires, that his should be branded with the indelible shame of being the offspring of a coward or a rebel?—No, this is, and ever will be the *viva voce* of an Englishman; OUR LAWS AND LIBERTY! LIBERTY AND OUR LAWS! Huzza! my boys; ere now I have assisted in defeating the army of Buonaparte, which are brave when compared with other nations, but cowards when compared to Englishmen. LIBERTY AND GEORGE! GEORGE AND LIBERTY!

Printed for JAMES ASPERNE, (Successor to MR. SEWELL,) at the Bible, Crown, and Constitution, No. 32, Cornhill, by S. ROUSSEAU, Wood Street, Spa Fields; Price One Penny, or 6s the 100.

Where may be had, at the same Price, SHERIDAN's Address to the People. Also a Collection of all the Loyal Papers that have been, or will be published.

---

* Noblemen, Magistrates, and Gentlemen, would do well by ordering a few Dozen of the above Tracts of their different Booksellers, and causing them to be stuck up in the respective Villages where they reside, that the Inhabitants may be convinced of the Cruelty of the CORSICAN USURPER.

[C. L., No. 30. Single sheet printed on one side, in two columns. 9½ × 15½. *Bibl. Lind.*, No. 1541.]

Epitaph

Underneath a GIBBET over a DUNGHILL, near
HASTINGS, close by the SEA BEACH.

UNDERNEATH this Dunghill
Is all that remains of a mighty Conqueror,
NAPOLEON BUONAPARTE,
Who, with inflexible Cruelty of Heart
And unexampled depravity of Mind,
Was permitted to scourge the Earth, for a Time,
With all the Horrors of War:
Too ignorant and incapable to do good to Mankind,
The whole Force of his Mind was employed
In oppressing the Weak and plundering the Industrious:
He was equally detested by all;
His Enemies he butchered in Cold Blood;
And fearing to leave incomplete the Catalogue of his Crimes,
His Friends he rewarded with a poison'd Chalice.
He was an Epitome
Of all that was vicious in the worst of Tyrants;
He possess'd their Cruelty without their Talents;
Their Madness without their Genius;
The Baseness of one, and the Imbecility of another.
Providence at last,
Wearied out with his Crimes,
Returned him to the Dunghill from which he sprung;
After having held him forth
On the neighbouring Gibbet,
As a Scarecrow to the Invaders of the British Coast.

This Beach,
The only Spot in our Isle polluted by his footsteps:
This Dunghill,
All that remains to him of his boasted Conquest.
Briton!
E're you pass by,
Kneel and thank thy God,
For all the Blessings of thy glorious Constitution;
Then return into the peaceful Bosom of thy Family,
and continue
In the Practice of those Virtues,
By which thy Ancestors
Merited the Favor of the Almighty.

Price 1d. or 9d. per Dozen.

Printed for J. HATCHARD, Piccadilly, by J. BRETTELL, Great Windmill-
Street, Haymarket

[C. L., No. 31. Single sheet printed on one side, in one column. 8½ × 12½. *Bibl. Lind.,*
No. 1492.]

Shakespeare's Ghost!

OUR immortal BARD,—who was as good an ENGLISHMAN as a POET, whose
Breast glowed as much with Enthusiastic LOVE OF HIS COUNTRY, as his
Fancy with Poetic Fire,—addresses his COUNTRYMEN in the following
animated Strain:

BRITONS!

BE STIRRING AS THE TIME; BE FIRE WITH FIRE,
Threaten the Threatener, and out-face the brow
Of bragging horror; so shall inferior eyes,
That borrow their behaviours from the great,

Grow great by your example, and put on
THE DAUNTLESS SPIRIT OF RESOLUTION.
Away, and glister like the God of War
When he intendeth to become the field:
Shew boldness, and aspiring confidence.
What! SHALL THEY SEEK THE LION IN HIS DEN?
AND FRIGHT HIM THERE; AND MAKE HIM TREMBLE THERE?
OH, LET IT NOT BE SAID!—Forage, and run
To meet displeasure farther from the doors;
AND GRAPPLE WITH HIM, ERE HE COME SO NIGH.—
—Shall we, upon the footing of our Land,
Send fair-play orders, and make compromise,
Insinuation, parley, and base truce
To Arms Invasive? Shall a . . . .
. . . . brave our fields,
And flash his spirit in a warlike soil,
Mocking the air with colours idly spread,
And find no check?—LET US TO ARMS!
. . . . Now on, you NOBLEST ENGLISH
Whose blood is fetch'd from Fathers of war-proof;
Fathers, that, like so many Alexanders,
Have on French soil from morn till even fought,
And sheath'd their swords for lack of argument.—
Dishonour not your Mothers; now attest,
That those, whom you call'd Fathers, did beget you.
Be copy now to men of grosser blood,
And teach them how to war. AND YOU GOOD YEOMEN,
Whose limbs were made in ENGLAND, shew us now
The metal of your Pasture: Let us know
That you are worth your breeding, which I doubt not:
For there is none of you so mean and low
That hath not noble lustre in your eyes;
I see you stand like Greyhounds in the slips,
Straining upon the start. THE GAME'S A-FOOT;
FOLLOW YOUR SPIRIT; and, upon this Charge,
Cry God for Us! For ENGLAND! and KING GEORGE.

BRITONS!

THIS ENGLAND NEVER DID (NOR NEVER SHALL)
LIE AT THE PROUD FOOT OF A CONQUEROR,
But when it first doth help to wound itself.—
    —Let come three corners of the World in Arms,
And we shall shock them: NOUGHT SHALL MAKE US RUE
IF ENGLAND TO ITSELF DO REST BUT TRUE.

SHAKESPEARE often delights us on the Stage in the Hour of Amusement,—let him now in the HOUR OF PERIL inspire us with that PATRIOTISM and COURAGE which animated our Forefathers to those DEEDS OF GLORY which he describes.— SHAKESPEARE now speaks in the Character of A TRUE ENGLISHMAN and A STURDY JOHN BULL, indignant that a FRENCH ARMY should WAGE WAR IN OUR ISLE: And in the Character of the heroic Harry the Fifth, who led our Forefathers to DEEDS OF GLORY in the HEART OF FRANCE—Deeds which no achievements have yet excelled, and which will ever honour our National Character, unless O'ERCLOUDED BY OUR WANT OF SPIRIT. Shall France, who acknowledged this Prince their Lord, now impose her Yoke upon Us? Need it be told that, led by this Royal Hero, an intrepid Band of Twelve Thousand Men, encountered and vanquished a Mighty Host of SIXTY THOUSAND?—These courageous Men were BRITONS— WE too are BRITONS;—Let, then, all who claim that Title, and whose Veins flow with BRITISH BLOOD, emulate the ARDOUR, the COURAGE, the GLORY of their ANCESTOR, and strive to preserve that Renown for their POSTERITY, which the HEROES of AGINCOURT and CRESSY have transmitted to us.—And MAY WE EQUALLY DESERVE THE ADMIRATION OF AFTER-AGES!   H.

———————————

Luke HANSARD, Printer, Great Turnstile, Lincoln's-Inn Fields, London.

[C. L., No. 32. Single sheet printed on one side, in one column. 17½ × 23½. *Bibl. Lind.*, No. 1513.]

LONDON, JULY 26, 1803

The Declaration of the Merchants, Bankers, Traders,

And Other Inhabitants of London and its Neighbourhood.

At a very numerous Meeting of MERCHANTS, BANKERS, TRADERS, and other INHABITANTS of LONDON and its Neighbourhood, held on the ROYAL EXCHANGE this Day, in Consequence of public Advertisement,

The following DECLARATION *was proposed, and unanimously resolved upon:—*

WE, the Merchants, Bankers, Traders, and other Inhabitants of London and its Neighbourhood, deem it our bounden Duty, at the present momentous Period, to make public our *unanimous* Determination to *stand* or *fall* with our *King and Country*.

The Independence and Existence of the British Empire— the Safety, the Liberty, the Life of every Man in the Kingdom are at Stake. The Events perhaps of a few Months, *certainly* of a few Years, are to determine whether we and our Children are to continue *Freemen* and *Members* of the most flourishing Community in the World, or whether we are to be the *Slaves* of our most implacable Enemies—*themselves* the *Slaves* of a foreign *Usurper?*

We look on this great Crisis without Dismay. We have the most firm Reliance on the Spirit and Virtue of the People of this Country. We believe that there exists a firmer as well as nobler Courage than any which Rapine can inspire; and we cannot entertain such gloomy and unworthy Apprehensions of the moral Order of the World, as to think that so admirable a Quality can be the *exclusive* Attribute of Freebooters or Slaves. We fight for our *Laws* and *Liberties*—to defend the *dearest* Hopes of our *Children*—to maintain the unspotted Glory which we have inherited from our Ancestors—to guard from Outrage and Shame those whom Nature has entrusted to our Protection—to preserve the Honour and Existence of the Country that gave us Birth.

We fight for that Constitution and System of Society, which is at once the noblest Monument and the firmest Bulwark of Civilization!—We fight to preserve the *whole Earth* from the barbarous Yoke of military Despotism!—We fight for the Independence of all Nations, even of those who are the most indifferent to our Fate, or the most blindly jealous of our Prosperity!

In so *glorious* a Cause—in the Defence of these dear and sacred Objects, we trust that the God of our Fathers will inspire us with a *Valour* which will be more than equal to the daring Ferocity of those who are lured, by the Hope of Plunder, to fight the Battles of Ambition.

His Majesty is about to call upon his People to arm in their own Defence. We *trust*, and we *believe* that he will *not* call on them in *vain*—that the Freemen of this Land, going forth in the righteous Cause of their Country, under the Blessing of Almighty God, will inflict the most signal Chastisement on those who have dared to threaten our Destruction—a Chastisement, of which the Memory will long guard the Shores of this Island, and which may not only vindicate the Honour, and establish the Safety of the British Empire, but may also, to the latest Posterity, serve as an Example to strike Terror into Tyrants, and to give Courage and Hope to insulted and oppressed Nations.

For the Attainment of these *great* Ends, it is necessary that we should not only be an *unanimous*, but a *zealous*, and *ardent*, and *unconquerable* People—that we should consider the public Safety as the chief Interest of every Individual— that every Man should deem the Sacrifice of his Fortune and his Life to his Country as nothing more than his Duty—that no Man should murmur at any Exertions or Privations which this *awful* Crisis may impose upon him—that we should regard Faintness or Languor in the *common* Cause as the basest Treachery—that we should go into the Field with an unshaken Resolution to *conquer* or to *die*—and that we should look upon nothing as a Calamity compared with the Subjugation of our Country.

We have most sacred Duties to perform—we have most invaluable Blessings to preserve—we have to *gain* Glory and Safety, or to incur indelible Disgrace, and to fall into irretrievable Ruin. Upon *our* Efforts will depend the Triumph of Liberty over Despotism—of national Independence over Projects of universal Empire—and, finally, of Civilization itself over Barbarism.

At *such* a Moment we deem it our Duty solemnly to bind ourselves to each other, and to our Countrymen, in the most sacred Manner, that we will employ all our Exertions to *rouse* the *Spirit*, and to assist the Resources of the Kingdom—that we will be ready with our Services of *every* Sort, and on *every* Occasion, in its Defence—and that we will rather perish together, than live to see the Honour of the British Name tarnished, or that *noble* Inheritance of Greatness, Glory, and Liberty destroyed, which has descended to us from our Forefathers, and which we are determined to transmit to our Posterity. JACOB BOSANQUET, CHAIRMAN.

LONDON: Printed for J. ASPERNE, Successor to MR. SEWELL, at the Bible, Crown, and Constitution, No. 32, Cornhill, by W. LANE, Minerva Office, Leadenhall Street.

[*Price Twopence, or Twelve Shillings per Hundred.*]

[C. L., No. 33. Single sheet printed on one side, in one column. 13 × 20½. *Bibl. Lind.*, No. 1533. Brit. Mus. *Catalogue, s.v.* "Bosanquet, Jacob."]

Union and Watchfulness,

BRITAIN'S TRUE AND ONLY SECURITY.

A few words to every British Subject inculcating this very important idea.

WE are fearless in War when happy in a King who reigns in the hearts of his People; and while he is beloved, honoured, and revered for his benevolence and clemency, we exclaim with M. Aurelius, "That where virtue hath acquired the love and affections of the subjects, there can be no want of men or treasure."

Self-interest, the bane of all great, and patriotic measures, must not be known, not even by name; for a King is never so rich as when he hath his People's hearts, nor they so happy as when for the Public good they cheerfully tender their persons and purses.

When menaced by an enemy, it becomes the duty of the threatened, to be on their guard and to strengthen themselves by every act of union against the common oppressor; especially HIM whose characteristic is never to want pretences of offence when they serve the purpose of insuring plunder; especially HIM who *cannot* err, but yet is never true to his promises, and is never destitute of insidious arts to inveigle the unsuspecting; especially HIM, who is like the wily fox and ravening wolf, that subject all to their devouring fangs they can either beguile or surprise. Therefore I say, by union and by council strengthen each other; for Union is the strongest Fortification, and Council surpasses Numbers. Being thus marshalled, and equipped with confidence and resolution, which are the best armour, we shall march on to success and prosperity.

Gallia's Arch Usurper is a declared tyrant over consciences, and is therefore a Usurper of GOD's prerogative; consequently his career will be but short.

This Usurper, like the father of usurpers, Satan, perseveres in fomenting discords, and makes the dire conclave resound with projected invasions, massacres, and violations; and in perspective feasts himself with the enormities to be inflicted upon those that his sanguinary mind has destined for his prey.

The would-be *Grande Nation*, like a herd of voracious wolves, have seized on their enfeebled neighbours' flocks; and while their hands are still dyed with unhallowed blood, hug themselves with the impious notion, that wicked enterprizes change their nature with their names, and hence are basely led to think that every proceeding is virtuous when attended with success.

How lost to reason and every thing great or good, and how forsaken by Providence, thus to be permitted to debase themselves lower than the irrational animals; for the generous lion disdains to make the mouse his prey; neither will the eagle catch flies.

It cannot be doubted, that a King is entitled to arm all for his own and his People's rights. The laws of God, of Man, and of Reason, sanction him, which are encouragers of self-preservation, even to the using of extremities.

Now is the momentous time, while threatened by an un-principled maurauder, for the defence of our King, our Country, our Altars, our Homes, our Families, our Property, and all that is near and dear to us. To suffer or to die in such a cause, is our first duty, and our highest honor.

We should be fortified against disappointments; for the most virtuous cause is not always crowned with immediate success; but patiently persevere and endeavour to deserve success, and ultimately your wishes will be realized, and your enemy discomfited.

As the long brooding storm cannot be dispelled, my Countrymen, stand prepared. Rally round the standard of Honor with alacrity. To be early in the field completely equipped, with minds cordially engaged in the cause, is a prominent advantage, for under such circumstances he that gives the first blow is more likely to renew his stroke, than he who is brought into the field by surprise and in disorder. Thus let us, brave Britons, meet the danger, or it will ferret us out, and be a mock to our reputation for courage and *power:* while the enemy may be emboldened to consider that a War tho' founded in injustice, if directed against a lethargic power cannot endanger his own success. But inspired by the glorious deeds of our brave ancestors, by our native pride, by our manly vigour, and by our hereditary spirit, let us rise up as one man to resist and conquer HIM, who vauntingly boasts, and ignorantly prides himself in his might, situation, numbers, riches, and above all in his past successes. Many heretofore who thought they stood have fallen. Neither success nor victory always serve the same master.

Brave and generous hearted Britons! promptly decide to die gloriously rather than tamely and ignominiously to *crouch* to the *grand Enslaver,* to be enfettered by his *galling* chains; —sacrifice every comfort, undergo any or every privation, rather than subject yourselves to the fraternal hug of those infernal miscreants, who can set no bounds to their ambition, nor impose any restraint upon their love of violence, plunder and desolation. Remember all lies at stake, LIFE, LIBERTY, and SAFETY, and remember these blessings of Providence, are threatened by those that have long since discarded HONOUR, disbanded MERCY, and who look upon JUSTICE, and the observance of Good Faith, as Plebeian virtues, deserving no place in *the glorious new order of things.*

Self defence is a dictate of nature, as is manifested among irrational creatures, so is it also in man; even the laws of nations will, that force be repelled by force. The hedge hog is ever armed against assailants; and there are but few animals that bear not their offensive weapon about them. The ox his horn; the boar his tusk, and the lion his paw.—Let the temerarious enemies of England, beware of the Lion's paw.

Lose no time was Caesar's motto. Delays are dangerous. It is the security of a State always to be watchful; and in a moment like the present, it is the greatest wisdom in ALL to be in readiness, and to have our magazines well stored with warlike implements, that in the hour of trial *none may be to seek, nor any thing be wanted.*

Sold by J. ASPERNE, (Successor to Mr. Sewell,) Cornhill, Price One Penny, or Six Shillings per Hundred; and may be had of the Booksellers, at the West-End of the Town, &c. &c.   *Page, Printer, Black Friars Road.*

[C. L., No. 34. Single sheet printed on one side, in two columns. 10½ × 15. *Bibl. Lind.,* No. 1521.]

The Duke of Shoreditch;
OR,
*Barlow's Ghost.

COUNTRYMEN:

AFTER my Spirit had rested in peace more than two hundred years, I was, in a manner, called from my grave by a report in circulation, that the French intended to invade the *now* United Kingdoms of England and Ireland. Presumptuous as they always were, they would not have dared to have thought of such an exploit in my time!

Why? you may probably ask. The answer is easy: Because, from our active exertions, we were always in a state of preparation to receive them.

However, hearing this report, I revisited Earth, and soon found that there was more truth in it than attends reports in general. The French about to invade this Kingdom! I said to myself; then the Inhabitants of every district, particularly that which I *still* call my own, are ready to meet them. But, how great was my surprise to find, that the exercise of Arms had been long laid aside, except upon particular emergencies;

---

* Barlow was a Shopkeeper in Shoreditch.

and that it was no longer considered as a sport and pastime, as we used to make it, in the district where I formerly resided! I remember that in my time, every one capable of using them, was provided with a Bow and Arrows, the weapons then most in request. All the Tradesmen, and Manufacturing Hands, used to parade in Finsbury Fields, on Thursday and Saturday Afternoons. *Butts* to shoot at were erected: the Inhabitants of the adjacent Parishes flocked to behold our military sports; the place was like a Fair. We soon became so expert at our exercise, that the fame of the *Finsbury Archers* reached the ears of his Majesty, King Henry the Eighth. The English Archers in general had long been celebrated all over Europe, as France had frequently found to her cost. Well; we were summoned to Windsor, and had the honour to be reviewd by the King, who was so pleased with our performance of the exercise, that he gave great praise and rewards to the whole Company. And, when he came to me, he said, "My good fellow, you have handled "your arms like a Duke: you shall be the Captain of this "warlike band, and shall be called the Duke of Shoreditch." Which was the title that the Captain of the Finsbury Archers ever after assumed, until, upon the introduction of fire-arms, the Company was dissolved.

I do not, Countrymen, remind you of these things out of vanity; for vanity cannot exist beyond the grave; but merely to stimulate you to the same endeavours, for which you have still greater occasion. I understand that our ancient enemy, the French, are now more formidable than ever; that a faction among them have barbarously murdered their good King, Queen, and part of their Family, with numbers of the Nobility; that they have ransacked Europe from one end to the other; and not only plundered the estates, and destroyed the lives, of the great, but, which must naturally follow, cut up by the roots, and totally annihilated, the comforts and happiness of the middle and lower orders of the People: Moreover, that they are now governed by the iron rod of a

Tyrant and Usurper, who, truly an Enemy to the Human Race, has spread destruction from Egypt to Switzerland.

He has, I am informed, stepped so far into Blood, that he cannot retreat, either with safety to his Person, or ease to his Conscience. The first will be sacrificed to the fury of a licentious Soldiery, hardened in scenes of devastation and carnage, if he refuses to lead them on to future depredation: and with regard to the latter, if his body remains inactive, it will present such horrors, such real *Blue Devils* to his mind, as will lead him to destroy himself. He therefore means to send, perhaps to conduct, these Savages of Europe, these modern Barbarians, cross the channel, which I hope and trust, will prove the RED SEA to them; and so, under Providence, it certainly will, brave Englishmen, if you do what my valiant companions and self used to do; namely, make yourselves Masters of the Manual Exercise, by which we acquired such Fame and Honor, not only, as I told you, from the King and Court, but from the Ladies of London; who used, as we marched along, to wave their handkerchiefs, and call us their Heroes, their brave Defenders. Nay, many a fair hand, which has so waved in approbation of our exploits, has been the reward of different youths who had borne away prizes in the field. I remember it was then the saying, that "the Archers of Finsbury took good aim, for they conquered both in Love and War."

I hope and believe, my valiant Compatriots, for so, though our alliance is distant, you certainly are, that neither your *Gallantry* nor your *Courage* is less than they were in my time. The Inhabitants of Shoreditch, Spitalfields, Finsbury, Clerkenwell, &c. &c. that used to compose our Companies, were Tradesmen and manufacturing Hands, the most useful hands in the Kingdom; as it was from those it derived its commercial opulence; and to those it looked for the support of its honor, and independence, as a Nation, in which support their own Independence, their glorious Constitution, every thing dear to Britons, as Men, as legal Subjects, as valuable

Members of Society, as Husbands, Fathers, Sons, Brothers, was involved.

If such, my friends, was our situation, and such our exertions to preserve our Monarch and Constitution, how much dearer must your present beloved Monarch and glorious Constitution be to you, who, under their benign influence, enjoy all the blessings I have enumerated; all those blessings of which the rest of Europe, through the operation of French Principles, is at this moment deprived, in a still greater degree. How anxious, therefore, must you be to defend your Country against the danger of subjugation with which it is threatened by an Enemy more wicked, unprincipled, ferocious, and, let me add, powerful, than any that ever before threatened or assailed it!

To do this, to be enabled to defend your Country with effect, let me advise you to repair to the Places which will soon be appointed in each of your respective Parishes; there enroll your Names in the honorable Lists of Heroes. Sacrifice all frivolous Amusements, take up your Arms: the time will be but trifling, if you make proper arrangements, that need be taken from your different pursuits: Yet, if you engage with Zeal and Ardour, of which I have no doubt, (for I do not believe that the Character of *Englishmen* has degenerated since my time,) you will soon be perfect. This Kingdom may then bid Defiance to "the World in Arms." You will deserve, and receive, the approbation of your Sovereign, of your Country, of your own Hearts: And, if I shall have had the good fortune, in the smallest degree, to have stimulated your endeavours, I shall rejoice that, upon this arduous occasion, the Perfidy of the *Corsican Usurper* BONAPARTE has raised

THE GHOST OF BARLOW.

London: Printed for J. ASPERNE, Successor to MR. SEWELL, at the Bible, Crown, and Constitution, No. 32, Cornhill, by T. MAIDEN.
[Price 1d. or 6s. the 100.]

[C. L., No. 35. Single sheet printed on one side, in one column. 10½ × 16¾. *Bibl. Lind.*, No. 1488. Brit. Mus. *Catalogue, s.v.* "Barlow (   )."]

Freedom or Slavery.

A NEW SONG.

Tune.—Rule Britannia.

I.

THE haughty French, with malice fraught,
   Swear to invade our blest domain;
   Swear to invade our blest domain;
But we will set their—will set their threats at nought,
   And boldly drive them back again.
Then arm, ye Britons, your happy Isle to save,
Britons never, never, never will be slaves.

II.

Shall gallant Britons ever yield,
   And bow beneath a tyrant's chain?
   And bow beneath a tyrant's chain?
No; we will perish—will perish on the field,
   Or boldly drive them back again.
Then arm, ye Britons, your happy Isle to save,
Britons never, never, never will be slaves.

III.

We'll shew them that the noble fame
   Our fathers won on Cressy's plains,
   Our fathers won on Cressy's plains,
Is not yet wither'd—not wither'd, but the same
   Bold spirit in our bosoms reigns.
Then arm, ye Britons, your happy Isle to save,
Britons never, never, never will be slaves.

IV.

Your wives and daughters call you on,
    To save them from rapacious lust;
    To save them from rapacious lust;
By all the glory—the glory you have won,
    Save them—on you alone they trust.
Then arm, ye Britons, your lovely females save,
Britons never, never, never will be slaves.

V.

Shall we, who long have been the dread
    And envy of surrounding shores,
    And envy of surrounding shores,
Bow to a foreign—a foreign yoke, our heads,
    And yield to yon Usurper's power?
Forbid it, Britons! still, still your country save,
Britons never, never, never will be slaves.

VI.

Arm, Sons of Freedom, in this cause,
    And let surrounding nations hear;
    And let surrounding nations hear;
We will defend our—defend our Country's laws,
    Britons never yield to fear.
Still shall Britannia—Britannia rule the waves,
Britons never, never, never will be slaves.

A FRIEND TO OLD ENGLAND.

LONDON: Printed for J. WALLIS, Ludgate Street; Price 1d.
or 8d. per Dozen.—
Where may be had, all the Loyal Papers that have been published.
Printed by J. Crowder and E. Hemsted, Warwick-Square.

[C. L., No. 36. Single sheet printed on one side, in one column. 10½ × 17½. Brit. Mus. *Catalogue, s.v.* "Freedom."]

Address to the People of Great Britain.

By W. J. DENISON, Esq.

YE gen'rous Youths who boast a Briton's name,
Alive to honour, and the blush of shame;
Shall GALLIA's slaves, who tremblingly obey
The haughty Corsican's relentless sway—
Who meanly cringe before his upstart throne,
Nor life nor liberty can call their own—
Dare to invade your smiling, happy Isle,
While LUST and RAPINE at their victims smile?
Dare to insult you with their vengeful ire,
Menace your harvest and your towns with fire?
To wrest from you the sceptre of the main,
Who basely kiss their Despot's iron chain?
Recall those heroes fam'd in days of old,
Your great Forefathers, hardy, free, and bold;
Recall those Chiefs, who nobly dar'd withstand
The base Oppressors of their Native Land;
Recall CARACTACUS's scythed car,
Who brav'd the terrors of a CÆSAR's war;
Recall great ALFRED's wise and awful ghost;
Recall great WALLACE, in himself a host;
Recall the Barons from fair Runnimede,
Resolv'd to conquer, or resign'd to bleed;
Recall the triumphs of ELIZA's reign,
The scourge of PHILIP and of haughty Spain!
Let not those Chieftains in oblivion lie,
Who oft have made the Gallic squadrons fly—
Who oft have made their trembling standards yield,
And dy'd with gore the long-remember'd field.

View your brave Prince, with sable shield and lance,
Whose feats surpass the pages of romance;
When Poctiers rivall'd Cressy's far-fam'd plains,
And hapless JOHN almost forgot his chains;
Let the fifth HENRY, drawn by FANCY's hand,
Lead on his martial and heroic band;
Let Agincourt each British heart inspire,
And embryo Patriots catch the Warrior's fire.
See your lov'd daughters, beauteous as the morn,
A prey to infamy, to lust, and scorn;
See curst Bastiles o'er ev'ry hamlet tower—
See vengeful harpies glut their love of power;
See the poor peasant plunder'd of his all,
And if he murmurs—meet the hostile ball;
See your fair towns in desolation laid,
And the fierce soldier to fresh carnage wade;
"Inur'd to blood, and nurs'd in scenes of woe,"
Your crafty, cruel, and vindictive foe,
Steel'd 'gainst the pleasures of the social bowl,
Or LOVE's soft fires, that melt the raptur'd soul;
His callous heart no gen'rous passions swell;
Within his breast REMORSE nor PITY dwell.
Go view at Jaffa (if you trust his word)
The pris'ners murder'd by his faithless sword;
Go view, where SMITH his daring feats display'd,
His soldiers poison'd, and his sick betrayed;
Go view, when Alexandria found her grave,
His troops forebade e'en helpless age to save:
View brave TOUSSAINT, transported cross the main,
Torn like a felon from Domingo's plain;
Torn from his home, his children, and his wife,
To close in fetters his eventful life.
View the Apostate steal from Egypt's sands,
The base deserter of his vet'rn bands:
His murd'rous dagger Pavia long shall weep;
He mocks her woes with—"DEATH's eternal sleep."

His broken faith let plunder'd Venice tell—
View how Batavia, how Helvetia fell;
Once bless'd like you, with all that life endears,
Abandon'd now to rapine, scorn, and tears!
Then, O my Country! must you feel the blow,
And be, like others, in your turn brought low?
Must you no more with gen'rous feeling beat,
Nor give MISFORTUNE a secure retreat?
Must all your social charities expire,
And your proud commerce feed the funeral fire?
Must you, renown'd for Probity and Laws,
Fam'd for your love of FREEDOM's glorious cause—
Must you relapse to what you were before,
A conquer'd province, and a barb'rous shore?—
No!—by those heroes, once your boast and pride,
Who oft for you have suffer'd, bled, and dy'd—
By great NASSAU, by HAMPDEN's spotless shade;
By BRUCE, whose laurels Time can never fade;
By Egypt's shores, and by Aboukir's wave;
By ABERCROMBY's much-lamented grave;
By Howe, by DUNCAN, by ST. VINCENT's name;
By WOLFE's great spirit, and by MINDEN's fame;
By that high Honour, which you must bequeath,
By SYDNEY's scaffold, and by RUSSELL's wreath;
By the still pang indignant VIRTUE feels;
By the firm spirit which the Patriot steels:—
Come when he will—elate in frantic pride,
With vassal kingdoms crouching by his side—
Deck'd with the pageantry of Eastern State,
Tortur'd with restless and malignant hate—
Drunk with success, array'd in hostile form,
OLD ENGLAND's Genius fearless meets the storm.
Tho' prostrate Senates their anath'ma's pour—
Tho' abject Priests their impious flatt'ries show'r—
Tho' dastard Courts the gen'rous strife forbear,
The plunder'd dole of guiltless neighbours share—

She spreads her Ægis o'er a sinking world,
Firm and erect, while all in ruin's hurl'd;
Calls her brave sons to grasp the shining spear,
Arrest the tyrant in his wild career—
Calls her bold Youth to train the martial steed,
Nod the plum'd helmet, and the Phalanx lead;
To grace the Poet and Historian's page,
Renown'd and honour'd to the latest age;
Again to rival Blenheim's glorious plain
While future MARLBROS equal trophies gain;
Again immortalize in Hist'ry's fight,
Boyne's rapid stream, or Calpe's tow'ring height.
Still shall your NELSONS guide the hardy Tar,
Teach him to wield the thunders of your war;
Extend the triumphs of your sea-girt isle,
From frozen Denmark to the sultry Nile.
Still shall your shores a safe retreat afford,
From the wide havock of the Gallic sword;
Grant an asylum to Distress and Woe,
And shield each suff'rer from his ruthless foe;
Still shall your Merchants distant seas explore,
And at your feet the wealth of India pour;
Still shall your Press, that bulwark of your Laws,
Protect, as ever, injur'd Virtue's cause;
Admir'd, while envied, by surrounding Slaves,
The dread of Despots, and the scourge of Knaves.
But if decreed by HEAV'N that fall we must;
And what she wills, is ever right and just;
If doom'd to swell (ordain'd by angry FATE),
This modern ATTILA's revengeful hate;
Then Europe's sun is set in endless night—
Then FAITH, then HONOUR, wing their hasty flight—
Then all the Ties of social life are o'er,
From Moscow's snows, to fair AUSONIA's shore—
Then Gothic DARKNESS spreads its baleful shade—
Then ART, then LEARNING, LAWS, and FREEDOM fade!

For happier climes they hoist th'indignant sail,
While savage FORCE and ANARCHY prevail—
While all the SCIENCE polish'd Greece bestow'd,
Of every Muse the once admir'd abode—
With all that GENIUS, all that TASTE inspire,
Sink in the flames to please a Despot's ire.
Long ere that moment let me meet my doom;
Grant me, great God, the refuge of the tomb!

Printed for JAMES ASPERNE (Successor to Mr. Sewell), at the Bible, Crown, and Constitution, No. 32, Cornhill; by W. Lane, Leadenhall-Street, Price One Penny each, or 6s. the 100.

Where may be also had, at the same price, Sheridan's Address to the People. Also a Collection of all the loyal Papers that have been, or will be published.

*⁎*Noblemen, Magistrates, and Gentlemen, would do well by ordering a few Dozen of the above Tracts of their different Booksellers, and causing them to be stuck up in the respective Villages where they reside, that the Inhabitants may be convinced of the Cruelty of the Corsican Usurper.

[C. L., No. 37. Single sheet printed on one side, in two columns. 11 × 17¾. Brit. Mus. *Catalogue, s.v.* "Denison, W. J."]

Corporal Trim on the Invasion.

As much of the public conversation is now engrossed with speculations on our means of defence against the threatened Invasion, it is vain to imagine that the ignorant and enlightened, the timid and the brave, will hold the same opinions; but that the majority of the most intrepid nation on earth can seriously entertain any apprehensions on that subject, appears to me utterly impossible. And I am one of those who place no less reliance in the perfect safety of conversing with the public on the subject, than I should in preparing the brave army destined for their defence to expect as

much danger as glory, their companionship being insepar-
able. When the object of a general is to make an attack upon
the enemy, secrecy must, for many obvious reasons, be held
sacred; on the other hand, when the general expects an
attack, he cannot be too explicit, both as to the nature of his
expectance, and in the means intended to frustrate the attempt; and in performing this duty nothing can be worse
policy than to attribute his security rather to the weakness
of the enemy than to his own superior means of defence; or
for him rashly to assert it is impossible the enemy should
carry that position, that they should be able to cross that
river, or to make a landing on the coast; because, if the reverse
took place, the troops would be disheartened, and naturally
lose their confidence in the general, whereas, every danger is
already half overcome when it is steadily looked in the face.
On the other hand, the greatest risk in war is acknowledged
to be the occurrence of any circumstance not expected; as for
example, it is known a corps of grenadiers will boldly advance
upon a battery in the mouth of the cannon, and bravely force
their way through the embrasures, yet if from an ambuscade
an unexpected fire of musketry was opened on their flank, it
is more than probable that a serious alarm would be the
consequence of the discovery of a danger they had not made
up their minds to. Therefore, though the most uncertain
military operation in the world is doubtless the invasion of
this country, yet we should be prepared to look the circumstance sternly in the face, and in this case our frown is perdition to the enemy. For though nothing can be more difficult
than to place an adequate defence on every part of an extensive coast, by the construction of forts, batteries, and
intrenchments, which can only take place in respect to particular points, and harbours; as the enemy floating at sea has
the choice of landing with a greater force than can suddenly
be opposed to him, under a superior fire from his shipping in
deep water, and from his gun-boats in shallow water; nevertheless, on being informed of the enemy's approach, it is

advisable to throw every obstruction in his way, and to cause as great destruction as possible; which the invaded troops may do with every advantage to themselves that soldiers can wish for, by marching down to the coast in different columns the moment when the enemy's boats stretch for the shore; at which favourable period our artillery may be advanced without being endangered from the fire of the shipping, which will be so masked by their own boats as to render it impossible for the ships to fire without endangering their own people; and if the boats, after suffering great loss from our guns, should still near the shore, the artillery may instantly be withdrawn to a more distant position, and the cavalry and infantry advance rapidly to cover the retreat of the guns, and to attack the enemy while in disorder. His loss will undoubtedly be ten times ours. Yet it is possible, that by very superior numbers, on a given point, he may be able to make good his landing, which in my mind will to him be no better than digging his own grave; or, in regard to his escape from our ships, be falling out of the frying-pan into the fire. As our generals will no doubt have taken such positions of communication as to secure the speedy assembly of a considerable body of troops and artillery, which, for the sake of argument, I now suppose to be assembled within five miles of the enemy's leading column, and that at a certain distance between them and the enemy a ditch be dug across the road, and extending to the right and left of it a considerable distance in the fields, obliging the enemy thereby to remain longer under the fire of our artillery, while the ground on which we decide to give battle be laid open to clear the way for the irresistible impetuosity of our cavalry. Meanwhile the horse-artillery and sharp-shooters are sent forward to salute the enemy in front, flank, and rear; who, exposed to this galling fire, must be reduced to the necessity of employing a considerable portion of his troops, provided with instruments, to clear away the hedges and ditches for his columns of march, or be confined to keep the high road in a single

column: in either case his movements must be greatly re-
tarded; and as cannon shot directed to large bodies will be
destructive at two miles distance, he will, when he arrives
within that range of fire, after passing through the ordeal of
the horse-artillery and sharp-shooters, be exposed to an ex-
terminating fire from our heavy artillery, which will so en-
filade his column, as that, according to his own favourite
phrase, the column will be *foudroyé*—a salutation he cannot
possibly return. As if it were practicable for him to land a
hundred guns, and their attendant ammunition carriages,
with horses to draw them, his ranks must still be devastated
by the irresistible thunder of a superior artillery, both as to
number, calibre, and celerity of movement, his guns would
soon be silenced without a capacity on his part of replacing
a shot he has fired, a man or horse that has been killed, or a
gun that has been dismounted. Pelted in this manner, with
an iron tempest in front, flank, and rear, the glitter of our
bayonets and the sound of our horses would be sufficient, and
he would scarcely venture within reach of our Egyptians;
and if he did, they have experienced what it is to *fear God* and
level low, and he has experienced also, that neither the possession of all the strong holds of the country, superior numbers united to a superiority of artillery and the means of its
movement, with every other advantage and resource, could
prevent their surrender to a handful of British troops, who
from this reason he endeavours to *underwrite*, as he did Suwarrow and the Russians. But his publications were in vain,
as it is well known the invincible citizens were constantly
averse to a close connexion with the Russians, though the
French generals as constantly pronounced them the worst
troops in the world, and the Russian generals the most un-
skilful. In spite therefore of these gasconades, the French are
very sensible that their march to the British capital will be
the most wearisome their infatuated Consul ever devised for
the victims of his ambition. Though by the boastful terms in
which the rapidity of his movements is described by hireling

writers, many of our old ladies are taught to believe that to march six and thirty miles a day is nothing for him; it may be so where there is no opposition. But however sorry I may be to differ from such respectable authority, it is my opinion that when the French van reaches London, their centre and rear will be eaten by the crows; and the Invincibles and Terribles be very glad to surrender their useless arms to *our Lambs* for the humble consideration of a dinner, which British magnanimity will not refuse.

I am, however, much afraid, from the natural partiality of our seamen to the inhabitants of their own element, that our poor crows will be cheated of their *French ragout*, and the *Armée d'Angleterre* be dished up to the fish, with broadsides and gunpowder sauce; in either case his Consular Majesty will be a welcome guest.

So Huzza for the Tight Little Island!!

Corporal Trim.

_____

Printed for JOHN STOCKDALE, 181, Piccadilly.—Price 1d. or 6d. per Dozen.
S. GOSNELL, Printer, Little Queen Street, Holborn.

[C. L., No. 38. Single sheet printed on one side, in two columns. 10¼ × 17¾. *Bibl. Lind.,* No. 1486. Brit. Mus. *Catalogue, s.v.* "Trim."]

_____

Citizens of England,

You Have Been Told That Bonaparte Will Not Attempt Invasion:

Read the following detailed Account of his Preparations, and ask yourselves whether those who tell you so are your Friends or your Enemies.

_____

"THE Alertness of our People, employed in the several Yards along the Coasts, never had a parallel. I reckon 11,000 Ship-Carpenters, and their necessary Assistants, Labourers, &c. employed here, and at *Calais, Dunkirk,* and *Ostend,* besides those at Work on the BOATS preparing at *Bruges, Ghent,* and *Antwerp.*

"At BOULOGNE, we have 36 GUN-BOATS ready, each carrying Three heavy Pieces or Ordnance, Two fore and One aft; besides 152 of what are called FLAT-BOTTOMED BOATS; but they are now generally *rounded below* and *keeled.* In Three Weeks Time we expect to have as many more in a State of perfect Readiness.

"At CALAIS, several of the FLOATING BATTERIES, that opposed LORD NELSON, when he attacked Boulogne, are now fitting up, and about 70 BOATS, that will carry 150 Men each.

"At DUNKIRK and the adjacent Canals there are 47 GUN-BOATS *ready,* with remarkable heavy Ordnance, and not less than 220 BOATS for carrying Men. They count upon being able to send 400 of these Vessels (great and small) to Sea, in less than Three Weeks.

"At OSTEND, the GUN-BOATS, FLOATING BATTERIES, and VESSELS *for carrying Soldiers,* that are now, and will be, completed during the present Month, amount to 487. They Work here during the Whole of the Moon-Light Nights.

"I cannot, at present exactly ascertain what Number of Men are employed, at *Bruges* and *Ghent;* but they are extremely numerous. Such is the Case at *Antwerp."*

Prepare then to meet this powerful and implacable Foe.—Lose not a Moment in your Preparations, and shew to the admiring Nations of Europe that, if the Desire of Plunder and the Ambition of the USURPER BONAPARTE *can call forth the Zeal of French Slaves, our Rights, our Liberties, our God, our Country, and our King, can unite Britons, and call forth a holy Enthusiasm sufficient to turn that Zeal into Dismay, Discomfiture, and Destruction.*

Printed for J. GINGER, 169, Piccadilly,
Price EIGHT-PENCE per Dozen, for Distribution,
IT IS PARTICULARLY RECOMMENDED, TO THOSE WHO CAN AFFORD IT, TO DISTRIBUTE THESE HAND-BILLS.

W. Marchant, Printer, 3, Greville-Street, Holborn.

[C. L., No. 39. Single sheet printed on one side, in one column. 10¾ × 17¼. *Bibl. Lind.,* No. 1484. Brit. Mus. *Catalogue, s.v.* "Napoleon I."]

A Peep into Hanover;

Or, *A Faint Description of the Atrocities Committed by the French in that City.*

"But if you can the mournful Pages read,
The sad Relation shews you such a Deed
As all the Annals of th' infernal Reign
Shall strive to equal or exceed in vain."

POMFRET'S POEMS.

IT will be remembered, that the Electorate surrendered without Resistance. This we do not mention, as encreasing our Compassion for the Inhabitants, which it certainly does not; but as increasing our Abhorrence of the Invaders, who, without Provocation or Pretext of Resistance, have perpetrated the Atrocities of which the following is a faint outline:

Ever since the Conquest the whole Electorate has been a scene of Pillage and Butchery, which is said to yield only to the Fate of Switzerland, in Spring, 1798. The French Soldiers have the most unbounded Indulgence of their ruling passions of *Rapacity*, *Cruelty*, and *Lust:*—IN THE CITY OF HANOVER, AND EVEN IN THE PUBLIC STREET, WOMEN OF THE HIGHEST RANK HAVE BEEN VIOLATED BY THE LOWEST OF THAT BRUTAL SOLDIERY, IN THE PRESENCE OF THEIR HUSBANDS AND FATHERS, AND SUBJECTED AT THE SAME TIME TO SUCH ADDITIONAL AND UNDESCRIBABLE OUTRAGES AS THE BRUTAL FURY OF THE VIOLATORS, ENFLAMED BY DRUNKENNESS, COULD CONTRIVE. We have seen the Names of some of these unfortunate Laides; but the Honour of their Families, and the Peace of their own future Lives, (if they can have peace,) forbid us to publish them. The Baron de K——, a well-known partisan of French Philosophy and Politics, went to the Commandant of Hanover, and claimed his Protection, as an Admirer of the French Revolution! but he found no more

favour in the Sight of the *Aga of Sultan* BONAPARTE's jani-
saries, than the most loyal *Noblemen in Hanover.* The French
Officer told him, *"All that Jacobinism is now out of Fashion—
Go about your Business!"* Nor have we heard, that the Philosophers of Gottingen, the *enthusiasts of Equality and Per-
fectability* have been at all better treated.—Such are the
tender Mercies of the Wicked! Such are the Gangs of ferocious Banditti, whom the MURDERER OF JAFFA let loose on
the civilized World! Such, and ten thousand times worse, is
the Fate prepared *for England, if the valour of her people do
not avert it; for England will assuredly be more oppressed in
proportion as she is more dreaded, envied, and hated.* To shew
any symptom of Neutrality in such a Cause, not to support
it with all our might, IS THE FOULEST TREASON AGAINST THE
PEOPLE OF ENGLAND; and, the poorest honest Labourer, who
has a Mother or a Sister, a Wife or a Daughter, has, in truth,
as much reason as the highest Duke in the Land to detest the
Traitor. Englishmen think of this and profit by Example.

BRITANNICUS.

Printed for J. GINGER, 169, PICCADILLY,
Price SIXPENCE per Dozen, for Distribution.

** *It is particularly recommended, to those who can afford it, to circulate this Hand-Bill.*

W. MARCHANT, Printer, 3, Greville-Street, Holborn.

[C. L., No. 40. Single sheet printed on one side, in one column. 10½ × 17. *Bibl. Lind.,*
No. 1507.]

Parody.

By AN HONEST ENGLISHMAN.

"ROUSE *Britannia*—dangers call thee,
  "Awhile thy tranquil state resign,
"Treach'rous friends and foes conspiring,
  "Now threat thy darling shores and mine.

"*France*, so deeply plung'd in horrors,
    "Aims, with joy, the threat'ned blow,
"Hopes at length for ample vengeance,
    "On her old, and deadly, foe."
—Thus with grief and sorrow pining,
    Did England's Guardian Angel say,
Where in Laurel Grove reclining
    All our *ancient Heroes* lay.
RUSSEL, KEPPEL, HOWE, BOSCAWEN,
    Former Guardians of the main,
MARLB'ROUGH, WOLFE, and ABERCROMBIE,
    So distinguished on the plain.
In the hour when gentle slumbers
    Seal in rest the guiltless mind,
Bonaparté, sleep deserted,
    Neither rest nor peace could find.
Round his couch stood Envy knawing,
    Pale-fac'd Guilt, and black Despair,
Discord high her *fire-brand* throwing,
    Cast around a dismal glare.
Then in council he sat working
    Horror's deeds, in *England's woe*,
With his Murmidons consulting
    How to give the *deadly blow*.
Fiends suggested acts of *Treason*,
    Which revolted Angels tell,
As a crime of deepest colour,
    Hurried them in chains to Hell.
When *two Forms* appear'd before him,
    Clad in robes of heav'nly light,
VIRTUE, led by ENGLAND'S GENIUS,
    Burst on his astonished sight.
—"Stay, rash man, thy horrid purpose,"
    Sternly thus the Phantom said,
"Stay, rash man, 'tis *Virtue* bids thee,
    "Tho', alas! to me thou'rt dead.

"Was thy youth for this so guarded?
"Horror scarcely dares to tell,
"How thy crimes, alas! would rival
"All the *blackest* deeds of Hell.
"Far, vain man, beyond thy malice
"Mounts GREAT BRITAIN's *glorious Name;*
"Hear how high it stands recorded,
"Mark'd for *everlasting Fame!*
"Long *we'll* guard *Old England's Glory.*
"Envious, hear what I relate;
"While *thy* sicken'd soul lies grov'ling,
"*Eternal* Honours ENGLAND wait."

Printed for J. GINGER, 169, *Piccadilly.* Price 6d. per Dozen, or 1d. each, by C. STOWER, Charles Street, Hatton Garden.

[C. L., No. 41. Single sheet printed on one side, in one column. 11 × 17½.]

The Prophecy!

Or, Bonaparte Killed at Last by His Own Troops!

A True Story, just brought from *Paris* by a Gentleman, who arrived in *England* only two Days ago. This Story is founded on a Dream of *Bonaparte,* which happened a Week since, and has greatly agitated his Mind, arising no doubt, from the inward workings of Conscience. This Dream he communicated to his faithful MAMELUKE, and some how or other it has transpired—perhaps by the secret intentions of Providence, whose Ways are inscrutable. The Dream is here given in Verse.

YE BRITONS, to your Country true,
In her *just* cause so *hearty,*
The French shall make *Invasion rue,*
And give *proud* Bonaparte
Such signs of Britons' *glorious* zeal,
When by *French slaves invaded,*
As soon shall make that *Tyrant* feel,
His *laurels* are all *faded.*

Blasted like his brilliant *fame*,
Which once shone with such *lustre*,
Patriots almost *ador'd* his name,
Who now *against* him muster.
His warmest friends, since he has chang'd,
The *Monster* detesting so;
They in the foremost ranks are rang'd,
To give to him his death-blow.

Shall Britons *court* a *Tyrant's smiles?*
Shall Britons, transform'd to *Slaves!*
Be *caught* by Bonaparte's *wiles?*
His *hypocritick knaves,*
Who *slily* say, "we only mean,
A hundred rich men to *kill,*
Frenchmen from *long experience* seen,
Too *mild, much blood* to *spill!*

"So *meek,* so *gentle,* they ne'er could,
Like the *base* English nation,
Embrue their hands in *guiltless blood;*
Britons in ev'ry station,
Characteris'd as *loving pain*
For *savage, barbarous* acts;
Whence they reject with high disdain,
Those *mild* laws *New* France enacts."

Freedom sure reigns in FRANCE *alone,*
For *only* the *Consul's free;*
But mark that *Tyrant* on his *throne,*
And him on his *pillow* see,
Where rack'd with *agonizing thought,*
At which his blood runs chill,
Murders he *plots,* who sleep has sought
In vain, the night to *kill.*

His *Death* see *Widows, Orphans pray*,
Carrying a *poison'd* bowl,
Whilst this, which some in *whispers* say,
Seems *thunder* to his soul:
"Thou *traitor* to thy *soldiers*, speak,
Nor feel refreshing sleep,
We now our *Husbands, Fathers* seek,
Thus doom'd by thee to weep.

"Where are thy *Fellow Soldiers*, say!
Whom thou, so trech'rous, slew?
Thou know'st at *Jaffa* long they lay
Expos'd to *public* view;
Till BRITONS, to their *foes humane*,
Gave them *sepulchral rite*;
For *they* with *sorrow, heartfelt pain*,
Beheld that *horrid sight*.

"But, *Monster*, know, 'tis *doom'd* by *Fate*,
Much longer thou shalt not *live*,
From *thy own troops just death* await,
They shall thy *death-blow* give:
Nor will those *guards* that round thy throne,
Have screen'd thee so long from death,
Their Consul's too just fate *bemoan*,
Or weep at his parting Breath,

"But *Terror fled*, shew *vast surprise*
Thou, Monster, liv'd so long;
That France did not *against* thee *rise*
In one promiscuous throng;
Thy stanch *Mam'lukes* too, shall cry out,
Thank God, the Tyrant's dead!!!
For *no more Consuls* Frenchmen shout,
But King Louis make your Head.

"With *Moreau, Minister* of *State,*
Not *mad Ambition's Fool,*
But choosing a much safer Fate,
Than over France to rule;
Frenchmen shall then this *blessing* see,
They've not *these twelve years* past,
Equality doth *best agree*
With *Governments* which *last.*"

"For though *Republics*, at first sight,
May *delusive Fancy* please,
They, closer seen, *mankind affright*,
And with so much *friction teaze*,
Faction against faction struggling,
Causing such *constant ferment*,
That with their arts of *patriot-juggling*,
A state's *vital strength* is *spent.*"

We BRITONS now, to our *good* King
Will *grateful* homage pay;
Nor *murmur*, tho' the war should bring
Fresh taxes ev'ry day!
Because they're rais'd but for the war,
When that's brought to an end,
Those *taxes cease* we *most abhor*,
And our *bad times* will *mend.*

Where we're tax'd too, *true Freedom* reigns,
And such *just laws* are *found;*
They can defy Old or Young PAINES,
And fight them on their own ground.
Their *Reason* would before our laws,
(Afraid with *Truth* to fight,)
Vanish in smoke, as the sun draws
The vapours of the night.

Printed for J. HATCHARD, 190, Piccadilly. 1d. each; 6d. per dozen; or, 3s. 6d. per 100. [BRETTELL, Printer.

[C. L., No. 42. Single sheet printed on one side, in two columns (poem). 13 × 14¾.]

Address to Irishmen

Residing in England.

Fellow Countrymen,

THE Calamities which have so lately threatened your native Country, by a few of your BRETHEREN being misled by the artful Designs of FRENCH SPIES; and which was so nearly, again bringing on the Name of IRISHMAN, a Stain which never could have been wiped away; shews to you the necessity for YOU, at this Moment, ONE and ALL, to step Forward in the Cause of *your best of* KINGS—*the Father of His People.*—Unite and associate—*be firm, as you are Brave;* suffer not the poisonous Language of the Enemies of their Country, however high in Rank, or the vain Promises of the designing SPIES of a CORSICAN USURPER and MURDERER, to deceive you, or to lead you from your Duty, to transgress the Laws of that Country which although not your native Land, protects and supports you, your Wives, and your Children in Happiness and Comfort;—but animated by the patriotic Language of a SHERIDAN (that Ornament of his Country) rally round the Standard of Loyalty, and be determined to CONQUER, or DIE, in fighting for *your King, your Country*, and *your God;* be *foremost* on the Shores of your Island, in repelling a BARBAROUS and FEROCIOUS ENEMY, and save your Wives and Children from their *savage Lust* and *murderous* HANDS—*then* will you redeem the Character of IRISHMAN—*then* will you share in the Glory of assisting to hand down to an ILLUSTRIOUS PRINCE, a CROWN UNSULLIED, and a CONSTITUTION UNBROKEN—*then* will you shew to such of *your Countrymen* as have been deceived by *French Perfidy*, an Example worthy of their Imitation, that they may see before it is too late their Error; and, by following your Steps, make Atonement to their insulted GOD, and their Sovereign. Let not an *Irishman* be seen, but in the Ranks, fighting for his King, despising all Promises—forgetting all Injuries—join against a cruel and barbarous Enemy—then will the Name of *Irishman* once again be renowned for its COURAGE, VALOUR, and LOYALTY.

An Irishman, and a Soldier.

CRAVEN HOTEL, STRAND, AUGUST 8, 1803.

LIST OF PATRIOTIC PUBLICATIONS,

By JOHN GINGER, No. 169, *Piccadilly.*

	s.	d.
Publicola's Addresses, stitched, price 3d. or . . .	2	6 per doz.
Dialogue between an English Soldier and a Taylor, price 2d. or	1	6 per doz.
Address to Mechanics, Labourers, &c. of England, price 2d. or	1	6 per doz.
Alfred's Address to the Ladies of England, price 6d. sewed, or	5	0 per doz.
Substance of Bonaparte's Hand-bills, price 1d. or .	0	6 per doz.
John Bull turned into a Galley Slave, price 1d. or .	0	6 per doz.
To the Infamous Wretch, &c. &c. price 1d. or . .	0	6 per doz.
Peep into Hanover, &c. price 1d. or . . .	0	6 per doz.
Men of England, by an English Woman, price 1d. or	0	6 per doz.
English Mastiffs, &c. &c. price 1d. or . . .	0	6 per doz.
Horrors upon Horrors, or the Blacksmith's Narrative, price 1d. or	0	6 per doz.
Fellow-Citizens, by a Shopkeeper, price 1d. or .	0	6 per doz.
Substance of Speech of Jacob Bosanquet, price 1d. or	0	9 per doz.
Bonaparte's Confession, &c. p. 2d. or	1	6 per doz.
Parody, by an Honest Englishman, price 1d. or .	1	6 per doz.
Britons Prayer, Address to Volunteers, price 1d. or	0	6 per doz.
Citizens of England, &c. price 1d. or	0	6 per doz.

Where all Patriotic Hand-Bills and Songs may be had assorted.

W GLINDON, PRINTER, 48 RUPERT-STREET, HAY-MARKET.

[C. L., No. 43. Single sheet printed on one side, in one column, except List of Publications, which is in two-column measure. 10½ × 17. *Bibl. Lind.*, No. 1540.]

The
Great Egyptian Gun,

WHICH now stands on the Parade, in ST. JAMES'S PARK, was taken at
ALEXANDRIA, in EGYPT, in the famous Battle of the 21st of March,
1801. It was at that Time TWENTY Feet in Length; but, being much
battered in the Muzzle, was cut down to sixteen Feet one Inch. It is
five Feet three Inches in Circumference, and seven Inches and a half
in the Bore; and weighs upwards of eighty-four Hundred-Weight. The
Carriage on which it stands is a new one, five Feet high, and about
fourteen Feet in Length; is elegantly carved, and so well painted, that
it is difficult to distinguish it from Bronze. Such is a brief Sketch of
that curious Piece of Ordnance, so gallantly obtained from the
FRENCH, who now threaten us with INVASION, headed by their diminutive Chief, THE CORSICAN BANTAM, BUONAPARTE. *Come when they
dare*, they may depend on receiving A WARM RECEPTION from THE

VOLUNTEERS OF ENGLAND.

AIR—"SUCCESS TO THE DUCHESS WHEREVER SHE GOES."

[*Broadside continues with song on following pages.*]

I.

YE Sons of BRITANNIA, alive to the call
   Of duty most sacred, of glory and honor,
Resolv'd with your Country to stand or to fall,
   Who gloriously croud to true LIBERTY'S BANNER.
          Thus loyal and free
          You always shall be;
Your KING and your COUNTRY rewards shall bestow,
          And gratitude raise
          The Song to your Praise:
May our VOLUNTEERS conquer wherever they go.

II.

In History's Volume the Sage shall record,
   How in Anarchy sunk, and led on by Distraction,
'Gainst this LOYAL KINGDOM that FRANCE drew the sword,
   Obeying the nod of vile Party and Faction.
          To your Country still true,
          To Arms strait you flew,
With ardor to combat the insolent Foe;
          While Britannia with pride,
          Triumphantly cried:—
May my VOLUNTEERS conquer wherever they go.

III.

Attach'd to our Country, our King, and our Laws,
   No Party shall rule us, no Faction dissever,
We'll conquer or perish in this glorious cause:
   Our Motto shall be, GEORGE AND FREEDOM FOR EVER.
          To win Glory's charms,
          More Brethren in Arms
Shall join us, as streams will enlarge as they flow.
          Be sacred their name
          In the RECORDS OF FAME:—
May our VOLUNTEERS conquer, wherever they go.

IV.

At College our Students the ardor have caught,
    Of Patriots distinguish'd in GREECE and in ROME;
By such bright examples, so gloriously taught,
    To fight for their COUNTRY in Life's early bloom:
            How, in every Age,
            The Hero and Sage,
United and conquer'd for FREEDOM, they know.
        For their Country enroll'd,
        Like the Patriots of Old,—
The LAUREL shall wreath them wherever they go.

V.

All Ranks, all Professions, shall boldly unite,
    The Lawyer, the Student, the Farmer, the Trader,
In one armed Host, for their COUNTRY TO FIGHT,
    Their Rights to preserve, and repel the INVADER.
            By this valiant Band,
            Protected we'll stand,
Long as Seas round the Shores of OLD ENGLAND shall flow.
        To them trophies raise,
        And the loud songs of praise:
May our VOLUNTEERS conquer our INSOLENT FOE.

LONDON:
Published by T. KAYGILL, 39, Upper Rathbone Place;

And sold by JOHN GINGER, 169, and HATCHARD, 190, Piccadilly; G. WALKER, 106, Great Portland-Street; LLOYD, Harley Street; TEGG and CASTLEMAN, Warwick Square; DWYER, 29, Holborn Hill; ROE, 90, Houndsditch; LEE, Ray Street, Clerkenwell; JAMES ASPERNE, (Successor to Mr. Sewell) 32, Cornhill; and other Booksellers.

[*Price* One Penny.]

W. S. Betham, Printer, 7, Furnival's-inn-court, Holborn.

[C. L., No. 45. Single sheet printed on one side; all but last stanza of verse in two columns. 8 × 13½.]

Navy of Britain,

Terror of Your Foes, and Wonder of the World! Brave, Magnanimous Sailors!

YOUR Country, no less confident in the future than grateful for the past, again calls upon you to crush and overwhelm the insulting pretensions of enslaved France and the ambitious projects of her *Tyrant Buonaparté*. Your fellow-countrymen on shore are prepared to give these vapouring invaders *a warm reception*, should they skulk over *in the night*, or be able to screen themselves from your vengeance *in a fog!* You will, I trust, however, meet them early, for they should be sunk mid channel, like another Spanish Armada! and it would be hard upon the Tars of Old England not to have the honor of sweeping from the sease *those Land Rats* who dare venture out of their element.

Their little Corsican task-master has driven them to the water edge, but finds it no such easy matter to tempt them in. They are apt to be *sea-sick*, and are aware that there is more room to make a retreat upon dry land than from *rafts or bum boats*. He finds it expedient, therefore, to *throw in a sop* to tempt them, and they, like true spaniels, who ever fawn and lick where they are worst treated, have, between kicking and cajoling, at length made the desperate determination of plunging in after it! And what, my brave fellows, do you think *this sop* is composed of?—read, and see to what atrocious excesses this *mongrel usurper* is carried by his craving ambition; he tells them, *when they have landed in this Country, that in order to make the booty the richer, no quarter shall be given to the base English, who fight for their perfidious Government, that they are to be put to the sword, and their property to be distributed among the soldiers of the victorious Army!!!*

These are his intentions, these his plans in the event of success: whether therefore he meet his fate on shore or on the waters, our vengeance must be proportioned to the enormity of his aggravating insults and bloody determination. *Our Country is threatened by a host of avowed Assassins*—our all is attacked: a war of plunder and massacre is waged against our Fields, our Homes, our Parents, Wives, and Children.—*Every Tar has his Sweetheart on shore, and even she is held out to the Republican Slaves as a lure to the venture;* every Landsman is the Sailor's friend, and every Landsman who defends his Country is threatened with death, as the reward of his patriotism, by this *Corsican Adventurer;* that redoubted Hero, whose name, though it strike terror among the timid ranks of his subjugated neighbours on the Continent, can never affect a British heart as long as the memory of a DRAKE, a RODNEY, or a HOWE lives in our breasts—as long as NELSON and ABOUKIR, ACRE and SIR SYDNEY are recorded and coupled with their *cause;* the *tyrant Buonaparté,* whose followers and creatures, to keep their hand in, are to be sent to this Country to renew their Egyptian cruelties, and most atrocious scheme of extermination. *Since his massacre of* 4000 *Turks in cool blood at Jaffa, and the poisoning of* 300 *of his own sick Soldiers, who had fought by his side, and been wounded in his cause,* little opportunity has occurred of extending these *Corsican tactics,* if we except *the sudden disappearance of Toussaint, the Black Chief, who gave himself up on French Honor, and has reaped the fruits of French Faith—"the Dead tell no tales!"*

You, my brave Seamen, are the peculiar objects of this man's rancour and inveteracy! an enviable distinction, which you have earned by your valour and intrepidity;—a distinction, which places you at the furthest possible distance from *French Fraternity,* whose kiss, like that of Judas, is meant to betray, and whose embrace is the signal for plunder and subjection. But why are ye thus selected and distinguished from surrounding people? Why? *Because you have never met his Fleets without blowing them out of the water; he has never planned an enterprize which you have not aided to baffle; nor has a vessel or ship of his been able for years to keep the Sea in the face of a cock-boat or a cockle-shell with the British Flag aboard!* Hate is always allied to Fear, and his venom is excited against you because you again threaten to overthrow all his plans and subvert all his machinations. Give him then, my gallant Fellows, abundant cause to continue this sentiment towards you—*sink and destroy his flat-bottomed Flotilla* to the tune of *Rule Britannia!*—Let the batteries open from our *Wooden Walls, and the Ditch will soon be filled with the Army of Republican Invaders!* and should the LITTLE UPSTART himself venture forth upon the expedition (which I very much doubt), *Jack* will, I am sure, throw him out a rope, to haul him aboard, and make *this speaker of lies for once speak truth perforce. Buonaparté shall land at Dover, and accompanied by the* real *Army of England, take up his quarters in the Tower of London, and call forth public rejoicings on his arrival in the capital!!*—This he has declared to be his purpose, and though vain boasters generally say more than they mean, you shall make him *for once* be as good as his word. *The British Navy is infallible*—Her Sons, like her Ships, are *Hearts of Oak*, and French iron, French steel, or even *French brass* are alike impotent in the attempt to penetrate either the one or the other—

> Strike then, my gallant Fellows! Rule the Waves!
> For BRITONS never, never will be SLAVES!!!

London, July 11, 1803.   PUBLICOLA.

Printed for J. GINGER, 169, Piccadilly, Price 6d. a Dozen for distribution; by D. N. SHURY, Berwick Street.

[C. L., No. 46. Single sheet printed on one side, in one column. 10½ × 17½. *Bibl. Lind.*, No. 1525. Brit. Mus. *Catalogue, s.v.* "Navy."]

John Bull Turned Into A Galley Slave;

Or, the Corsican Bonaparte, (The Grand Subjugator's) New Plan for Raising an Army of British Volunteers,

By which he Means first to give Liberty to Poland,
and then Conquer Prussia, Austria, and Russia.
Being the Sequel to an Address to the
Mechanics, Artificers, &c.

IN addition to what I have already stated, one more circumstance has occurred to me, and though *last*, will certainly not be found the *least*. It is this—admit for a moment, (though God forbid that so dreadful and improbable an event should ever happen) that this country, or even the smallest part of it, should be conquered, what would be the inevitable consequence, in addition to the horrid miseries I have before described? It would, beyond all doubt, be this: Bonaparte's first object would necessarily be to recruit his army, in order to replace the many thousands that he must have lost. For, should the Tyrant have conquered but part of England, he will feel the absolute necessity of raising fresh troops to incorporate with his own, in the hope of being enabled to subdue the remainder; and should he have conquered the whole, what finer troops could the world afford to this cruel and insatiable monster of ambition, for the conquest of Austria and Prussia, than an army composed of Britons,—a nation which experience has taught him is the bravest and most formidable he ever had to cope with. Here then would be no *volunteering*, no *ballotting*, unless, indeed such *Volunteers* as were raised in France for the conquest of St. Domingo. And how were these raised? Why by every man having a bayonet put to his breast, being seized by force, and then *chained in couples like dogs*, and drove down in a string to the coast for embarkation like so many *Galley-slaves*. This, though it may sound incredible to an Englishman's ear, is a fact known to all Europe.

Such my brave Countrymen, would be your dreadful fate, could this blessed island be once subjugated to that haughty and merciless Tyrant, the Corsican Bonaparte. Where then is the man who would not die a thousand and a thousand deaths sooner than submit to so cruel and unnatural a fate?

Think well of this, brave Britons, 'ere it be too late; and if it be our lot to fall individually in this glorious cause, let us remember that we shall have, at least contributed our part to save our Country, and that we shall die with the blessings of our dear Countrymen.

Printed for JOHN GINGER, No. 169, Piccadilly.

Price SIXPENCE *per Dozen*.

N. B. It is earnestly requested that those who can afford it, will distribute these Papers among them who cannot.—*Ladies*, and Women of all ranks think of this!

W. FLINT, Printer, Old Bailey.

[C. L., No. 47. Single sheet printed on one side, in one column. 11 × 17. *Bibl. Lind.*, No. 1499. Brit. Mus. *Catalogue, s.v.* "Bull (John)."]

English Mastiffs,

WE, by this Address, publicly and solemnly, before God and our Country, pledge our Fortunes, Persons, and Lives, in the Defence of our Sovereign and all the Blessings of our glorious Constitution.

There is not a Man that hears me, I am persuaded, who is not prompt and eager to redeem that pledge. There is not, there cannot be a Man here, who would leave undefended our good, tried, and brave OLD KING in the Hour of Danger.

No, Sir! we need now no Warning-voice; no string of Eloquence; no Thoughts that heat, and Words that burn, are necessary to raise a Host of hardy Men, when the King, the Parliament, and the Country are in Distress. CALL OUT TO YORKSHIREMEN, "COME FORTH TO BATTLE!"—our Answer will be, One and All—"WE ARE READY!—*There is the Enemy! —Lead on!*"—Sir; that Enemy is not far off; a very numerous, well-appointed, ably-commanded Army, to whom is promised the Plunder of England, are now hovering round, and Part of them in daily Sight of the promised Land. They view it, like as many famished Wolves, Cruel as Death, and Hungry as the Grave, panting for an Opportunity, at any Risk, to come into our Sheep-Fold;—*but*, and if they should, is it not our Business, our first Duty, to have such a Guard of old faithful ENGLISH MASTIFFS, of the old Breed, as shall make them quickly repent their temerity.

The CHIEF CONSUL of France tells us, that we are but a Nation of Shopkeepers: let us, Shopkeepers, then melt our Weights and our Scales, and return him the Compliment in Bullets. SIR; we may have a firm reliance on the Exertions of as gallant a Fleet as ever sailed; but the Fleet cannot perform Impossibility; it cannot be in two Places at once; it cannot conquer the Winds and subdue the Storms. Though our old TARS can do much, they cannot do every Thing; and it would be unsafe and dastardly to lie skulking behind them. With the Blessing of GOD, and a good Cause, we can do Wonders; but, if we depend upon our Naval Prowess only we have much to fear. No, SIR: England will never be perfectly safe, until she can defend herself as well by *Land* as by *Sea;* until she can defy the haughty Foe: if there was *even a Bridge* between CALAIS and DOVER, and that Bridge in Possession of the Enemy, still she can say in the Language of a good *English Boxing Match*, "A FAIR FIELD AND NO FAVOUR!"

Printed for J. GINGER, 169, Piccadilly,
Price SIXPENCE per Dozen, for Distribution.

WHERE MAY BE HAD ALL THE PATRIOTIC PAPERS PUBLISHED, PROPERLY ASSORTED.   W. MARCHANT, Printer, 3, Greville-Street, Holborn.

[C. L., No. 48. Single sheet printed on one side, in one column. 11 × 17. *Bibl. Lind.*, No. 1489. Brit. Mus. *Catalogue, s.v.* "English."]

Brave Soldiers, Defenders of Your Country!

THE road to glory is open before you—Pursue the great career of your Forefathers, and rival them in the field of honour. A *proud and usurping* TYRANT (a name ever execrated by Englishmen) dares to *threaten our shores with* INVASION, *and to reduce the free-born Sons of Britain to* SLAVERY *and* SERVITUDE! Forgetting what English Soldiers are capable of, and ranking them with the Hirelings of the Powers who have fallen his prey on the Continent, he supposes his threat easily executed. *Give him a lesson, my brave Countrymen, that he will not easily forget, and that France may have by heart for a Century to come!* Neither the vaunting Hero (who deserted his own Comrades and Soldiers in Egypt), nor the French Army, have ever been able to cope with British valour when fairly opposed to it. Our ancestors declared, that ONE ENGLISHMAN *was ever a match for* THREE FRENCHMEN—and that man to man was too great odds in our favour. We have but to feel their sentiments to confirm them;—you will find that their declaration was founded on experience; and that even in our day, within these three years, an army of your brave Comrades has convinced its admiring Country that the balance is still as great as ever against the enemy. *Our* EDWARD, *the illustrious Black Prince, laid waste the Country of France to the Gates of Paris, and on the Plains of Cressy left* 11 *Princes and* 30,000 *men dead upon the Field of Battle—a greater number than the whole English Army boasted at the beginning of the action.* The same heroic Prince, having annihilated the Fleet of France, *entirely routed her Army at Poictiers, took her King prisoner, and brought him Captive to London,* with thousands of his Nobles and People, and *all this against an Army* SIX TIMES AS NUMEROUS AS THAT OF THE ENGLISH! Did not our Harry the Fifth invade France, and at Agincourt *oppose an Army of* 9000 *men, sickly, fatigued, and half starved, to that of the French amounting to* 50,000: and did he not leave 10,000 of the enemy dead upon the field, and take 14,000 prisoners, with the loss of only 400 men?

Have we not, within this century, to boast a MARL-BOROUGH, who (besides his other Victories) at Blenheim slew 12,000 of the French, and made 14,000 Prisoners, and *in less than a month conquered* 300 *miles of Territory from the enemy?*

And are not the glorious of our ABERCROMBY *and the gallant* ARMY OF EGYPT fresh in your minds? *An Army of* 14,000 *Britons, who landed in the face of upwards of* 20,000 *troops of France,* and drove from a country, with whose strong holds they were acquainted, and whose resources they knew how to apply, a host of Frenchmen enured to the climate, and veterans in arms? *Did they not cut to pieces that vaunted Corps of Buonaparte's, whose successes against other Powers had obtained it the appellation of* INVINCIBLE—and is not their Standard (all that is left of it) a trophy at this moment in our Capital?

The Briton fights for his Liberty and Rights, the Frenchman fights for *Buonaparté*, who has robbed him of both! Which, then, in the nature of events, will be most zealous, most active, and most terrible in the Field of Battle?—the independent supporter of his country's cause, or the Slave who trembles lest the arms of his comrades should be turned against himself; who knows that his Leader, his General, his *Tyrant, did not hesitate, after having* MURDERED 4000 *disarmed Turks in cool blood, to* POISON 300 *of his own sick Soldiers, of men who had been fighting his battles of ambition, and been wounded in his defence.* English Soldiers will scarcely credit this, but it is on record not to be doubted, never to be expunged. But more; read and blush for the depravity even of an enemy. It is not that these bloody deeds have been perpetrated from necessity, from circumstances however imperious at the moment; they were the acts of cool and deliberate determination, and his purpose, no less sanguinary, is again declared in the event of success in his enterprize against this Country. Feeling that even the slavish followers of his fortune were not to be forced to embark in this ruinous and destructive expedition, he declares to them in a public proclamation, or decoy, that *when they have landed in this Country, in order to make the booty the richer,* NO QUARTER *shall be given to the* BASE ENGLISH, *who fight for their perfidious Government—that they are to be* PUT TO THE SWORD, *and their Property distributed among the Soldiers of the Victorious Army!!!* Say is this the conduct of a Hero? is this the man who is destined to break the spirit of Englishmen? *shall we suffer an* ASSASSIN *to enter our blessed Country, and despoil our fields of their produce—to massacre our brave Soldiers in cool blood, and hang up every man who has carried arms?* Your cry is Ven-

geance for the insult—and vengenace is in your own hands.
It must be signal and terrible! Like the bolt from Heaven let
it strike the devoted Army of Invaders! *Every Frenchman will
find his Grave where he first steps on British ground, and not a
Soldier of Buonaparte's boasted Legions shall escape the fate his
ambitious Tyrant has prepared for him!*

Britons Strike Home!

Or your Fame is for ever blasted,—your Liberties for ever lost!!!

PUBLICOLA.

—————

Printed by D. N. SHURY, Berwick Street, Soho,
for J. GINGER, 169, *Piccadilly; Price 6d. a Dozen for distribution.*

[C. L., No. 49. Single sheet printed on one side, in one column. 10½ × 17½. *Bibl. Lind.*,
No. 1481. Brit. Mus. *Catalogue, s.v.* "Publicola."]

—————

Invasion!

—————

*A Familiar Letter from John Bull
to his Countrymen, on the Report of an Invasion.*

My FRIENDS and COUNTRYMEN,

WE are once more threatened with an Invasion from our
Neighbours, the French. Were I to offer an opinion, I should
say, they will not dare to make so rash an attempt. But
whatever may be your opinion and mine, on the subject, it
should operate no further, than to give us confidence in our
means of Defence, and in the Valour and firmness which will
be displayed by us all, should the Enemy presume to put the
matter to the test. We have nothing to fear, if we are

UNANIMOUS and WELL PREPARED.

But strong as we are, we cannot answer for the event, if by a misplaced confidence we take no precautions, or by our indifference, we suggest to our enemy a chance of success, to which he will never look, if he finds we are ready to receive, and determined to repulse his attack.

NOW is the TIME,

therefore to open your purses, and to Volunteer your Persons in the Defence of your Country. An efficient, and quick Disciplined Army, produced by British Energy and Patriotism, will not fail to carry dismay into the Hearts of your Enemies, and Teach them to Pause, before they Rashly Invade the Territory and Rights of ENGLISHMEN!!

They may tell you, they are come to Redress your Grievances, to give you Plenty, to Disburthen you of your Taxes, and to equalize your Rights. But will you believe them? Have the French acted that part towards other Countries which they have Conquered? Did they Invade Egypt, Switzerland, Holland, and Hanover, for the purpose of giving Freedom, to the Inhabitants of those Countries? Has the Government of France conferred that advantage even on its Own Subjects? No! There is no Civilized Country in Europe, under a more Arbitrary Government, than France is at present. How then can it be expected, that the French should act so favourably towards the People of England, whom they have always looked upon with the most jealous eye, and by whose Virtue and Valour, they have been prevented from enslaving all Europe. Would they not rather retaliate upon us for our opposition to their views, than come over as Friends to relieve the Distresses of the Poor, and give them Freedom, Plenty and a Peace. Could we be weak and blind-sighted enough to offer them a favourable reception, can it for moment be supposed, that they would be so *Kind and Neighbourly*, as to pay us a *Friendly* Visit at their own expence? No! The least-informed of us all, must know, that *Retribution* would be their first object, and that not a trifling one, to reimburse the immense expense, which they now incur to menace our Coasts.

It is true the articles of life, particularly Provisions, are high in price, beyond all former precedents; the Taxes are heavy to an extreme degree; and many of us are at a loss to subsist ourselves and Families; even upon the smallest scale. But why should we despond? It has been the characteristick of the English, particularly during our late contest, to bear such inconveniences with firmness and resignation; virtues which reflect more lustre upon their character, than all the Trophies which decorate the conquests of their Enemies. Then surely our pride will not allow us to lose what we have so honourably acquired; or to give way to despair, when the prospect is brightening, and when by a steady perseverance, we shall ultimately conquer all our difficulties. Have not we a favourable season before us, and a plentiful harvest? You may tell me there are Monopolists, regraters and the like, who will keep up the price of Provisions, even in the midst of Plenty. It may be so; but it cannot be supposed that they will carry their Speculations beyond their own interests; or if they do, that the Government, whose wisdom and solicitude for the Public Good, have been so conspicious, will pass over unnoticed, the wants of the People, when it is fully convinced, that the Country can relieve them. Will the *French* give you plenty by bringing an immense Army into the Country, to feed upon its produce, which but lately was incapable of supplying its own inhabitants? Will your Harvest be benefited by the march of such an Army over your Corn-fields; by numerous Encampments; or by the depredations always attached to a Military life on service, and to a French Army beyond all others? Will your Taxes be reduced, or your Property secured, by French retribution, and a confiscation of all Property? The result of a successful Invasion, is too obvious to need an inference. But there is one argument, which I am convinced, will have weight in the mind of an Englishman, should every other fail: and this is the disgrace of allowing himself to be conquered by an enemy, whom he has always regarded with contempt; whose disposition, sentiments, and habits are in direct opposition to his own; and who by destroying the National Character, which so long has preserved the honour of our Country, would endeavour to convert our Sons into *Petit Maitres, our Wives and Daughters, into Kept Mistresses.*

I am convinced that while I am thus indulging my own reflections, there are few of my Countrymen, who have not made similar ones, or who do not agree with me, that whatever may be our grievances, we shall forget them the moment the Enemy appears upon our Coast, and by a

VIGOROUS EXERTION,

consider only, how we can contribute to his discomfiture and defeat,

JOHN BULL.

July 5th 1803.

———————

Printed by A Seale, 15, Terrace, Tottenham
Court Road: for Mr. West London Street.

[C. L., No. 50. Single sheet printed on one side, in one column. 10½ × 17¾. *Bibl. Lind.,* No. 1523. Brit. Mus. *Catalogue, s.v.* "Bull (John)."]

English, Scots, and Irishmen.

A Patriotic Address to the Inhabitants of the United Kingdom.

By John Mayne.

English, Scots, and Irishmen,
All that are in valour's ken!
Shield your King; and flock agen
   Where his sacred Banners fly!
Now's the day, and now's the hour,
Frenchmen wou'd the Land devour—
Will ye wait till they come o'er
   To give ye Chains and Slavery?

Who wou'd be a Frenchman's slave?
Who wou'd truckle to the knave?
Who wou'd shun a glorious grave
   For worse than death, for—infamy?
To see your Liberties expire—
Your Temples smoke, your Fleets on fire!
That's a Frenchman's sole desire—
   That's your fate, or—Liberty!

Robb'd of all that sweetens life,
Tranquil home and happy wife!
Reeking from the villain's knife,
   Yonder harmless Peasant see—
Prostrate near him on the heath,
A ruin'd Daughter gasps for breath!
Frenchmen riot in their death—
   That's to them a luxury!

In fancy'd conquest over you,
The Tyrant tells his tyger-crew—
If chains will not your minds subdue,
   Nor exile, stripes, and poverty,
Then, when the Land is all defil'd,
He'll butcher woman, man and child—
He'll turn your gardens to a wild—
   Your Courts, to caves of misery!

Mothers, Sisters, Sweethearts dear,
All that VIRTUE gives us here!
Can your Sons or Lovers fear
   When Frenchmen threaten slavery?
O! no!—In hosts of VOLUNTEERS,
The GENIUS of the ISLE appears!
With dauntless breast, BRITANNIA rears
   Her arm, and points to VICTORY!

IRISH, SCOTS, and ENGLISHMEN,
All that WORTH and VALOUR ken!
Shield your KING; and flock agen
   Where his sacred Banners fly!
Now's the day, and now's the hour,
Frenchmen wou'd the Land devour—
To arms! to arms! and make them cow'r,
   Or meet their certain destiny!

PRINTED BY A. WILSON, WILD COURT, LINCOLN'S INN FIELDS,
FOR W. J. AND J. RICHARDSON, ROYAL EXCHANGE.
JULY 1803.

[C. L., No. 51. Single sheet printed on one side, in two columns. 10 × 17. Brit. Mus. *Catalogue*,
s.v. "Mayne (John) of Dumfries."]

The Menaces of Bonaparte.

What Strange Things are Come to Pass!!

A LITTLE insignificant Man, not more than fifty inches high, with an half starved Army, that would faint at the sight of an English Bull, has dared to say that he will

Conquer Four Millions of Englishmen!!

ENGLISHMEN, whom the brave Romans themselves, that subdued the rest of the World, could hardly conquer!! Englishmen, whose name is feared and respected over the whole Universe.

CONQUER FOUR MILLIONS OF ENGLISHMEN!! What can this mean? Why it means that this presumptuous little man conceives that Englishmen are dead to every sense of Virtue; that the love of their Country, no longer animates their breasts; that the courage for which heretofore they have been so preeminent, has forsaken their hearts; and that, without a struggle, they will tamely and basely lay down their arms upon the TYRANTS approach. In short, that the

BRITISH LION

is become as docile and tame as a LADY'S LAP-DOG, and that he will allow himself to be kicked, buffeted, and trampled upon, without even a growl to shew that he feels the foot of his oppressor. Good Heavens what an imputation!! Can you set down with an appetite to your meals, can you retire quietly to rest, can you follow your daily occupations, under such a charge, and not move one step to express your indignation? Does not your blood boil at the very idea of Englishmen's patriotism being so questioned? Can you indifferently allow yourselves to be accused of forgetting the enjoyments of your mild laws, which equally afford to every man protection to his property and person; of your fertile soil which rewards the labourer's toil with plenty; of your extensive commerce which conveys to your hands, riches, and all the luxuries of the World; and of your beautiful Women, who to every domestic comfort; bring you strong and Virtuous Children, to hand down to posterity the honourable name and qualifications of ENGLISHMEN? All these, and a great many more blessings will you lose, if you do not hastily step forward to prove, that you have hearts to vindicate the charge, and hands to protect your Country, and its Rights, against all Aggressors. But if you can quietly set down with such glaring insults, then shall I say that ENGLISHMEN are

CONQUERED!

then may the USURPER Sheath his Sword, and put by the implements of destruction, with all the Paraphernalia of War, and with a few of   His Banditti

only, come over to receive the degraded submission of CONQUERED BRITAIN!! But this shall never happen. Sooner may the avenging hand of Heaven avert the disgrace, and by one grand concussion destroy every vestige, that could hand down to Posterity, the name, or recollection of such a race, as ENGLISHMEN.   THE BRITISH LION.

Price One Penny, or 6d. per Dozen for distribution.—Printed by A. Seale, 15, Terrace, Tottenham-Court-Road.

[C. L., No. 52. Single sheet printed on one side, in one column. 10½ × 17. *Bibl. Lind.*, No. 1502. Brit. Mus. *Catalogue, s.v.* "Napoleon I."]

Advice

Suggested by the State of the Times.

By William Wilberforce, Esq.
Member of Parliament for the County of York.

IT has been maintained, and will not be disputed by any sound or experienced politician, that they who really deserve the appellation of TRUE CHRISTIANS are always most important members of the community. But we may boldly assert, that there never was a period wherein, more justly than in the present, this could be affirmed of them, whether the situation, in all its circumstances, of our own country be attentively considered, or the general state of society in Europe. Let them on their part seriously weigh the important station which they fill, and the various duties which it now peculiarly enforces on them. If we consult the most intelligent accounts of foreign countries, which have been recently published, and compare them with the reports of former travellers, we must be convinced, that Religion and the standard of morals are every where declining, abroad even more rapidly than in our own country. But still, the progress of irreligion, and the decay of morals at home, is such as to alarm every considerate mind, and to forebode the worst consequences, unless some remedy can be applied to the growing evil. We can depend only upon *true Christians* for effecting, in any degree, this important service. Zeal is required in the cause of Religion; they only can feel it. The charge of singularity must be incurred; they only will dare to encounter it. Uniformity of conduct, and perseverance in exertion, will be requisite; among no others can we look for those qualities.

Let *true Christians* then, with becoming earnestness, strive in all things to recommend their profession, and to put to silence the vain scoffs of ignorant objectors. Let them boldly assert the cause of Christ in an age when so many, who bear the name of Christians, are ashamed of Him: let them consider as devolved on Them the important duty of suspending for a while the fall of their country, and, perhaps, of performing a still more extensive service to society at large; not by busy interference in politics, in which it must be confessed there is much uncertainty, but rather by that sure and radical benefit of restoring the influence of Religion, and of raising the standard of morality.

Let them cultivate a catholic spirit of universal good will and amicable fellowship towards all those, of whatever sect or denomination, who, differing from them in non-essentials, agree with them in the grand fundamentals of Religion. Let them countenance men of real piety wherever they are found, and encourage in others every attempt to repress the progress of vice, and to revive and diffuse the influence of Religion and virtue. Let their earnest prayers be constantly offered, that such endeavours may be successful, and that the abused long-suffering of God may still continue to us the invaluable privilege of vital Christianity.

Let them pray continually for their country in this season of national difficulty. We bear upon us but too plainly the marks of a declining empire. Who can say but that the Governor of the universe, who declares himself to be a God who hears the prayers of his servants, may, in answer to their intercessions, for a while avert our ruin, and continue to us the fulness of those temporal blessings, which in such abundant measure we have hitherto enjoyed? Men of the world, indeed, however they may admit the natural operation of natural causes, and may therefore confess the effects of Religion and morality in promoting the well-being of the community, may yet, according to their humour, with a smile of complacent pity, or a snear of supercilious contempt, read of the service which *real Christians* may render to their country, by conciliating the favour, and calling down the blessing of Providence. It may appear in their eyes an instance of the same superstitious weakness, as that which prompts the terrified inhabitant of Sicily to bring forth the image of his tutelar saint, in order to stop the destructive ravages of Ætna. We are, however, sure, if we believe the Scripture, that God will be disposed to favour the nation to which his servants belong; and that, in fact, such as They have often been the unknown and unhonoured instruments of drawing down on their country the blessings of safety and protection.

But it would be an instance in myself of that very false shame which I have condemned in others, if I were not boldly to avow my firm persuasion, that *to the decline of Religion and morality our national difficulties must both directly and indirectly be chiefly ascribed; and that* MY *only solid hopes for the well-being of my country depend not so much on her fleets and armies, not so much on the wisdom of her rulers, or the spirit of her people, as on the persuasion that she still contains many, who, in a degenerate age, love and obey the Gospel of Christ, on the humble trust that the intercession of these may still be prevalent, that for the sake of these, Heaven may still look upon us with an eye of favour.*

Published by J. HATCHARD, 190, *Piccadilly;* J. ASPERNE, *Cornhill;* J. DOWNES, *Temple Bar;* J. SPRAGG, *King Street, Covent Garden;* W. DWYER, 29, *Holborn;* and E. BURNS, 54, *Tottenham Court Road;* where may be had the following new Publication, Price 3d. each Number, or 2s. 6d. a Dozen; (to be continued every Saturday;) The LOYALIST: containing original and select Papers; intended to rouse and animate the British Nation, during the present important Crisis; and to direct its united Energies against the perfidious Attempts of a malignant, cruel, and impious Foe. Addressed to all patriotic Persons; especially, to the Soldiers, Sailors, and Loyal Volunteers, throughout England, Wales, Scotland, and Ireland. Recommended for liberal Distribution in every City, Town, Village, Camp, and Cottage of the United Kingdom.

Price 9d. per Dozen for Distribution, or 1d. each.

S. GOSNELL, Printer, Little Queen Street, Holborn.

[C. L., No. 53. Single sheet printed on one side, in two columns. 11 × 17½. *Bibl. Lind.,* No. 1475. Brit. Mus. *Catalogue, s.v.* "Wilberforce (William)."]

Freedom and Loyalty:
WITH A NEW SONG.

IN every Nation the COMMON PEOPLE must unavoidably become the first Victims of a violent or protracted WAR; because they always constitute the bulk of a nation, and are least able to bear the hardships of Plunder and Desolation. When the Rich are pillaged, the Poor lose the price of their labour: and when daily employment fails, Death stares the poor in the face. *To you, therefore, my countrymen, I particularly address myself.*

WE are now engaged in a cause which no less concerns the Peasant in his Cottage, than the Prince on his Throne. We are contending against an INVETERATE FOE, who aims at the Destruction of everything dear to you as ENGLISHMEN. We are threatened on our own Shores, and in our own Houses. Our domestic, civil, and religious Privileges are ALL at stake. The existence of our Wives, our Children, our Relations, our Friends, our Family comforts, our Freedom, our Trade, and our Property, may depend on your immediate exertions.

Let BRITONS, at this awful moment, consider how much they may lose, and against whom they are contending. *Did not that cruel Deceiver, Bonaparte, when in Egypt, coolly* MURDER *his Captives by Thousands? Did he not even poison 580 of his wounded Companions, who had faithfully been fighting his Battles?* Does he not still enslave, imprison, and export the FRENCHMEN, who dislike his vile Tyranny? And has he not increased the Taxes *fourfold* in every part of his Dominions? What then have Free-born BRITONS to expect? The CONSUL himself has told you—FIRE, and SWORD, and PLUNDER, *wherever he finds the English in Arms!!!* How implacable is his hatred! He invites and stimulates his Soldiers to the present War by promising to afford

"No Quarter to the English, who defend their Country"!

And if you do but once receive the Invader, *forget not the* CHAINS *he has prepared for Yourselves, your Wives, and your Children.* Remember the SWISS, the DUTCH, and the HANOVERIANS, whose lives he has spared to make them his *obedient Vassals.* But, especially, my Countrymen, recollect that BONAPARTE so envies your Liberty, your Commerce, your Trade, your Greatness, your Privileges, your Happiness, and your PATERNAL KING, that nothing short of utter Ruin, and inevitable Death is held out as our Portion.

Awake, then, my Friends; be roused, *and shew yourselves* MEN. Who can decline to meet such an ENEMY on our own SHORES? Who does not burn to repel this CORSICAN INVADER? If he *dare* to send his Armies, and to head those deluded Slaves, let the BRITISH LION arise to devour them. GOD HELPING US, we WILL arise, and unite as one Man:

Like our Fathers of old, We will Unite and Conquer.

GREAT GEORGE: A NEW SONG.

To the Tune of *"God save the King."*

1

FAME, let they trumpet sound,
Tell all the world around,
  Great George is King;
Tell France, and all her train,
Britannia scorns their chain,
All their vile arts are vain,
  God spares our King.

2

May Heav'n his life defend,
And make his race extend
  Wide as his fame.
Thy choicest blessings shed
On his most favour'd head,
And make his foes to dread
  Great George's name.

3

He peace and plenty gives;
While Bonaparte lives
  But to destroy.
Then let his people sing,
God save great George the King,
From whom our comforts spring,
  Freedom and joy.

JULY 30, 1803.   BY A TRUE BRITON.

N. B. All true Britons are very earnestly desired to read "Important Con-siderations for the People of this Kingdom": Sold by J. DOWNES, Temple Bar; J. SPRAGG, King Street, Covent Garden; J. ASPERNE, Cornhill; J. HATCHARD, Piccadilly; and E. BURNS, 54, Tottenham Court Road. Price 2d. or 1s. 6d. per Dozen.

Printed for E. BURNS, 54, Tottenham Court Road;
by S. GOSNELL, Little Queen Street, Holborn:
Price 9d. per Dozen for Distribution, or 1d. each.

[C. L., No. 54. Single sheet printed on one side, in one column; except first two stanzas of verse. 11 × 17. *Bibl. Lind.*, No. 1537. Brit. Mus. *Catalogue, s.v.* "Freedom."]

THE CONSEQUENCES OF
Buonaparte's Succeeding
IN HIS DESIGNS AGAINST THIS COUNTRY.

Universal Pillage.
Men of all Parties Slaughtered.
Women of all Ranks Violated.
Children Murdered.
Trade Ruined.
The Labouring Classes thrown out of Employment.
Famine, with all its Horrors.
Despotism Triumphant.
The remaining Inhabitants carried away by
　　Ship-loads to Foreign Lands.

Britons! Look before you;

AND REMEMBER, that by Combined and Vigorous Re-sistance, under GOD, You may prevent all these Evils: Yet do not trifle with Your Danger; for nothing short of this may be sufficient for Your Security. Although these Horrors be threatened, Your Cause is Good, and Your Resources are great: Let Your Courage be equal to the Magnitude of the Evil, the Goodness of Your Cause, and the Strength of Your Resources.

See a small Tract entitled the "Prospect," in which the Arguments, on which the above mentioned Consequences are grounded, are Calmly and Freely stated. The Tract is Sold at Messrs Rivington's, St. Paul's Church-Yard, and at Hatchard's, Piccadilly, price *Threepence.*—Of the latter may be had an extensive Assortment of Tracts, Posting-Bills, Songs, &c. calculated to shew the horrid Consequences of French Invasion; and that the only Means, under God, of preventing it is our all UNITING as ONE MAN, in Defence of Our Beloved King and unrivalled Constitution.

London. Printed by J. Hales, Old Boswell Court, for J. Hatchard, *Piccadilly. Price* Sixpence *per Dozen.*

[C. L., No. 55. Single sheet printed on one side, in one column. 10½ × 17. *Bibl. Lind.,* No. 1485. Brit. Mus. *Catalogue, s.v.* "Napoleon I."]

THE ANTIGALLICAN CLUB.

For Our Country.

Held at the Sign of the *British Lion,* in OAKLAND.

PRESENT,

Crispin Heeltap, *Cobler,* in the Chair.

Toby Tun, *Landlord.*

Charles Caxon, *Barber.*	Matt Manchet, *Baker.*	Paul Pitt, *Tanner.*
Harry Hobnail, *Farrier.*	Kit Crossbones, *Sexton.*	Tom Tray, *Butcher.*
Ben Button, *Taylor.*	Moses Medley, *Shopkeeper.*	Peter Ploughshare, *Farmer.*
Frank Fell, *Currier.*	Sam Sledge, *Smith.*	Adam Amen, *Clerk.*

Constable, and Others.

Scene, the Front Room at the Lion. *Time, Evening.*

Cobler. CALL Landlord!   [*Bell rings.*

The Landlord *enters.*

Cobler. My friend, *Toby Tun,* I am, by the unanimous vote of the Club now present, directed to thank you for fitting up this room for their reception. Egad, Pound'em, the 'Pothecary, seeing the bow window open, and smoak issuing out, said, as he came up the hill, that this was the Lion's Mouth, and the upper story his Nostrils.

Landlord. Nobody's better at a *story* than little Pound'em; ours is *raised*, his are generally *long*. But, with respect to the appellation, I must differ from my learned friend, as I did when he said I had fortified my house, because I hoisted the colours, and planted a few cannon to fire on the king's birthday, &c. I then told him, we did not mean to be cooped up in garrison; that our hearts were our best fortifications; that we had as much right to guns as he had to mortars. Therefore, Gemmen, as I know both your courage and generosity, I have christened this club-room the Lion's Den.

All. That's right, Uncle Toby.

Cobler. Let this be written over the door.

Clerk. Amen!

Cobler. Now to business. Were any minutes taken when we met under the great tree in the church-yard, to determine *upperleather* and *sole*, to oppose the Corsican Usurper, who threatens to take our *alls*, and make an *end* of us?

Landlord. If any *minutes* were taken, they were turned into *hours*, and merrily spent here, and at the Royal George, in drinking *tory-rory*, and singing GOD SAVE THE KING, and BRITON'S, STRIKE HOME.

Sexton. After debating upon *grave* subjects, we came here, and passed a jolly evening.

Barber. Our ancestors and friends laid snug and quiet, and we had no fears that they would rise to haunt us, as they say the Egyptian Ghosts do the Murderer of Jaffa; and the Spirits of his Comrades, the Poisoner of the sick Soldiers in the Hospitals. Heavens! my countrymen, what a fellow is this Bonaparte? To think of coming here, indeed! Did not Pound'em say that, wheresoever he goes, he's attended by three thousand eight hundred mummies? The very idea makes one's *hair* stand an end! and that all that he has murdered, appear in succession, and shake their gory *locks* at him. Some Africans, frizzled like the head of Mungo, and others, European, strait as the tuft of *hair* that hangs from the end of my *pole*.

Cobler. That's all true, Master Caxon.

Barber. In fact, by his wishing to be at the *head* of every thing, I take the dog to be a Whig; or rather, after he had given his Egyptian army the *bag*, a dictator to all the Whigs of Europe. The Dutch he considers as *full bottoms:* the Germans, as *majors*, *brigadiers*, and *ramilees:* the Swiss as *perriwiged* with snow: the Flemings, as *collyflowers*, which he can cabbage whenever he pleases. Has he not clap'd a *tye* upon the *head* of the Spaniards, given the Portuguese a *bob*, crop'd all the ancient nobility of France, and made *Brutuses* of all his associates? Does he not now threaten to furnish us with plenty of *scratches:* to bring his *curling-irons*, and *powder*, and *dress* us? Has he not been preparing *puffs* and *powder-machines* for several months? Therefore, can our countrymen be such *blocks* as not to be convinced that he has formed a *meal-tub* plot against this kingdom?

Cobler. Did not Primer, the School-master, tell us last night, that Italy was in the shape of a large *boot*, and that Bonaparte has been stretching it till the *stitches* cracked again? Has he not considered the Popedom as the *calf*, and got *his leg* into it? and will not his *foot* reach to the kingdom of Naples and Otranto, its *instep*, *sole*, and *heelpiece?* If he comes to our shop for some *Royal Brunswick Blacking* for it, we must take care not to let him have any: for though he has pummeled many like a piece of leather upon a *lapstone*, and reduced them from *shoes* to *slippers*, I hope here he will turn out to be of my profession, a *Cobler*, and find us the toughest job he has ever undertaken.

Currier. He brags, neighbour Heeltap, that he has cut down whole forests, to make wooden shoes for us, merely to spoil your trade and mine.

Tanner. And mine also; for which I wish I had him in one of my *Tan-pits*.

Farmer. I hear he means to *harrow* up our native land, to *mow* us down, and to take our *stacks* into his *granaries*.

Miller. Yes, and to take treble *toll*, and then grind us to powder.

Butcher. He will make us eat *soup maigre*, which you are to understand, Gemmen, is a pound of lean beef, perhaps, from the land of Pharoah, boiled in a pail of water; so that it looks in the dish, like the Island of Malta in the midst of the Mediterranean Sea.

Baker. Though we may have plenty of *dead men*, yet, if he comes here, he will not only take our *tallies*, but our *bread*.

Farrier. He means to *rowel* us; he has kept our wounds open, and now provokes *a discharge*.

Smith. He has forged a thousand lies of our good King and his administration; therefore, let's stop his *wind holes*, and strike while the iron's hot.

Fidler. The dog said he would make us *dance* without a fiddle. Did you ever hear of such a thing, Gemmen? But if we take our *instruments* in hand, I believe that we shall *tune* him.

Shopkeeper. We shall soon settle the Balance of Power: I fancy his *scale* will kick the *beam*.

Sexton. If he falls, he will have no mourners: I should like to provide him a *patent coffin* of cast iron.

Smith. Right: That would be for the good *of trade;* I'll *rivit* him into it gratis.

Constable. That is the only way to *bind* him to keep *the peace;* you all know that he forfeited his former *recognizance,* and his *sureties* proved insufficient.

Smith. Therefore, as this man has more *vices* than are to be found in my shop, I move, while this *heat* is upon the anvil, that he may be beaten.

Cobler. There is but one way: as we have got to our *last*, let us stick as close as *wax* to each other. Your houses, my friends, are your castles, and so is my stall. If Bonaparte comes, I can tell you, he will pay no more respect to the stall of the poorest cobler, than to that of the richest canon; we shall all fare alike. The crown is in danger; the church is in danger; the constitution, which comprehends both, is in danger; your wives and daughters are in danger: let us, therefore, like true Antigallicans, turn out Volunteers, heart and hand, to defend our king and country, our religion and families. I hate conscriptions as much as I do prescriptions. I hope Pound'em does not hear me. Let us not be forced to the drill.

Taylor. No; for if we are not quick in our *measures*, the Corsican will come with his long *needles*, and *drill* holes thro' us. He'll pink our doublets, and sit upon our skirts.

Cobler. Therefore, let us take a glass round to the health of his MAJESTY, and then go and enroll ourselves in the honourable list of heroes that stand forth at this perilous crisis to defend their king and country.

Landlord. I move an amendment: let us take another glass to our good queen, and our lovely princesses, the patroness and representatives of the virtues and beauty of the ladies of the united kingdom; another to the Prince of Wales, and his royal brothers, representatives of the courage and honour of the gentlemen; another to administration; another to the wooden walls of Old England; and another to the volunteer corps of this kingdom.

Barber. I second the amendment. Fidler, strike up GOD SAVE THE KING.

Clerk. And, as in duty bound, I say, AMEN!

Printed for JAMES ASPERNE, (Successor to Mr. SEWELL,) at the Bible, Crown, and Constitution, No. 32, Cornhill, by T. MAIDEN, Sherbourn Lane; Price One Penny, or 6s. the 100.

*** *JAMES ASPERNE respectfully informs Noblemen, Magistrates, and Gentlemen, that he keeps ready assorted, a Collection of all the Loyal Papers that have been or will be published. He at the same Time takes the Liberty of suggesting, that they would do their Country an essential Service, if they would order a few Sets of their respective Booksellers, and cause them to be dispersed in the Villages where they reside, that the Inhabitants may be convinced of the perfidious Designs of BONAPARTE against this Country; and to expose the Malignant, Treacherous, and Cruel Conduct of the* CORSICAN USURPER *to the various Nations that have fallen beneath his tyrannical Yoke.* [*August 23d,* 1803]

[C. L., No. 56. Single sheet printed on one side, dialogue in two columns. 10¾ × 17½. Bibl. Lind., No. 1545. Brit. Mus. *Catalogue, s.v.* "Antigallican."]

[THREE SONGS]

From the British Neptune, Sunday, Sept. 11, 1803.

The Ploughman's Ditty:

BEING AN ANSWER TO THAT FOOLISH QUESTION,

"WHAT HAVE THE POOR TO LOSE?"

To the Tune of—"*He that has the best Wife.*"

1.

BECAUSE I'm but poor,
And slender's my store,
That I've nothing to lose is the cry, Sir;
Let who will declare it,
I vow I can't bear it,
I give all such praters the lye, Sir.

2.

Tho' my house is but small,
Yet to have none at all
Would sure be a greater distress, Sir;
Shall my garden so sweet,
And my orchard so neat,
Be the prize of a foreign oppressor?

3.

On Saturday night,
'Tis still my delight,
With my wages to run home the faster;
But, if Frenchmen rule here,
I may look far and near,
For I never shall find a pay-master.

4.

I've a dear little wife,
Whom I love as my life,
To lose her I should not much like, Sir;
And 'twould make me run wild,
To see my sweet child,
With its head on the point of a pike, Sir.

5.

I've my Church, too, to save,
And will go to my grave,
In defence of a church that's the best, Sir;
I've my King, too, God bless him!
Let no man oppress him,
For none has he ever opprest, Sir.

6.

British laws for my guard,
My cottage is barr'd,
'Tis safe in the light or the dark, Sir;
If the 'squire should oppress,
I get instant redress,
My orchard's as safe as his park, Sir.

7.

My cot is my throne,
What I have is my own,
And what is my own I will keep, Sir;
Should Boney come now,
'Tis true, I may plough,
But I'm sure that I never should reap, Sir.

8.

Now do but reflect,
What I have to protect,
Then doubt if to fight I should chuse, Sir;
King, Church, Babes, and Wife,
Laws, Liberty, Life;
Now tell me I've nothing to lose, Sir.

9.

Then I'll beat my ploughshare,
To a sword or a spear,
And rush on these desperate men, Sir;
Like a lion I'll fight,
That my spear now so bright,
May soon turn to a ploughshare again, Sir.

———

The Committee of the Patriotic Fund, at Lloyd's, have directed, that, in future, a List of the Subscribers of both Subscriptions, now open at that Coffee-House, be published, every Sunday and Monday, in the BRITISH NEPTUNE.—*To be had at the Office, No.* 5, *James-Street, Covent-Garden;* BOOTH'S, *Bookseller, Duke-Street, Portland-Place;* GINGER'S, 169, *Picca-dilly; likewise of all Booksellers, Newsmen, &c., in the United Kingdom.*

———

FROM THE BRITISH NEPTUNE, SUNDAY, AUG. 28, 1803.

———

The Island of Britain.

A LOYAL SONG.—1803

Tune—"Hearts of Oak."

I.

MY friends, ye have heard, in the late British wars,
Of our navy—our admirals—brave British tars!
But the ship I would bring to your notice and view
Is THE ISLAND OF BRITAIN, *her Captain and Crew.*
Heart of oak is this ship,
Hearts of oak are our men:
We always are ready, steady boys, steady;
We'll fight and we'll conquer again and again.

2.

For ages safe moor'd, in the Channel she's laid,
Made fast to a rock, of no danger afraid;
But now she is threatened to stay there no more,
To be boarded and plunder'd, or driven on shore.
 Heart of oak is this ship, &c.

3.

Her CAPTAIN, God bless him! is lov'd by us all;
With HIM we're determined to stand or to fall;
United in hand and in heart we await
The lot which Great Providence seals as our fate.
 Heart of oak is this ship, &c.

4.

But the means in our hands we will ardently use;
We'll fight—and no danger or hazard refuse;
For our lives—for our property—children and wives
We'll fight—for the old British spirit survives.
 Heart of oak is this ship, &c.

5.

The ship is staunch good, and her timbers are sound;
Still fast to the rock we trust she'll be found;
Her hull, stores, and rigging all malice defy;
I name not her sails—*for she don't mean to* FLY!
 Heart of oak is this ship, &c.

6.

Then clear ship, my boys! and each man to his gun;
If they board us, UNITE, and we'll soon make them run;
And ages to come shall still have in view
THE ISLAND OF BRITAIN, *her Captain, and Crew.*
 Heart of oak is this ship, &c.

FROM THE BRITISH NEPTUNE, SUNDAY, SEPT. 4, 1803.

NEW

God Save the King.

SOUND trumpets, beat your drums,
See our lov'd Sov'reign comes,
        Long may he reign.
Oh! may his virtues find,
True friends in all mankind;
Sure, he's by heav'n design'd
        All hearts to gain.

See the *Corse* threat'ning stands,
Midst all his fire-brands,
        Vomiting flame!
Soon shall his insolence,
Sink into impotence;
Britannia's sure defence
        Is GEORGE's name.

O Lord, our God, arise,
Scatter his enemies,
        And make them fall;
Cause civil broils to cease,
Commerce and trade t'increase,
With safety, joy, and peace,
        God bless us all!

Bounteous to this bless'd isle,
On our lov'd Sov'reign smile,
        With mildest rays;
Oh! let thy light divine,
On Brunswic's Royal Line,
With fadeless lustre shine,
        To latest days!

God save great George, our King,
Long live our noble King,
　　　　　God save the King:
Send him victorious,
Happy and glorious,
Long to reign over us,
　　　　　God save the King!

PRINTED FOR J. GINGER, 169, *Piccadilly*,

Price 2*s*. 6*d*. for Fifty, or 4*s*. per Hundred, for Distribution,—
where may be had all the Patriotic Publications, properly assorted.

Marchant, Printer, 3, Greville-Street, Hatton-Garden.

[C. L., No. 57. Single sheet printed on two sides: on one side, "The Ploughman's Ditty," in two columns; on the other, "The Island of Britain" and the new "God Save the King," in two columns. 8½ × 11.]

Fellow Citizens,

BONAPARTE threatens to invade us: He promises to enrich his soldiers with our property: To glut their lust with our Wives and Daughters: To incite his Hell-hounds to execute his vengeance he has *sworn* to permit every thing. Shall we merit, by our cowardice, the titles of sordid Shopkeepers, Cowardly Scum, and Dastardly Wretches, which in every proclamation he gives us: No; we will loudly give him *the lie:* let us make ourselves ready to shut our Shops and march to give him the reception his malicious calumnies deserve: Let every brave young fellow instantly join the *Army* or *Navy;* and those among us, who, from being married, or so occupied in business, cannot, let us join some Volunteer Corps, where we may learn the use of arms and yet attend our business; let us encourage recruiting in our neighbourhood, and loudly silence the tongues of those whom Ignorance or Defection (if any such there be) lead them to doubt of the attempt to invade, or inveigh against the measures taken to resist it.— By doing this, and feeling confidence in ourselves, we shall probably prevent the attempt, or, if favoured by a dark night, the enemy should reach our shores,—our Unanimity and Strength will paralize his efforts and render him an easy prey to our brave *Army*. Let *us*, in our families and neighbourhood, thus contribute to so desirable an event, and the *blood-stained banners of the vaunted Conquerors of Europe will soon be hung up in our Churches, the honourable Trophies of our brave Army:*—an Army ever Victorious when not doubled in numbers; and the only Army who can stand the charge of Bayonets.—What *Army* ever stood THEIRS!!!—*Let the welfare of our Country animate all—and "come the World in Arms against us, and we'll shock 'em!"*   A SHOPKEEPER.

> Thee, Haughty Tyrants ne'er shall tame,
> All their Attempts to pull thee down
> Shall but arouse thy gen'rous flame
> To work their woe and thy renown.—
> RULE BRITANNIA.

Printed for J. GINGER, 169, Piccadilly, Price SIXPENCE per Dozen, for Distribution. W. MARCHANT, Printer, 3, Greville-Street, Holborn.

[C. L., No. 58. Single sheet printed on one side, in one column. 11 × 17. *Bibl. Lind.*, No. 1493.]

A Word of Advice

TO THE SELF-CREATED CONSUL.

As a plain Man, permit me to give you a Word of Advice, if your Arrogance and Presumption have not put you above it. I was one of the Number, who, but a few Years back, was deceived by your alluring and specious Pretensions, and then thought you a Friend to Mankind. I wish I could have found your Conduct such as would have made me continue so; but your Cruelties, your insatiable Thirst for *extensive Dominion, and arbitrary and overbearing Power*, has raised up against you *Enemies* in *every Friend to Virtue, Truth, Religion, Morality, Order, Freedom, and Independence.*

You set forward promising Freedom to the World—Look at Holland, Switzerland, Helvetia. You caused the Tree of Liberty to be planted; but wherever it has taken Root, it has produced the most baneful and deadly Fruit. You *promised*, whereever you went, to treat the People with *Humanity* and *Mercy*—Look at the *Massacre of your Prisoners*, and the *poisoning Part of your own Troops;* the remainder of whom you, in the most *Cowardly* and *Dastardly* Manner, abandoned, in an ungenial and unhealthy Clime. Your *Treachery*, in this Instance, will be an eternal Stigma upon you; and while your own Minion may fawningly applaud your Conduct, the Patriot Soldier will ever view it with Infamy and Disgrace.

You threaten to Invade our Country—you Promise your Soldiers the Pillage of our Property—to load them with the Spoils of Englishmen—to abrogate our Laws—to give us French Fraternity—and to gratify their lustful Passions with the Violation of the Chastity of our Wives and Daughters.— But here, THOU DESPOILER OF THE REPOSE OF THE WORLD, hast thou raised the Dagger against thyself; the Bloody Weapon which thou would carry to other Nations, must (DREADFUL TO HUMANITY) recoil upon yours; and would to God upon YOU ONLY might be the fatal Stroke.

The Tameness, the tardy Negligence of other Nations, will not be found among *Englishmen:* they will ever be found at the Post at the Hour of Danger; they will present to your *Front* a MILLION OF FREE PEOPLE, armed in the Cause of VIRTUE, ORDER, and MORALITY; acting as ONE MAN, and guided by ONE HEART, in Defence of that KING, that CONSTITUTION which gives EQUAL LAWS, and dispenses EQUAL HAPPINESS, to every Subject. Compare this with a People borne down with the TYRANNIC HAND *of* ARBITRARY *and* DESPOTIC POWER; a People who have nothing left to Fight for, and who are kept in Order by the *Coercive Mandates* of an Usurper—the

Point of a Bayonet, or the Fear of being immured in loath-some Dungeons. Look at a *mild* and *beneficent Sovereign*, reigning in the *Hearts* of a *free People*, who are *rallying round his Standard for his Defence*—and then see the *horrid Reverse* of your own Case—a *Foreign Usurper*, flying like the *Leader of a Banditti of Plunderers* at unstated Periods, anticipating the Deserts of his oppressive Conduct. Think of this, and know, what *must be the Fact*, of your *deceived Army*, seeking in *France that Plunder* which was *not to be obtained from a free People*.

Wishing you an early Enjoyment of all the Happiness you may deserve in another World, I remain

ONE OF THE OLD MINORITY;

But now one of the largest Majority ever leagued under the Banners of any Sovereign.

London: Printed for J. ASPERNE, Successor to MR. SEWELL, at the Bible, Crown, and Constitution, No. 32, Cornhill, by T. MAIDEN.
August 10th, 1803.   [Price 1d. or 6s. the 100.]

[C. L., No. 59. Single sheet printed on one side, in one column. 11 × 17½. *Bibl. Lind.*, No. 1542.]

A Relish for Old Nick.

SONG ON THE THREATENED INVASION.

Tune.—Vicar and Moses.

I.

ARM Neighbours at length,
And put forth your strength,
Perfidious bold France to resist;
Ten Frenchmen will fly
To shun a black eye,
If one Englishman doubles his fist.

II.

But if they feel stout,
Why, let them turn out,
With their maws stuff'd with frogs, soup, and jellies,
Brave Nelson's sea thunder
Shall strike them with wonder,
And make the frogs leap in their bellies.

III.

Their impudent boast
Of invading our coast,
Neptune swears they had better decline;
For the Rogues may be sure,
That their frenzy he'll cure,
And he'll pickle them all in his brine.

IV.

And when they've been soak'd
Long enough to be smok'd,
To the regions below they'll be taken;
And there hung up to dry,
Fit to boil or to fry,
When OLD NICK wants a rasher of bacon.

A LOYAL SUBJECT.

Printed for J. WALLIS, Ludgate Hill, Price 1d. or 8d. per Dozen, by J. Crowder and E. Hemsted, Warwick Square.

[C. L., No. 60. Single sheet printed on one side, in one column. 10¾ × 17¼.]

People of the British Isles.

LET none affect to despise the idea that WE SHALL SHORTLY BE INVADED. Our Foe has pledged himself to it. He is at this moment disengaged from every Continental Enemy—he is supported, he exists only by warfare and plunder. Our Naval Victories have sufficiently taught him to despair of ever withstanding us on the Watery Element, and consequently the only possibility of any success rests in conveying his Land Forces on our Shores; and that this is by no means impracticable, is the opinion of the first Military Characters.

Let us therefore make known to Frenchmen that whatever difference in Political opinions may arise among ourselves, that when *our beloved Country is menaced by Invasion*, WE WILL AND HAVE RESOLVED ONE AND ALL, to defend with bravery and vigor its Honour, Freedom, and Independence.

> "Death is the worst, a fate which all must try,
> But for our Country 'tis a bliss to die.
> The gallant man, tho' slain in fight he be,
> Yet leaves his Children safe, his Country free,
> Entails a debt on all the grateful state,
> His own brave friends shall glory in his fate;
> His wife live honor'd, all his race succeed,
> And late posterity enjoy the deed."

But let us pause, and contemplate for a moment what we have to defend.

We have to defend from brutal violation the British Fair, whose unrivalled beauty so far from protecting them, will add proportionably to their misery. We have to defend (and transmit unimpaired to our children) those Rights and Liberties for which our Ancestors have so often bled, from time to time, and even sacrificed their lives to preserve to us.

We have to defend and to maintain, such glorious privileges as collectively no other nation on earth can boast of possessing. We have a MAGNA CHARTA and a FREE PRESS; but above all, our glorious and invaluable Constitution, the admiration and the wonder of the world.

What ardor will not the first consideration alone inspire in the breasts of our British Youths? What hitherto unheard of prodigies of valour, what feats of Courage may we not expect, in A CAUSE, SO TRULY GRAND—SO TRULY JUST.

"Rely on fate, whose out-stretch'd hand
Shall still preserve thee from the hostile steel,
For scenes of future bliss.—Think on the day
When with a victor's emulation swoln
Thine arms shall clasp a mistress' throbbing breast,
When tears of joy shall grace thy mother's eye,
And rapt'rous smiles, to view a conquering son,
Play on her aged brow! O think—
And let the contemplation chear thy heart."

It is hoped and trusted therefore, that every individual, in proportion to his means, will imitate the glorious example of the Merchants and others of the City of London.

"Those generous traders who alike sustain
Their nation's glory on th'obedient main,
And bounteous raise affliction's drooping pain."

A Volunteer.

Published by J. Ginger, 169, Piccadilly.
Price One Penny, or Ninepence the Dozen.
Nicholson, Printer, Clerkenwell.

[C. L., No. 62. Single sheet printed on one side, in one column. 10½ × 17½. Bibl. Lind., No. 1509. Brit. Mus. Catalogue, s.v. "Volunteer."]

Horrors upon Horrors;

Or, What are the *Hellish Deeds* that can surprise us, when committed by the *Blood-Hounds* of that *Arch-Fiend* of Wickedness, the Corsican Bonaparte?

BEING

A true and faithful Narrative of the Sufferings of a Hanoverian Blacksmith, who *died raving Mad*, in consequence of the dreadful Scenes of Barbarity, of which he had been late an Eye-witness, in his own Country.—For the further Particulars of this horrid Scene, *vide* The British Neptune, from whence this Relation has been extracted.

". . . . . If these be Men,
I'll hie me to the Woods, there dwell with Beasts."

THE following dreadful Narrative has been just communicated to us, and this in so *unquestionable* a shape, and from such authority, that we loose not a single moment in laying it before the public. We shall now, without farther comment, give to our readers, *verbatim*, the narrative delivered to us:

"One evening, as I was sitting at supper, in a paltry inn, at a small village, when, on my road to Toningen, a wretched looking man, apparently half frantic, and almost disfigured by dirt, rushed suddenly into my chamber. Before I had time to recover from my surprize, the poor creature was at my feet, embracing my knees so closely, that I could with difficulty disengage myself. He addressed me in German, and could not be prevailed on to rise from the floor until I had promised him what he was pleased to call my protection; in short, every assistance in my power. I then got him to take a basin of soup, and recommended him to go quietly to bed, which I had ordered to be prepared for him in the garret. This he at length acceded to, but not until I had declared to him, on the *word of an Englishman*, that I would take him with me to England, that he might never more be on land which was not separated by water from France. When the poor creature left me, his eyes had so wild an appearance, that I own, notwithstanding the compassion which I naturally felt for his sufferings, I was heartily glad to get him fairly out of the room.

"The tale of this unfortunate man was of so simple a nature, that, the moment he left me, I thought I could not do better than to commit it to paper, as nearly as I could recollect, in his own words. But, before I enter upon this, I must acquaint you that I had not been in my bed two hours, before my servant came to inform me, that the poor Blacksmith had become *raving mad*, and that the people of the house had been obliged to tie him down to the bed. I immediately flew to the chamber, sent instantly for the best medical assistance that could be procured; and, in the mean time, endeavoured, by soothing and every humane effort, to tranquillize the wretched sufferer's mind: but all was to no purpose, for the poor man went off in a dreadful delirium, in less than eight hours, never ceasing, for one moment, to execrate the French as the most horrid monsters the world ever saw."

The Blacksmith's Narrative.

I am by trade a Blacksmith, and my name is John Wardack; I kept my shop hear Harbourgh, and was gaining my bread honestly, by the sweat of my brow, when the French army entered the country of Hanover. Shortly after, I was seized by a party of French soldiers, dragged out of my shop, had my hands tied behind me, and was driven forward by the point of the bayonet, expecting every moment would be my last. On turning round my head, to beg my guards to be a little more merciful, and not to prick me as they were doing for their fun, I perceived that the infernal villains had set fire to my house and shop, and that the whole was in flames. On the road to Harbourgh, we passed the shop of a person who sold sausages, hams, herrings, and suchlike eatables. The door was shut, but this was instantly burst open, by the but-ends of the soldiers muskets. Here we saw a decent good-looking woman suckling her infant, whilst four other little children, who had been playing round her, had now fled to her for shelter, having been terrified by the noise of bursting open the door. In an instant, three of these monsters flew at the poor woman, like so many tigers, whilst another of them, seizing the poor innocent, dashed it against the floor, saying something, at the same time, in French, that I did not understand, though it must have been some jest, as it made them all laugh heartily. What I now beheld is almost too shocking to relate, but what cannot, and what will not Frenchmen do! Whilst the unhappy woman was in vain struggling to resist their villainous embraces, the children were filling the chamber with their mournful cries, when the eldest of them, a boy about six years of age, flew like a little tiger upon the

corporal, who was violating his poor mother, and in a moment set his face in the gore of blood with his little nails.
This so enraged the monster, that he called out something to
his comrades, when in an instant the whole of these dear
innocent babes were bayoneted, and thrown out of the door
upon a dung-hill. As soon as all these wretches had satisfied
their monstrous lust, the shop was stripped by them to the
very last article, and then, to complete the whole, they set
fire to the house, leaving it to Providence to spare or destroy
the unhappy victim of their savage barbarity, whom they
had left senseless. Shortly after, nearly a similar tragedy was
acted by these wretches, but suffice it to say that savage
ferocity, plunder, and bloodshed, marked their footsteps,
wherever we passed.—Oh, how my poor brain boils, whilst I
think of what I have of late seen! Here the poor creature
dropped down in an agony on the floor.—On recovering himself, he continued his narrative thus:—

On my arrival at Harbourg, I was told, by the officer, that
I was a fine young fellow, and just the sort of man that
Bonaparte wanted to send to St. Domingo to conquer the
Blacks, that I need not make myself uneasy, as I should have
many hundreds of my countrymen to keep me company, as
the Grand Consul could not spare a single Frenchman, at
present, from the Army of England, in which country he
hoped soon to have better *sport* than they had ever had in
Hanover; for, you know, added he with a hellish grin, that in
that country the women are all pretty, and the men are all
rich, or fit to recruit our victorious armies. These devils, sup-
posing me safely secured, now all left me to go in quest of
fresh plunder. By God's good providence, a German soldier,
who had been forced into the French service, happened to
pass that way, and, on hearing my lamentations, and be-
holding the piteous state I was in, he humanely cut the cords
that bound me, at the hazard of his life. I instantly fled and
hid myself in a hay-loft until night, when, by the darkness
and heaven's assistance, I escaped from the clutches of these

devils in human shape. Thus, hiding myself by day, and travelling by night, I am at length, thank heaven, safely arrived here, and my great object now is to embark for England, where I will live and die, it being now the only free and happy country that is left in all Europe.

PRINTED FOR J. GINGER, 169, PICCADILLY,
Price SIXPENCE per Dozen, for Distribution, or one PENNY each,

Where may be had the following:—Publicola's Addresses to the People of England, to the Soldiers and the Navy;—John Bull turned Galley-Slave;—Bonaparte's Hand-Bills;—An English Taylor equal to Two French Grenadiers;—A Peep into Hanover;—An Address to the Ladies of England, &c. &c.;—where all the Patriotic Hand-Bills and Books may be had, properly assorted.

W. MARCHANT, Printer, Greville-Street, Hatton-Garden.

[C. L., No. 63. Single sheet printed on one side; narrative in two columns. 10¾ × 16¾. *Bibl. Lind.*, No. 1495.]

SUBSTANCE OF THE

Corsican Bonaparte's Hand-bills;

OR, A

Charming Prospect for John Bull
and his Family.

BRITONS AWAKE!

AND though it may be galling to your feelings, and make your blood boil with indignation, to read that which is to follow, it is surely far better that you should experience this, than the direful effects of that ruin and destruction with which you are now menaced, and which must inevitably be your lot, should you not rouse and meet the danger with one hand and with one heart.

Know then

That the Corsican Bonaparte, the *grand Subjugator of the great French Nation*, has at length thrown off the mask. This relentless Tyrant, this insatiable Monster of cruelty and ambition, this eternal enemy to the repose and happiness of all mankind, no longer conceals his long buried rancorous designs of annihilating this truly happy country, the envy of all Europe.

This atrocious intention he has not only made known to Mr. Marcoff, the Russian Ambassador at Paris, in an affected fit of merriment; but he has proclaimed it by *hand-bills* in every hole and corner of France. There is not a Town or Village, between Paris and Calais, where may not be read hand-bills to the following effect:—

Road to England!

But now mark, my brave Countrymen, what follows. It is an invitation to every dastardly Frenchman, whose courage is only to be roused by the hopes of plunder, to enlist for the *Army of England;* which country, the haughty Tyrant boastingly tells them, shall be devoted to its Conquerors as their just reward. Behold, says this rapacious Plunderer and Assassin, the *Paradise of the World!* the richest and most flourishing Nation the sun ever blest with its beams! Nature and art seem here to have combined to leave nothing wanting to its happiness.—Observe the riches of her plains; not an acre but what is covered with grain and matchless cattle. Towns, villages, stately mansions, beautiful country-seats, villas, gardens, orchards.—Was there ever beheld so enchanting, so lovely a scene! Brave Frenchmen! could you but see the interior of these invaluable towns and happy dwellings, you would there find not only every desirable comfort of life, even among the very lowest classes of the people, (I mean compared with your own wretched hovels) but go but one or two steps higher, and there you would discover almost every article which industry can produce, or luxury ever thought of. But from whence flow all this superabundant riches? The answer is plain—'tis their industry and commerce; 'tis their manufacturing towns that are her inexhaustable mines; and these are the *true seed* of her *boasted British Oak;* that *insolent and unconquerable* Navy, which has set all Europe at defiance for ages past.—

But let England boast her Sheffield and her Birmingham; her Liverpool and her Bristol; her Newcastle and her other numberless rich towns and cities!—All these, brave Frenchmen, shall be yours!—aye, I repeat it, they shall be yours— Nay, your reward shall not end here; for though the haughty Britons must *bite the dust,* their wives and daughters must be spared—for what purpose, I need not tell you. Rouse, rouse then, brave and heroic Frenchmen; brave all dangers, and look to your reward; for, spite of that ridiculous lying song, *Rule Britannia,* I now announce to you, that Britains shall be *Slaves;* and what is more, they shall be the most *abject Slaves* to all-powerful and all-conquering France.

Such, Britons, is the Boast of the Corsican Tyrant, the grand *Subjugator of the great French Nation;* and such are the Hand-bills spread throughout France. I do not say that the above are the very words; but I say such are their true sense and meaning.

What answer, my gallant Countrymen, shall we give to this? Surely there can be but one; and that, thank Heaven! will be found engraven on the bottom of your hearts.—*"Or Death or Freedom";* or in other words, *Annihilation to every Frenchman, who shall dare to set his cloven-foot on these happy and matchless shores.* Let this bloody-minded Corsican then dare to land on British ground, with his thousands and hundreds of thousands of his hell-hounds at his back, and he shall find, that that same spirit and bravery that enabled our gallant Egyptian Army to compel double its numbers of French to lay down their arms, shall now again, with the blessing of the Almighty, drive our enemies into the sea, whenever their rapacity or temerity may tempt them to reach our shores.

A true Friend to OLD ENGLAND.

N.B. *It is earnestly recommended to the Editors of the Sunday Papers to insert the above Hand-bill.*

Printed for J. GINGER, 169, Piccadilly, Price 6d. per Dozen, or 1d. each,
BY C. STOWER, CHARLES STREET, HATTON GARDEN.

† It is earnestly recommended to those who can afford it to distribute this Hand-Bill.

[C. L., No. 64. Single sheet printed on one side, in one column. 10¾ × 17. *Bibl. Lind.*, No. 1515.]

Twenty Thousand Pounds Reward.

MIDDLESEX (to wit)

> *To all Constables, Headboroughs, Tithing-Men, and other Officers of the County of Middlesex, and to every of whom it may concern.*

WHEREAS a certain ill-disposed Vagrant, and common Disturber, commonly called or known by the Name of NAPOLEON BONAPARTE, *alias* Jaffa Bonaparte, *alias* Opium Bonaparte, *alias* Whitworth Bonaparte, *alias* Acre Bonaparte, by the instigation of the Devil, and with malice aforethought, hath lately gone about swindling and defrauding divers Countries, Cities, Towns, and Villages, under divers various and many false and wicked pretences, out of their Rights, Comforts, Conveniencies, and CASH, AND WHEREAS the said NAPOLEON BONAPARTE, *alias* Jaffa Bonaparte, *alias* Opium Bonaparte, *alias* Whitworth Bonaparte, *alias* Acre

Bonaparte, still continues so to go about, *craftily* and *subtilly* endeavouring to deceive and defraud the peaceable and well-disposed Subjects of divers Realms: AND WHEREAS it has been signified to Us, that the said NAPOLEON BONAPARTE, *alias* Jaffa Bonaparte, *alias* Opium Bonaparte, *alias* Whitworth Bonaparte, *alias* Acre Bonaparte, hath been guilty of divers Outrages, Rapes, and Murders, at *Jaffa*, *Rosetta*, and elsewhere: AND WHEREAS It is strongly suspected, that the said NAPOLEON BONAPARTE, *alias* Jaffa Bonaparte, *alias* Opium Bonaparte, *alias* Whitworth Bonaparte, *alias* Acre Bonaparte, hath in contemplation at the Day of the Date of these Presents, to land in some (but what part is not yet known) of Great Britain or Ireland: WE DO hereby will and require, that in case the said NAPOLEON BONAPARTE, *alias* Jaffa Bonaparte, *alias* Opium Bonaparte, *alias* Whitworth Bonaparte, *alias* Acre Bonaparte, shall be found to *lurk* and *wander* up and down your Bailiwick, that you bring before us the Body of the said NAPOLEONE BONAPARTE, *alias* Jaffa Bonaparte, *alias* Opium Bonaparte, *alias* Whitworth Bonaparte, *alias* Acre Bonaparte, on or before the Morrow of All Souls, that he may be forthwith sent to our Jail for WILD BEASTS, situate, standing, and being over Exeter-'Change in the Strand, without *Bail* or *Mainprize;* and that he be there placed in a certain IRON CAGE, with the Ouran Outang, or some other ferocious and voracious animal like himself, for the purpose of being tamed, or until a Warrant shall issue to our beloved subject *Jack-Ketch*, to deal with him according to Law and the *Virtue* of his Office; and this in no-wise omit at your peril. Witness our hands,

JOHN DOE and RICHARD ROE.

The said NAPOLEON BONAPARTE, *alias* Jaffa Bonaparte, *alias* Opium Bonaparte, *alias* Whitworth Bonaparte, *alias* Acre Bonaparte, is a Corsican by birth, about five feet four inches in height, of a swarthy black complexion, dark hair and eye-brows, and resembles a great deal in person a Bear-leader, or one of the Savoyards who play on the reeds at Vauxhall: He is remarkable for walking fast, and taking long strides, and has been thought to squint, though it is in fact no more than a *cast* in the left eye, with looking too much on one object—Old England—to which over application he also owes being afflicted with the JAUNDICE.

The above Reward will be paid by the County immediately on apprehension. _____

London: Printed for S. HIGHLEY, No. 24, Fleet-Street; by B. McMILLAN, Bow-Street, Covent-Garden (price 1d. or 9d. per dozen).

Where may be had BONAPARTE; or, THE FREEBOOTER; a Patriotic Drama, price One Shilling.

[C. L., No. 65. Single sheet printed on one side, in one column. 10 × 16. *Bibl. Lind.*, No. 1520.]

_____

Men of England!

_____

IT is said that some of you are so discontented that you would join the Enemies against your Country—Is it possible that you are so misled, as to believe that the Enemies to England would, whatever they pretend, be friends *to you*. Be assured, if you are so persuaded, that you are grossly imposed upon. What should make them your friends—What ties should bind them?—Think a little; and a very little proper reflection will be sufficient to make you see, that the Invaders of your Country, in their hearts, hate the inhabitants of it; and will, in the end, themselves betray the Traitors to it.

The Invaders would nearly desolate your country—and if Provisions are dear now, what would they be when numberless stacks of hay and corn were burnt—the cattle destroyed, and a horrid legion of desperate faithless, lawless Invaders to be maintained?—who would trample upon every tie, break all promises, make *tools* of you first, but soon sacrifice your wives, your daughters, your families, and yourselves, when you had served their purpose. If any few among you were guilty of plunder, you would yourselves soon be plundered and destroyed.

It has been the necessity of defending our country against its enemies that has made provisions dear; but your wages have been increased in proportion—and though you may sometimes, in the course of events, suffer some hardships, as *every body* in their turn must do, you may, unless it be your own faults, enjoy the greatest comforts—a peaceable home—a happy family—a quiet country, whose trade and consequence is envied by all the world—plentiful harvests—a government that respects you, and that your fore-fathers would have defended with the last drop of their blood—you have an excellent and lawful King, who will protect you; and above all, you may have a blessing from God, who will reward you hereafter, if you do your duty *here*. But from a Usurper and Invader you can have nothing to expect but the being slaves to his lawless schemes for power. Let who will tell you the contrary, he comes only for plunder and revenge upon the only nation he fears. Will you be his instruments, his tools? Can you, as Englishmen, lower yourselves in such a manner, —to such a mean Usurper. Heaven, from the beginning, intended you should have kings and superiors—Equality never was intended—it never can be on this earth—Heaven and reason forbid it—and Bonaparte himself has shown you how little he intended to establish it. Your fore-fathers call to you from their graves—their warning voice tells you, that you would soon find the perfidy of his heart. The wretched condition you would bring yourselves and your families into, you would repent too late—deprived of every friend, but sure of ample punishment here and hereafter.

People of England!—Sons of my beloved glorious Country! You are now called upon by the Women of your country to protect them.—Can you refuse to hear us?—Can you bear the thought of not only seeing *us* used with insult and barbarity,—of seeing your country bleed at every pore, but of being the occasion of these dreadful evils, in consequence of your mistaken opinions, and by suffering yourselves to be deceived and cajoled by foreign ill-designing wretches, who have only our, and your ruin at heart.

Attend, Men of England,—you who may give conquest to your country, safety to us, and everlasting glory to yourselves.—Attend, Men of England, to the *solemn* truths told you by an honest

Englishwoman.

Printed for J. GINGER, 169, Piccadilly
Price 6d. per Dozen or 1d. each.
Where may be had all the Patriotic Papers that have been published, properly assorted.
C. STOWER, PRINTER, CHARLES-STREET, HATTON GARDEN

[C. L., No. 67. Single sheet printed on one side, in one column. 11 × 17. *Bibl. Lind.*, No. 1501.]

To the Infamous Wretch,

If there be such an one in England, who dares to talk of, or even hopes to find *Mercy* in the Breast of the *Corsican Bonaparte*, the *eternal sworn Foe of England*, the Conqueror and Grand Subjugator of France.

IF there be any Englishman so base, or so foolish, as to wish to trust to the *Mercy* of a French INVADING ARMY, let him read that which follows:—The accuracy and veracity of the account cannot be doubted, it being an Extract from a Book, not only written under the Inspection of the French Government, but, moreover, dedicated to the *Grand Consul*.

I shall make no comment on this most scandalous public avowal, or rather boast of so inhuman and atrocious a proceeding, as the simple Fact sufficiently speaks for itself.

"We, who boasted that we were more just than the Mamalukes, committed daily and *almost necessarily* a number of iniquities; the difficulty of distinguishing our Enemies, by their Form and Colour, made us, every day, *kill innocent Peasants;* the Soldiers took Caravans of *poor Merchants* for enemies, and, before justice could be done them (*when there was time to do it*) *two or three of them were shot,* a part of their cargo was *pillaged or destroyed,* and their Camels exchanged for those of ours, which had been wounded. The Fate of the People, *for whose happiness we no doubt came to Egypt,* was no better. If, at our approach, terror made them leave their houses, they found, on their return, nothing but *the Mud of which the Walls were composed:* utensils, ploughs, gates, roofs, every thing served as fuel to boil our Soup; their pots were broken, their grain was eaten, their fowls and pigeons roasted, and nothing was left but the carcases of their dogs, *when they defended the Property of their Masters.* If we remained in their Villages, the wretches were *summoned to return,* under pain of being treated as *Rebels,* and, in consequence, *double Taxed;* and when they yielded to these Menaces, *came to pay their Tax,* it sometimes happened, that, from their great Number, they were taken for a body of Revolters, their sticks for arms, and they received *some discharges of Musketry before there was time for explaining the Mistake;* the Dead were enterred, and we remained friends, till a safe opportunity for revenge occurred. It is true, that when they staid at home, *paid the Tax, and supplied all the wants of the Army,* they were saved the trouble of a Journey to Residence in the Desert, *saw their Provisions consumed with regularity,* and were *allowed* a Part of them, preserved some of their gates, sold their eggs to the Soldiers, and had BUT FEW OF THEIR WIVES AND DAUGHTERS VIOLATED!"*

* Denon's Travels in Egypt, translated from the French. *See London Quarto Edition,* Vol. i. *p.* 256, &c.

Such was the Treatment which Egypt experienced; a Country which the French were desirous to possess and to conciliate; very Different is their Design upon Great Britain, which it is their avowed Intention to RAVAGE, PLUNDER, and DESTROY.

Printed for J. GINGER, 169, PICCADILLY,
Price SIXPENCE per Dozen, for Distribution.

N. B. It is earnestly requested that those who can afford it will distribute these Papers to those who cannot. Ladies and Women of all Ranks think on this!

W. MARCHANT, Printer, 3, Greville-Street, Holborn.

[C. L., No. 68. Single sheet printed on one side, in one column. 11 × 17. *Bibl. Lind.*, No. 1518.]

Most Wonderful Wonder of Wonders!!

JUST arrived, at Mr. BULL's MENAGERIE, in BRITISH LANE, the most renowned and sagacious MAN TIGER, or OURANG OUTANG, called

NAPOLEON BUONAPARTE;

HE has been exhibited through the greatest Part of Europe, particularly in HOLLAND, SWITZERLAND, and ITALY, and lately in EGYPT.—He has a wonderful Faculty of Speech, and undertakes to reason with the most learned Doctors in Law, Divinity, and Physic.—He proves incontrovertibly that the strongest POISONS are the most sovereign Remedies for Wounds of all Kinds; and by a Dose or two, made up in his own Way, he cures his Patients of all their Ills by the Gross.—He PICKS the POCKETS of the Company, and by a ROPE suspended near a LANTERN, shews them, as clear as Day, that they are all richer than before.—If any Man in the Room has empty Pockets, or an empty Stomach, by taking a Dose or two of his POWDER of HEMP, he finds them on a sudden full of Guineas, and has no longer a Craving for Food: If he is rich, he gets rid of his *taedium vitæ;* and if he is over-gorged, finds a perfect Cure for his Indigestion.—He proves, by unanswerable Arguments, that SOUPE MAIGRE and FROGS are a much more wholesome Food than BEEF and PUDDING—and that it would be better for OLD ENGLAND if her Inhabitants were all MONKEYS and TIGERS, as, in Times of Scarcity, one half of the Nation might devour the other half.— He strips the Company of their Cloathes, and when they are stark naked, presents a PAPER on the POINT of a BAYONET, by reading which they are all perfectly convinced that it is very pleasant to be in a State of Nature.—By a kind of hocus-pocus Trick, he breathes on a CROWN, and it changes suddenly into a Guillotine.—He deceives the Eye most dex-terously; one Moment he is in the Garb of the MUFTI; the next of a JEW; and the next Moment you see him the POPE.—He imitates all Sounds; bleats like a LAMB; roars like a TIGER; cries like a CROCODILE, and brays most inimitably like an ASS.

Mr. BULL does not chuse to exhibit his MONKEY's Tricks in the puffing way, so inimitably played off at most foreign Courts; as, in trying lately to puff himself up to the Size of a BULL, his Monkey got a *Hernia,* by which he was very near losing him.

He used also to perform some wonderful Tricks with GUN-POWDER; but his Monkey was very sick in passing the Chan-nel, and has shewn a great Aversion to them ever since.

ADMITTANCE, ONE SHILLING AND SIXPENCE.

N. B. If any Gentlemen of the CORPS DIPLOMATIQUE should wish to see his OURANG OUTANG, Mr. BULL begs a Line or two first; as, on such Occasions, he finds it necessary to bleed him, or give him a Dose or two of cooling Physic, being apt to fly at them if they appear without such Prepa-ration.

TO THE PUBLIC.

The very great Demand for the *Spirited* and *Loyal Patriotic Papers* lately published by Mr. GINGER, Piccadilly, has induced him to print NEW EDITIONS, at a considerable Expense.—NOBLEMEN, GENTLEMEN, and others, who are desirous of serving their Country, would do well to embrace the present Opportunity. The following are selling at the very low Price of *One Penny, or for Distribution Four Shillings per Hundred*.

1 Address to the Women of England, on their contributing to the Patriotic Fund at Lloyd's.
2 Substance of Corsican Buonaparte's Hand-Bill.
3 John Bull turned into a Galley Slave.
4 To the Infamous Wretch (from Denon's Travels).
5 Horrors upon Horrors, or the Blacksmith's Narrative.
6 English Mastiffs.
7 Peep into Hanover, or a faint View of the Cruelties committed by the French.
8 To the Men of England, by an English Woman.
9 A Parody, by an honest English Woman.
10 The Shopkeeper's Address to his Fellow Citizens.
11 The Briton's Prayer, and Address to Volunteers.
12 Account of Buonaparte's Preparations for Invasion.
13 Address to Irishmen residing in England, by an Irishman and a Soldier.
14 People of the British Isle.
15 Mr. Pratt's (author of the Gleanings) Address to his Countrymen.
16 To the Volunteers of England, a new Song.
17 My Friend and my Country, by an old Whig.

Price One Penny, or Six Shillings per Hundred.

18 The Alarum Bell.
19 Twenty Thousand Pounds Reward.
20 Union and Watchfulness.
21 English, Irish, and Scotch, a new Song.
22 A full, true and particular Account, Life, Character, &c. of Buonaparte, the Corsican Monster.
23 Substance of the Speech of Jacob Bosanquet.

Price Twopence, or One and Sixpence per Doz. Fifty for Six Shillings.

24 Address to Mechanics, Artificers, Labourers, &c. of England. 4th edit.
25 An English Taylor equal to two French Grenadiers.
26 British Patriot's Catechism, 2nd edit.

27 British Moral and Political Creed, 2nd edit.

28 Home Truths, or a Collection of undeniable Facts.

29 French Catechism, or a Dialogue between an Eng. Volunteer & a
     French Prisoner.

Price 3d. each, or 2s. 6d. per Dozen.—9s. for Fifty.

30 Publicola's Address to the People of England, to the Soldiers and
     Sailors; to which is added his Postscript.

31 Address to the Inhabitants of Britain, founded on the Advice of Ne-
     hemiah to the Jews, recommended by the Rev. Mr. Evans, M. A.
     author of Sketch, &c. &c. 2nd edit.

32 The Warning Drum, by T. Newenham, Esq.

33 Piety and Courage, by the Rev. John Crofts, M. A. 2nd edit.

Price Sixpence each, or Five Shillings per Dozen.

34 Alfred's Address to the Ladies of England.

35 A few Words, resist or be ruined.

36 The Volunteer's *Vide-Mecum*, by an Officer.

37 History of Buonaparte, large sheet, with wood cut.

38 Dramatic Dialogue between an Englishman and a Frenchman.

39 The Anti-Gallican, published in numbers every Saturday, 6d. per
     number.

Songs at Fifty for 1s. 6d. or One Hundred for 2s. 6d.

40 Mr. Boney's hearty Welcome to Old England.

41 Britons Unconquerable.

42 Buonaparte answered, or the Briton's War-Song.

43 Britons Strike Home, a new Song.

44 Eve of Invasion.

45 Song for all true Britons.

46 John Bull's Invitation to Buonaparte.

47 The Minor's Soliloquy.

48 Britons' Defiance to France.

49 Song for all true Britons, tune Rule Britannia.

WHEELER, PRINTER, 57, WARDOUR STREET, SOHO;
FOR J. GINGER, 169, PICCADILLY.

[C. L., No. 69. Single sheet printed on one side, in one column; list of new editions in two
columns. 11 × 17. *Bibl. Lind.*, No. 1503.]

Buonaparte and Talleyrand.

It is well known that Monsieur TALLEYRAND *always objected to the Invasion of England, as a mad Attempt, that must end in the Destruction of the Invaders. Having been favoured with a Note of a Conversation between him and the Chief Consul on this Subject, I have attempted, for the Entertainment of my Countrymen, to put it into Rhyme.*   A.S.

BUONAPARTE.

TALLEYRAND, what's the state of my great preparation,
To crush, at one stroke, this vile, insolent nation,
That baffles my projects, my vengeance derides,
Blasts all my proud hopes, checks my arrogant strides,
Boasts a *press unrestrain'd*, points its censure at ME,
And while Frenchmen are slaves, still presumes to be free?

TALLEYRAND.

In a month, Sire, or less, your magnanimous host,
Their standards shall fix on the rude British coast.

BUONAPARTE.

'Tis well—let the troops be kept hungry and bare,
To make them more keen—for that island's good fare.
Give them *drafts upon London*, instead of their pay,
And rouse them to *ravish, burn, plunder,* and *slay.*
Prepare too,—*some draughts,* for the sick and the lame;
You know what I mean—

TAL.—*As in Syria?*

BUON.—*The same!*

That *England I hate*, and its armies subdued,
The *Slaughter of Jaffa* shall there be renew'd.
Not a wretch that presumes to oppose but shall feel
The flames of my fury, the force of my steel.
Their daughters and wives to my troops I consign;
So shall vengeance, sweet vengeance deep-glutted, be mine.
Their children—

TAL.—What, massacre them, my dread Lord?

BUONAPARTE.

Why not? with *me* PITY *was never the word!*
That island once conquer'd, the world is my own,
And its ruins shall furnish the base of my throne.

TALLEYRAND.

What a project! how vast!—yet allow me one word;
Sir; the English are brave, and can wield well the sword.
In defence of their freedom, their *King*, and their soil,
Not a man but will dare the most perilous toil.
Should our troops but appear, they will rush to the field,
And will die on the spot to a man ere they yield.
In defence of their honor, their women will fight,
And their navy triumphant still sails in our sight.

BUONAPARTE.

Hush, hush, say no more, lest some listener should hear,
And our troops should be taught these fierce Britons to fear.
They are brave; and my soldiers have felt it—what then?
Our numbers are more—to their five, we are ten.
Say their sailors are skilful, oak-hearted, and true,
One army may fail, yet another may do.
And though thousands should fatten the sharks in the sea,
There are thousands remaining, *to perish for me.*
In a night or a fog we will silent steal over,
And surprize unexpected, the Castle of Dover.
Then to gull the poor dupes of that navy-bound land,
You have lies ready-coin'd—*'tis your trade*, at command.
We will tell them, and swear it, our sole end and aim
Is to make them all equally rich—all the same.
I see by your smile you interpret my meaning,
That where'er my troops reap, they leave nothing for gleaning.
They soar at a palace, they swoop at a cot.
And plunder—not leaving one bone for the pot.
Now, Sir, to your duty, your business prepare,
Leave the rest to *my* genius, *my* fortune, *my* care.
　　[*Exit Buonaparte, Talleyrand looking after him.*

TALLEYRAND.

Your fortune, I fear, Sir, will play you a trick;—
Notwithstanding his vaunts, he is touch'd to the quick.
What folly! what madness, this project inspires,
To conquer a nation, whom liberty fires.
E'en now from their shores, loudly echoed, I hear
The song of defiance appalling mine ear.
Their spirit once roused, what destruction awakes!
What vengeance, the wretched invaders o'ertakes.
Prophetic I plead, but my warning is vain,
Ambition still urges, and maddens his brain:
Fired with hopes of rich booty, his soldiers all burn,
THEY MAY GO, SOME MAY LAND, BUT NOT ONE WILL RETURN.

Printed for J. HATCHARD, Piccadilly, Price 6d. per dozen, by
J. BRETTELL, Great Windmill Street.

[C. L., No. 70. Single sheet printed on one side; dialogue in two columns, rest in one.
10¾ × 17½. Brit. Mus. *Catalogue, s.v.* "Napoleon I."]

NOTES TO THE BROADSIDES

Under this heading will be found explanatory annotations affecting the individual broadsides. Annotations having reference to two or more broadsides are entered under the "Guide to Persons, Places, and Societies," pages 263–280 below.

No. 1. *Publicola's Postscript to the People of England.*

Dated July 18, 1803.

Single sheet, 17 × 21; printed on one side, in two columns.

Catalogue of English Broadsides: *Bibliotheca Lindesiana*, No. 1527.

British Museum, *Catalogue of Printed Books*, *s.v.* "Publicola." In the same catalogue, and assigned to the same author, appears the following entry: Publicola's addresses to the people of England, to the soldiers, and to the sailors. To which is added his Postscript to the People of England. London, 1803. 12°.

No. 46 and No. 49 in this book seem to be from the same hand. Cf. the printer's advertisement to No. 69.

No. 2. *To the Inhabitants of the British Isles.*

S. sh., 10½ × 17¾; one side, two columns.

Bibl. Lind., No. 1519.

Ptolemais (Ptolomais) is the ancient name of Acre.

Hume, David (1711–1776), *The History of England from the Invasion of Julius Caesar to the Abdication of James II, 1688* (Boston, 1849), Vol. I, p. 374. Hume's History was the first great English history and long the most popular general history of the country. The quotation in the broadside consists of parts of two separated sentences.

Brissot, Jacques-Pierre, *dit* de Warville (1754–1793). Journalist, pamphleteer, and humanitarian, he was one of the leaders of the Girondists who demanded war to spread the French Revolution. The Jacobins overthrew the Girondists and executed Brissot.

The Shakespearean lines are from John of Gaunt's valedictory in *King Richard the Second*, Act II, scene 1.

Father Paul. Paolo Sarpi (1552–1623). The motto "Esto perpetua" is from Father Paul's *Dying Apostrophe to Venice*, January 15, 1623. In the struggle between Venice and Rome, Sarpi championed the cause of Venice. His last words, "May she live forever," formed a prayer for the welfare of the Adriatic city. See Andrew D. White, *Seven Great Statesmen*, p. 36.

No. 3. *A Letter to the Volunteers.*

S. sh., 10½ × 18; both sides, two columns.

Bibl. Lind., No. 1500; tentative dating, June, 1803.

Brit. Mus. *Catalogue*, *s.v.* "Letter"; tentative dating, 1803.

On Talleyrand's demand for the suppression of certain pamphlets, see the Supplement to Volume III of *Cobbett's Annual Register*, cols. 1003–1007 (letter dated August 17, 1802).

Jenkinson, Robert Banks, first Baron Hawkesbury and second Earl of Liverpool (1770–1828). British statesman who served as Foreign Secretary in Addington's administration, from 1801 to 1803, later as Home Secretary and Secretary for War, and as Prime Minister from 1812 to 1827.

Bantry Bay, Ireland. A deep inlet in county Cork, where, in December, 1796, a large French fleet of ten ships and seventeen transports, with about 15,000 troops, brought aid to an Irish uprising by anchoring in the Bay for a week. General Hoche and his admiral became separated from the squadron, the army did not land, and later a storm drove the expedition back to France.

Windham, William (1750–1810). A leading Whig who joined Burke in going over to Pitt in 1794. Windham served as Secretary for War, 1794–1801, and was an opponent of the Peace of Amiens. According to a report of the debate in the House of Lords on December 12, 1803, Windham objected to the raising of a volunteer force because laborers would thereby be taken from their proper tasks and the military system would be mischievously democratized by "making officers of low mechanics"; *Gentleman's Magazine* (January, 1804), Vol. LXXIV, Pt. 1, p. 69. Various speeches by Windham are reprinted in *Cobbett's Annual Register* (1803), Vol. III, cols. 929–939. See also cols. 953–960 for further commentary on the bill.

Marengo, Battle of. In this village in Piedmont, Italy, Napoleon turned apparent defeat into complete victory over the Austrians on June 14, 1800.

Masséna, André (1758–1817). An Italian, often called the ablest of Napoleon's marshals, who served with distinction in Italy, Switzerland, Austria, and Spain. He was unable to defeat Wellington in Spain.

Harold the Saxon (1022–1066). Became king on the death of Edward the Confessor. He was defeated by William the Conqueror, the "Norman Duke" of the broadside, at the Battle of Hastings, and there lost his life.

The "parliamentary officers during the usurpation" were the officers of Cromwell's army.

Frederick II (Frederick the Great, 1712–1786), King of Prussia, 1740–1786. The ablest of the benevolent despots of the eighteenth century, Frederick was well known in England as the chief ally of Britain in the Seven Years' War (1756–1763). Supported by the elder William Pitt with subsidies, he fought France, Austria, and Russia to a standstill, a success which enabled England to secure the domination of North America and India. His picture, and that of the elder Pitt, were commonly hung together in the American Colonies.

Bird-cage Walk. Bordering St. James's Park, London, to the south, the walk was so called from the cages for birds and beasts kept there for the amusement of Charles II. The region was presumably used as a drill ground for troops. Wellington Barracks occupies adjoining areas to the west.

This Letter, with its practical military counsel, may be compared with similar advice offered by Corporal Trim in No. 38.

No. 4. *The Tender Mercies of Bonaparte in Egypt! Britons, Beware.*

S. sh., 18 x 21; one side, two columns.
Bibl. Lind., No. 1529; tentative dating, July 24, 1803.

Sir Robert Wilson's *History* is noticed at some length, and with copious extracts, in the *Monthly Review* for March, 1803, pp. 281–288. Among the passages quoted is one giving the details of the mortal wounding of General Abercromby, who is mentioned in our No. 37, No. 41, and No. 49. Another review appears in the *Monthly Mirror* for January, 1803, pp. 105–112. The full title of the work: *History of the British Expedition to Egypt: To which is subjoined, a Sketch of the present State of that Country, and its Means of Defence.* By Robert Thomas Wilson, Lieutenant-Colonel of Cavalry in his Britannic Majesty's Service, and Knight of the Imperial Military Order of Maria Theresa. (London, 1802; also issued at Philadelphia, 1803.)

The entire broadside appears under the title, "Bonaparte in Egypt," in the *European Magazine and London Review* (June, 1803), Vol. XLIII, pp. 433–437. From this printing and from the broadside itself is omitted the following footnote from Wilson's *History*, relating to Napoleon's conduct at Jaffa:

"Buonaparte pleaded that he ordered the garrison to be destroyed because he had not provisions to maintain them, or strength enough to guard them; and that it was evident if they escaped, they would act against the French, since amongst the prisoners were five hundred of the garrison of El Arish, who had promised not to serve again (they had been compelled in passing through Jaffa by the commandant to serve;) and that he destroyed the sick to prevent contagion, and save themselves from falling into the hands of the Turks; but these arguments, however specious, were refuted directly, and Buonaparte was at last obliged to rest his defence on the positions of Michiavel. When he afterwards left Egypt, the Scavans [*sic*] were so angry at being left behind, contrary to promise, that they elected the physician president of the Institute; an act which spoke for itself fully."

Assalini, Paolo (1765 ?–1840). An Italian physician who served with the French army in Egypt in 1798 and afterward as First Surgeon to the

Court, by Napoleon's appointment, and as surgeon-in-ordinary to the viceroy Eugène. He published *Observations on the Disease called the Plague* ... in 1803.

Carrier, Jean-Baptiste (1756–1794). A French Jacobin, who in 1793 was sent as a deputy on a mission to Nantes, where he executed from 2,800 to 4,600 prisoners and citizens without trial. After the fall of Robespierre, he was tried and executed.

On the uncompromising physician, a correspondent subscribing himself E. O. E. writes to the *Gentleman's Magazine*, October 4, 1803, a plausible tale as follows: "An English medical gentleman carried with him on a visit to Paris a letter of introduction to the very surgeon who had refused to be the tool of Napoleon in poisoning the sick. The French practitioner, in the subsequent conversation, said that Bonaparte had 'wanted to prescribe for his patients,' a suggestion to which the doctor refused to accede." E. O. E. adds that the French surgeon had in effect later been retained by Napoleon to write an account of the Egyptian campaign, from which the recital of the reprehensible incident was to be sedulously omitted. The horrid fact, concludes E. O. E., is nevertheless beyond dispute.

The Institute at Cairo, or Institute of Egypt. A society of French savants created by Napoleon, whose duty it was to study the monuments of Egyptian civilization.

The Copts. A Christian community in Egypt, which today forms 8 per cent of the Egyptian population and numbers about one million members. They owe allegiance to a patriarch at Alexandria, who derives his title in an unbroken line since 452. They are the descendants of the ancient Egyptians.

Andréossy (Andreossi), Antoine-François (1761–1828). As the French ambassador to England during the Peace of Amiens, he repeatedly warned Napoleon that, should French expansion continue, the British would fight.

The "late Official Correspondence" is printed in *Cobbett's Annual Register*, Vol. III. The quotation from General Andréossy appears in col. 1056 of the correspondence.

Sebastiani, Horace-François (1772–1851). French marshal and diplomatist whose "commercial" mission to Algiers, Egypt, Syria, and the Ionian Islands was chiefly concerned with fortifications, troops, ships of war, and the feelings of the natives. Accepted as evidence of Napoleon's expansionist plans, his report contributed to the reopening of the war in May, 1803. Colonel Sebastiani's "Report," translated into English, is printed in *Cobbett's Annual Register* (1803), Vol. III, cols. 1087–1100.

In the Sebastiani report appears an account of the Colonel's visit to

Dgezzar (Djezzar) Pasha at Acre on November 20, [1802]. The Pasha
treated Sebastiani coldly but, according to the report:

"... from the whole of his demeanour it could easily be seen, that he wished to be on good
terms with the First Consul, and that he stifled his resentments.—The following is the
apologue, which he used to demonstrate the causes of his resistance [against the French at
Acre]. 'A black slave,' he said, 'after a long journey, in which he had suffered the greatest
privations, arrived at a little field of sugar canes—he stopped therein and indulged himself in partaking of the delicious liquor they afforded, and at length was determined to
remain on the spot. Very soon after, two travellers, who had followed him came up. The
first said to him, *Salamaltee* (the mode of wishing health). The devil take it, answered the
black. The second traveller then approached, and inquired why he had answered in such
a way to so good a wish. I had very good reason for it replied he; if I had answered in a
friendly manner, the man would have entered into conversation with me, and afterwards
sat down beside me; he would have partaken of my refreshments, and finding them desirable, would have endeavoured to obtain exclusive possession.' " (See *Cobbett's Annual
Register*, Vol. III, col. 222.)

The "gallant and estimable British General" against whom Sebastiani
directed his insinuation—that of counseling assassination—was Sir John
Stuart (1759–1815). General Stuart held command of the British troops
at Alexandria; he was promoted major general on April 29, 1802. On
October 17, 1803, he was assigned to lead defense forces gathered in Kent
to repel the threatened invasion, a post he retained until March 24, 1805.
Lord Whitworth, in a despatch to Lord Hawkesbury dated February 3,
1803, reports that Sebastiani, in a conversation with Whitworth, had
retracted his charges against General Stuart. See Oscar Browning's *England and Napoleon in 1803*, p. 59.

The Latin passage at the end of Wilson's letter is from Horace's *Odes*,
II, 13. Horace, having narrowly escaped death by the fall of a tree,
cursed planter and tree alike, with an allusion to the classical poisoner
Medea, as capable of every crime.

No. 5. *The British Flag Maintained.*

S. sh., 6 × 11; one side, one column.
Cymon (Cimon; d. 449 B.C.). An Athenian general, naval commander,
and statesman, who fought the Persians at Salamis and conquered Asia
Minor. His successes on land and sea are told in Plutarch's *Lives*.

No. 6. *Britons! to Arms!!!*

S. sh., 13 × 15; one side, two columns.
Brit. Mus. *Catalogue, s.v.* "Britons."
Fitzgerald, William Thomas (1759 ?–1829). A popular versifier, who
frequently recited his own compositions on public occasions. This poem
he read at a meeting of the Literary Fund, of which he was one of the

vice-presidents, on July 14, 1803. In 1814 he issued a collected edition of his poems against Napoleon. A brief account of Fitzgerald appears in the *Dictionary of National Biography*.

The poem is printed in the *Gentleman's Magazine* (July, 1803), Vol. LXXIII, Pt. 2, p. 665, and in John Ashton's *English Caricature and Satire on Napoleon I*, pp. 172–173.

The date of Blenheim, given in the third note of the broadside as 1706, should be 1704.

The *Gentleman's Magazine*, as above, prints a fourth footnote, on the " 'bawbling' Vessels from the Main," as follows, with a reference to Shakespeare,

A bawbling vessel was he Captain of,
For shallow draught, and bulk unprizable.

Another of Fitzgerald's poetic effusions against the "Tyrant," read at the anniversary of the Literary Fund on April 12, 1804, may be found in the *Gentleman's Magazine* (May, 1804), Vol. LXXIV, Pt. 1, p. 452.

The Literary Fund (later, the Royal Literary Fund). Founded in 1790, by Dr. David Williams, as a benevolent institution for the relief of needy writers. For a general account of the society, see the *Dictionary of National Biography*, under the founder's name. A more detailed history of the Fund appeared in the *Athenæum*, May 1, 1841.

Queen Anne (reigned 1702–1714). Last of the Stuarts, daughter of James II and Anne Hyde, and granddaughter of the Earl of Clarendon, Anne played a vital part in the government of England. In 1710 she dismissed Marlborough's Whig ministry and put the Tories in power. The Tories ended the War of the Spanish Succession by the Peace of Utrecht in 1713.

Tallard, Camille d'Hostun, duc de (1652–1728). French marshal and diplomat who negotiated the treaties of partition that preceded the War of the Spanish Succession. He was defeated by Marlborough at Blenheim.

No. 7. *Buonaparte's Confession of the Massacre of Jaffa.*

S. sh., 17½ x 23; one side, two columns.

Bibl. Lind., No. 1478; tentative dating, June, 1803.

Sir Robert Wilson's testimony regarding Jaffa is set forth in No. 4; Dr. Wittman's, in No. 26.

Morier, John Philip (1776–1853). His "assertions" are no doubt contained in his *Memoir of a Campaign with the Ottoman Army in Egypt from February to July, 1800; containing a description of the Turkish army, journal of the march from Syria to Egypt, general observations on the Arabs, and on the treaty of El-Arish, etc.* (London, 1801.) The *European Magazine* (November, 1801), Vol. XL, pp. 360–361, in a review states that the work deals at length with the story of Jaffa. Pillage and murder, according to Morier's assertion, continued for twelve hours, the 4,500 troops of the garrison were "murdered" by the bayonet, and "all their wounded and sick were poisoned by order of the General" (quotation drawn from the *Memoir*, p. 67).

Bruce, Thomas, seventh Earl of Elgin (1766–1841). Appointed to the embassy to the Ottoman Porte, 1799. His archeological interests culminated in the removal to England of sculptures from the Parthenon, known to fame as the "Elgin Marbles." Departing from Turkey in 1803, Lord Elgin was among the Englishmen detained in France by Napoleon. The *European Magazine* (July, 1801), Vol. XL, pp. 66–67, contains selections from the correspondence of Lord Elgin, in Constantinople, to Lord Hawkesbury, relating to information brought by Mr. Morier on his return from Egypt.

Bonaparte's "Confession," in an official form, may be read in the *Correspondance de Napoléon I* (No. 4035: *Au Directoire Exécutif;* dated March 13, 1799), Vol. V, pp. 361–362. The broadside omits certain portions of the text as it appears in this source.

Pièces officielles de l'Armée d'Egypte. The French version of Napoleon's account of Jaffa, as cited by the broadside, appears in *Pièces diverses et Correspondance relatives aux opérations de l'Armée d'Orient en Egypte* (Paris, 1801), pp. 94–96. A section of this book, which does not include the cited quotation, is headed "Pièces officielles de l'Armée d'Egypte" (pp. 229–344).

The *Moniteur.* The French official organ, which, founded in 1789, throughout its existence (to 1868) published a record of the debates in the French legislative chambers. By 1800, with the suppression of most of the French press, it had become Napoleon's official journal.

Lasne (Lannes), Jean (1769–1809). One of the ablest of the French marshals, for whom Napoleon had real affection. After following his leader through all of the campaigns, Lannes fell mortally wounded in the Battle of Aspern-Essling, near Vienna, in 1809. Napoleon called Lannes "at once the Roland of the army and a giant in capacity. He had been in 54 pitched battles."

The Kurds. A Moslem people, found scattered through Asia Minor, Syria, and the upper Tigris-Euphrates valleys. Today they number about one and one-half millions. They are closely related to the Persians racially and ethnically. The Albanians, about a million in number, have their chief homeland on the eastern side of the Adriatic. Mohammedan in religion, they have been repeatedly conquered by numerous invaders. "Natolians" are no doubt the inhabitants of Anatolia. The Turkish army had recruits from all parts of the Empire, as well as from Aleppo, Damascus, etc. Leon Dominian, a leading modern authority on the people of Turkey, has described the Syrian region and peoples as a "motley population containing representatives of every race," in *The Frontiers of Language and Nationality in Europe* (New York, 1917), pp. 271–272. A colored map, with a key of the Turkish Empire including Syria, showing the distribution of the peoples, occurs opposite p. 274.

Duroc, Géraud-Christophe-Michel (1772–1813). A French marshal, the son of an officer, educated at the military schools of his native town and of Châlons. Becoming aide-de-camp to Napoleon in 1796, he distinguished himself in the Italian campaigns of 1796–1799. He served in Egypt and was seriously wounded at Aboukir. As aide-de-camp (1798) and general of brigade (1800), he served with Napoleon through the Battle of Marengo. Later, he was sent on private missions to Vienna, St. Petersburg, Stockholm, and Copenhagen. After Austerlitz, he was employed in the negotiations with Frederick William of Prussia and the Elector of Saxony. He was mortally wounded at the Battle of Bautzen in Saxony.

Rambaud (Rambeaud), François (1745–1799). A French general. In the Syrian campaign he led a party of two hundred men into the city at the assault on Acre. Cut off from the rest of the division, they took refuge in a mosque, and Rambaud died there with most of his men on March 8, 1799.

No. 8. *Proclamation ... to Every Man.*

S. sh., 7½ × 12¼; one side, one column.
Bibl. Lind., No. 1538; dated August 1, 1803 (note the date in the extended title).

No. 9. [Six songs.]

S. sh., 17 × 21; an undivided sheet as it came from the press, containing six songs, printed in rows of three, head to head, each song occupying one of three columns to the half sheet (folio). Each piece of verse is separately priced and evidently intended to be cut singly for distribution. In the Clark Library copy the several items have been individually lettered for convenience of reference.

In the *Catalogue* of the British Museum may be found an entry, *s.v.* "Napoleon I" (1803), for three of the poems on one folio sheet, our numbers 9 d, 9 e, and 9 f, apparently one half of the printer's larger sheet.

9a. *Britons' Defiance of France.*

Brit. Mus. *Catalogue, s.v.* "Britons"; tentative dating, 1803.
The tune, "Can of Grog," is from Charles Dibdin's *Yo Yea;* see the Brit.

Mus. *Catalogue of Printed Music*, and Grove's *Dictionary of Music and Musicians* under the name Charles Dibdin.

9 b. *Britons Unconquerable!*

The Clark Library broadside No. 10 appears to be another printing, on paper of a different color, of 9 b.

9 c. *John Bull's Invitation to Bonaparte.*

The tune "A Cobler there was" appears in two forms in Chappell, *Popular Music of the Olden Time*, pp. 348–352. See, besides the references given by Chappell, a printing of his second tune in *The Universal Musician* (London, 1738), Vol. I, p. 9, in the setting of Mr. [Richard] Leveridge.

9 d. *Bonaparte Answered; or, The Briton's War Song.*

Brit. Mus. *Catalogue*, *s.v.* "Napoleon I" (1803).

This piece is printed in the *Gentleman's Magazine* (July, 1803), Vol. LXXIII, Pt. 2, pp. 665–666, with the following title and headnote: *"War Song.* Written in May, 1803, on Bonaparte's telling Lord Whitworth that England could not, single-handed, cope with France, and threatening invasion.

> 'What! shall he seek the Lion in his den,
> And fright him there! and make him tremble there!
> O let it not be said!—
>   —Nought can make us rue,
> If England to herself shall be but true!
>   Shakespeare, *King John*.' "

At the head of the first two stanzas, the Magazine places the words, "Bonaparte speaks"; before the last two, "Englishman."

The Magazine also has the following notes in explanation of the passages in the poem:

On "him who triumphed": "Lord Nelson";

on "him who died": "Abercrombie";

on "him whom Acon's turrets raise": "Sir Sidney Smith";

on "Acon's": "Bonaparte's siege of Acre, from whence was driven by Sir Sidney Smith";

on "Richard's": "Richard the First, called the Lionhearted."

See Lord Whitworth's despatch of February 21, 1803, in Oscar Browning's *England and Napoleon in 1803*, pp. 78 ff.

9 e. *Britons Strike Home!*

Brit. Mus. *Catalogue*, *s.v.* "Britons"; tentative dating, 1803. Cf. the general note to No. 9.

This song is printed, with Purcell's air fitting only the refrain, in Ashton's *English Caricature and Satire*, pp. 164–166. For the original air, with words, see Purcell's *Works* (Purcell Society), Vol. XVI, Pt. 1, pp. 80–83. The music was written by Purcell in 1695 for a set of words interpolated in an adaptation of Beaumont and Fletcher's play, *Bonduca*. The whole of Purcell's music to *Bonduca* was printed (1842) for the members of the Musical Antiquarian Society. The words of the original song ran as follows:

> Britons strike home! Revenge your country's wrongs;
> Fight and record yourselves in Druids' song.

The piece appears in Purcell's *Orpheus Britannicus* (2d ed., 1706–1712) as a two-part song.

9 f. *Invasion. A New Song.*

Brit. Mus. *Catalogue, s.v.* "Napoleon I" (1803); see page 228 above.

No. 10. *Britons Unconquerable!*

This piece appears to be another printing of No. 9 b, on paper of a different color; it is therefore not printed here. No. 10 is on a single sheet, 6 × 10¾; one side, one column.

No. 11. *Old England to Her Daughters.*

S. sh., 11 × 17½; one side, two columns.
Bibl. Lind., No. 1506; tentative dating, June, 1803.

This frank recognition of caste in English society is interesting for the integration of the various ranks that are mentioned; the broadside thus reveals the solidarity of a caste society not by concealment but by open avowal. Moreover, the author assumes that there is no conflict of interest between the sexes and boldly states that women have acquired all the rights they could possibly want. In the light of the publications of William Godwin and Mary Wollstonecraft on women's rights and the later indictment of the masculine social order by John Stuart Mill in *The Subjection of Women* (1869), this blanket statement on the emancipated woman is a bit startling. The industrialization of society had not yet occurred and the author of the broadside can therefore assume the complete identity of women with men, and their equal responsibility in repelling the invader. The measured and intelligent hostility of the women would, he says, virtually make the conquest of the country by Napoleon impossible.

The social distinction, here between Ladies, Women, and Labouring Women, to be noticed in the text of the broadside, appears from time to time in the printers' advertisements. "*Ladies*, and women of all ranks" are requested to assist in the distribution (No. 47, No. 68); "Noblemen,

Magistrates, and Gentlemen" are similarly exhorted (No. 17, No. 30, No. 37, No. 56); finally, "Noblemen, Gentlemen, and others" are urged to serve their country by extending the circulation of the sheets (No. 69).

Halsewell Indiaman. The loss of the Halsewell Indiaman, referred to in this broadside, occurred on January 6, 1786, just off St. Albans. According to an account appearing in the *Gentleman's Magazine* (January, 1786), Vol. LVI, Pt. 1, pp. 75–76, "Capt. Pierce, a little while before the ship went down, called Mr. Meriton [the first mate] into his cuddy, where his two daughters, two nieces, and three other beautiful young ladies were clinging round him for protection, and on being told it was impossible for the ladies to escape, he nobly resolved to share their fate, and addressing himself to his daughters and enfolding them in his arms, he said, Then, my dear children, we will perish together. The ship disappeared in a few minutes." Captain Pierce was the oldest Captain in the service of the East India Company.

Ackland, Lady Christian Henrietta Carolina, generally called Lady Harriet Acland (1750–1815). She accompanied her husband, Major John Dyke Acland (also spelled Ackland), on General Burgoyne's ill-fated expedition to America in 1777. Her memoirs of her sufferings during the campaign have been often printed both in England and America. On her return to England her portrait as she stood in a boat with a white handkerchief in her hand as a flag of truce was exhibited at the Royal Academy.

Cortez, Ferdinand (Sp., Hernán Cortés) (1485–1547). Spanish conquistador, conqueror of Mexico. The Indian girl, Marina, "betrayed" her country by acting as an adviser and interpreter throughout his career. The conquest was made possible by the division of the tribes in Mexico.

Genoa. A fortified seaport of northern Italy, which came under Roman dominion in the 3d century B.C., and achieved its independence in the 10th century. Genoa lost her republican independence in 1797 when Napoleon incorporated the Genoese dominions into the Ligurian Republic.

Milan. The most important of the episcopal sees in the 4th century, Milan had, by the 12th century, become the most powerful of the city-republics. From 1499 to 1525 it was repeatedly in the hands of the French, and in 1535 it went to Charles V of Spain. In 1713–1714 it was ceded by Spain to Austria. Milan was the capital of the short-lived Kingdom of Italy (1805–1814) established by Napoleon.

No. 12. *A Full ... Account of the ... Life ... of Napoleone Buonaparte.*

S. sh., 7½ × 14½; one side, two columns.
Bibl. Lind., No. 1494; tentative dating, June, 1803.
Corsica. The island off Italy on which Napoleon was born. In the course of its earlier history it was successively under the sway of Vandals,

Goths, Saracens, Lombards, Franks, and Genoese. The Corsicans, sturdy, rustic, largely Italian, revolted in the 18th century. In 1768 France annexed the island. An insurrection (1793–1796) gave a short period of liberation before French authority finally became paramount.

Autun, Brienne, Paris. At Autun from December, 1778, to April, 1779, the young Napoleon was afterward transferred to the Ecole Militaire at Brienne, where he remained for five years. His proficiency in mathematics made him one of five students who, in October, 1784, were sent to the Ecole Militaire at Paris, from which he graduated a year later, at 16, in September, 1785. Without the usual three months of preliminary service, he was immediately commissioned a junior lieutenant in the Army. An interesting sidelight on his schooling is the fact that at Paris he was a classmate of Louis-Edmond Le Picard de Phélipeaux, who was an engineer for the British troops at Jaffa and thus fought against Napoleon and the French.

Ajaccio. A seaport and the capital of Corsica. The house where Napoleon was born is still standing, and there are numerous monuments in the city to him and his family.

Bastia. A fortified seaport in Corsica, on the northeast coast, sixty-seven miles from Ajaccio. It is the wealthiest and most populous city on the island.

Toulon, Nice. Early in the year of terror and civil war in France, from the middle of 1793 to the middle of 1794, the British occupied Toulon. The city was retaken by the French on December 19, 1793. Napoleon, beginning his career, was at this time merely commander of a battalion under General Dugommier. There is a discussion of the Toulon episode in August Fournier, *Napoleon I*, Vol. I, pp. 55–56. The reference to Nice concerns Napoleon's close association with Robespierre during the Revolution. When Robespierre was guillotined, on July 27, 1794, Napoleon was deprived of his rank as general, arrested at Nice, and imprisoned. His Jacobin enemy, Saliceti, vouched for him, and on August 20, 1794, he was released, and, on September 14, restored to his rank as general of the artillery. See Fournier, *Napoleon I*, Vol. I, pp. 58–61.

Hood, Samuel, first Viscount (1724–1816). Hood, second in command of Rodney's North American fleet during the American Revolution, was conspicuous in the destruction of De Grasse's fleet in the West Indies in 1782. In 1793 he captured Toulon and demolished Corsica's fortifications.

Badharness, Sukey. No doubt a reference to the Empress Joséphine, who, as Joséphine Beauharnais, married Napoleon. Her son, Eugène Beauharnais, was loyal to Napoleon to the end.

Lugo, Italy. Fourteen miles west of Ravenna, this town is important as a place of trade, and has a large annual fair. Benasco (Binasco) is a small village eleven miles from Pavia. When, on May 15, 1796, Napoleon marched triumphantly into Milan, the insurgents of Pavia, having imprisoned 300 French soldiers, revolted, expecting the Milan insurgents to revolt, too, and pushed 800 men to Binasco. There they were met by Lannes, who "took the village, pillaged and set fire to it." Napoleon hastened to Pavia with 1,500 men and 6 fieldpieces, and ordered the city pillaged as an example to the rest of Italy. See William Hazlitt, *The Life of Napoleon Bonaparte* (New York, 1902), Vol. II, pp. 53–54.

Foxe, John (1516–1587). His *Actes and Monuments of these Latter Perilous Times touching Matters of the Church* (commonly called the Book of Martyrs) commemorates the martyrs of the Christian church from earliest times, with special emphasis on the Protestant martyrs of Mary Tudor's reign. Published at Strasbourg in Latin in 1559, the work appeared in English in 1563.

Jerusalem. This Biblical city is mentioned in Egyptian records as early as 1400 B.C. Under King David it became the capital of the Hebrew monarchy. In 70 A.D. the city was destroyed by the Romans under Titus. Established by the Crusaders as the capital of the Christian kingdom, Jerusalem since 1516 has been for the most part in the hands of the Ottoman Turks.

Liberty of the press. The regulation of radical newspapers during this period was accomplished by Parliamentary legislation and by legal prosecution entailing heavy penalties. The Rev. Gilbert Wakefield, in 1799, was heavily fined (£5,000 was subscribed for him) and imprisoned in Dorchester gaol on a charge of criticizing the Emperor of Russia for various acts of tyranny and for preventing the export of timber and other products to Britain. In the same year another judge condemned the *Courier* for expressions that might displease Russia. These precedents had already been established when Napoleon, during the Peace of Amiens, asked that criticism of him by the English Press be restrained. To this Lord Hawkesbury replied, August 28, 1802, that the liberty of the press was secured by the Constitution and that the Government could not interfere. He qualified this statement by adding that the Courts could "investigate and punish not only libels against the Government and magistracy of this Kingdom, but, as has been repeatedly experienced, publications defamatory of those in whose hands the administration of foreign Governments is placed." Under this reservation, the libeler of a foreign power could be arraigned; the French émigré, Jean Peltier, was brought to trial by the Attorney-General and convicted, but the sentence was not carried out because the war with France was renewed.

The trial is famous for the defense of Peltier by Sir James Mackintosh, whose arguments became fundamental in the development of free speech and a free press. Sheridan expressed the English view when he said: "Give me but the liberty of the press, and I will give the Minister a venal House of Peers—I will give him a corrupt and servile House of Commons—I will give him the full swing of the patronage of office—I will give him the whole host of Ministerial influence—I will give him all the power that place can confer upon him to purchase submission, and overawe resistance; and yet, armed with the liberty of the press, I will go forth to meet him undismayed: I will attack the mighty fabric he has reared with that mightier engine: I will shake down from its height corruption, and lay it beneath the ruins of the abuses it was meant to shelter." *Parliamentary Debates*, 1st Ser., Vol. XV, p. 341. See Sheridan's broadside, this collection, No. 16.

For a discussion of the press and liberty of opinion, consult Sir Thomas Erskine May, *The Constitutional History of England*, Vol. II, pp. 1–68, esp. pp. 60–68. An account of the Peltier trial appears in the *European Magazine and London Review* (March, 1803), Vol. XLIII, pp. 214–225. The jury, out one minute, brought in a verdict of guilty. References to liberty of the press appear in Nos. 3, 12, 15, 21, 37, 62, and 70.

No. 13. *My Friends and Countrymen.*

Dated July 27, 1803.
S. sh., 9 × 10¾; one side, one column.
Bibl. Lind., No. 1534.
Brit. Mus. *Catalogue, s.v.* "Friends."
Little Britain is a district in London.

No. 14. *Countrymen!*

S. sh., 18 × 21½; one side, dialogue in three columns, rest in one column.

This dramatic passage is taken, with some omissions, from Philip Massinger's (1584–1640) play, *The Bondman*, Act I, scene 3. See *The Plays of Philip Massinger*, ed. W. Gifford.

Timoleon (*ca.* 411–*ca.* 337 B.C.). A Greek statesman and general. When Syracuse (Sicily) appealed to her mother city, Corinth, against the Carthaginians, Timoleon hastened to her aid. He introduced 10,000 additional Greek colonists and endowed them with a democratic constitution. He suppressed later assaults by tyrants of other Sicilian cities. The grateful Syracusans erected a statue and a gymnasium in his honor. His Life was written by Plutarch and by Cornelius Nepos. The writer of broadside 27 subscribed himself TIMOLEON.

Thersites. A scurrilous Greek soldier at the siege of Troy. His foul mouth brought about his death at the hands of Achilles.

No. 15. *Song.*

S. sh., 8 × 12¾; one side, one column.

The tune "Heart[s] of Oak" may be found in Chappell's *Popular Music of the Olden Time*, p. 716. The original words were written by David Garrick for his *Harlequin's Invasion* (1759); the air, by Dr. William Boyce (1710–1779). Many other songs have been written to this popular air. One such on the theme of the invasion, under the title "The Voice of the British Isles," appeared in the *Gentleman's Magazine* (July, 1803), Vol. LXXIII, Pt. 2, pp. 666–667. In the same periodical (November, 1803), p. 1056, there is a longer anonymous poem entitled "Harlequin's Invasion," in which Napoleon takes on the dimensions of the famous pantomimic.

The play, *Harlequin's Invasion,* an anomalous pantomime with words, was produced at the height of a theatrical rivalry in which John Rich's pantomimes had become dangerous to the popularity of Garrick's Shakespearean stage. At the end of a nonsensical plot the forces of pantomime, undertaking to invade Parnassus, lose their fleet in a storm. Mercury adjures their leader, Harlequin, who has been presented as a Frenchman, to "beware encroachment and invade no more." Mercury waves his caduceus and, as the stage direction has it, "Shakespear rises: Harlequin sinks."

The text of *Harlequin's Invasion* may be found in David Garrick, *Three Plays,* ed. Elizabeth P. Stein; the "Heart of Oak," presumably because it was an occasional song, appears not to have been a part of the manuscript from which this edition is printed. See also Miss Stein's *David Garrick, Dramatist.*

No. 16. *Sheridan's Address to the People.*

S. sh., 8 × 13; one side, one column.
Bibl. Lind., No. 1514; tentative dating, June, 1803.
Sheridan, Richard Brinsley (1751–1816). The Dublin-born dramatist and statesman. His dramatic reputation rests mainly on his brilliant comedies, *The Rivals* (1775) and *The School for Scandal* (1777), and on his management, as Garrick's successor, of the Drury Lane Theater (1776 et seqq.). Entering Parliament in 1780, he took an active part thereafter in affairs of state; he held office as Under-Secretary for Foreign Affairs (1782) and as Treasurer of the Navy (1806). He opposed the war in America (1775–1783). He disapproved of the union of Great Britain and Ireland, except by the free consent of the two Parliaments. During the French Revolution, he maintained, with Fox, the right of the French to form a government to their own liking, but became a vigorous oppo-

nent of the aggressive designs of France. Although he demanded proof in Parliament of the imminence of a French invasion in 1796, when similar apprehensions arose in 1798, and particularly in 1803, he was a stout advocate of defense measures, urging Parliament to support the Volunteers and himself becoming a Lieutenant Colonel in the St. James's Volunteer corps. His last speech in Parliament was a vigorous plea for resistance against Napoleon, resting upon the conviction that should England fall the liberties of the world would fall with her.

Sheridan is held up to Irishmen as a model patriot in our No. 43. In a fanciful invasion sketch printed in Ashton's *Dawn of the Nineteenth Century* (pp. 83–88), Sheridan, with Lords Nelson, St. Vincent, and Duncan, Messrs. Addington, Pitt, and certain other peers and commoners, is charged with insurrection against the French occupation authorities, sentenced to be shot, and summarily executed in Hyde Park.

The substance of Sheridan's "Address" may be found in his *Speeches* (Bohn edition, 1842), Vol. III, pp. 89, 240, 417–458.

No. 17. *A Farce . . . The Invasion of England.*

S. sh., 16½ × 23; one side, one column.
Bibl. Lind., No. 1516; tentative dating, June, 1803.

The broadside is printed in full in Ashton's *English Caricature and Satire*, p. 154; also in *The Spirit of the Public Journals for 1803* (pp. 336–337), a miscellany, being, as runs the subtitle, "an impartial selection of the most exquisite essays and *jeux d'esprits;* principally prose, that appear in the newspapers and other publications." For other sham playbills, see Ashton, *Dawn of the Nineteenth Century*, pp. 89–90.

According to serial notations in the "Theatrical Register" columns of the *Gentleman's Magazine* (1803–1804), Colman's play titled *John Bull* was presented at Covent Garden on March 5, September 14, 21, 28, November 8, December 1, 8, 30, 1803, and January 4, June 5, 14, 1804.

No. 18. *Countrymen!* (Omitted, as a duplicate of No. 14.)

No. 19. *Epilogue to the New Play of* The Maid of Bristol.

S. sh., 10 × 14; one side, one column.
Brit. Mus. *Catalogue, s.v.* "Boaden, James," as follows: "The Maid of Bristol: a play [in three acts and in prose], with . . . an epilogue, written by George Colman, the Younger. *London,* 1803. 8°."

The Maid of Bristol was first performed at the Haymarket Theater, August 24, 1803; other performances followed, August 29, September 1, September 7, to fix the earlier dates. Genest's outline of the play (*Some Account*, Vol. VII, p. 592) does not indicate a patriotic plot.

Colman's "Epilogue" is printed in the *Gentleman's Magazine* (Supplement for 1803), Vol. LXXIII, Pt. 2, p. 1238; in the *European Magazine* (August, 1803), Vol. XLIV, p. 218; and, with immaterial changes, in the *Monthly Mirror* (September, 1803), Vol. XVI, pp. 205–206.

Boaden, James (1762–1839). English writer, known especially for his dramas and theatrical biographies.

Colman, George, the Younger (1762–1836). English actor and playwright who succeeded his father (1733–1794) as director of the Haymarket Theater in 1785. He wrote many popular comedies. For *John Bull* he received the largest sum ever paid up to that time for any drama.

Elliston, Robert William (1774–1831). A celebrated English actor who ran away from school and made his debut at the Haymarket Theater in 1796. In 1803 he was the principal actor and actor-manager of the Haymarket Theater.

No. 20. *Britons Triumph or Bonapartes Knell.*

S. sh., 7½ × 12; one side, one column.
Brit. Mus. *Catalogue, s.v.* "Napoleon I"; tentative dating, 1803.

The power of France under Napoleon, in geographical extent, in wealth, and in population, was so great that Switzerland, disunited Italy, Belgium, and Holland, after having been softened by the French Revolutionary crusade, inevitably became satellite states of France. An attack on any one or on all of them, or on the German states along the Rhine, upset the balance of power in Europe and menaced Britain. Spain could never quite make up her mind whether to direct her hostility against France or against Britain, and might, therefore, fight first on the one side and then on the other. Having lost her navy in the French interest at Trafalgar (October, 1805), she played a major part, after 1808, in the final overthrow of Napoleon.

No. 21. *Bonaparte's True Character.*

S. sh., 17½ × 22½; one side, one column.
Bibl. Lind., No. 1480.

The Polish Legion. Two half-brigades from the Polish Legion, originally intended for the French service in Italy, were induced, in part by their own Republican sympathies, to engage in the campaign against the rebels in Santo Domingo. Some 6,000 men in all, under the command of General Jablonowski, departed for the Caribbean early in 1802. Decimated more by disease than by the casualties of battle, only 300 of them returned from the abortive campaign. See *The Cambridge History of Poland, 1697–1935*, p. 225; also A. M. Skalkowski, *Polacy na San Domingo, 1802–09.*

No. 22. *Plain Answers to Plain Questions*.

S. sh., 17½ × 21; one side, dialogue in two columns, rest in one.
Bibl. Lind., No. 1510; tentative dating, June, 1803.
Brit. Mus. *Catalogue*, *s.v.* "Bull (John)"; tentative dating, 1803.
The references to September, October, foggy weather, long nights, indicate Napoleon's stated preference for autumn and winter as a period suitable to invasion, a predilection which his unfortunate experiences of the season 1803–1804 led him to abandon. Cf. Desbrière, *Projets et tentatives*, Vol. III, *passim*.

100,000 men. An early reference may be found in Napoleon's address to the five Swiss delegates at Paris, in January, 1803: "I solemnly declare that I would prefer to lose 100,000 men than to suffer an intervention of England in your affairs." See Paul Frischauer, *England's Years of Danger* (New York, 1938), p. 125. In the *Gentleman's Magazine* (May, 1803), Vol. LXIII, Pt. 1, p. 471, Napoleon is quoted as having said "to the English Ambassador that he would sacrifice 100,000 men to invade Britain."

No. 23. *Citizens of London!*

S. sh., 17½ × 21½; one side, one column.
For contemporary songs on the Armada, see *The Roxburghe Ballads*, ed. Ebsworth (Ballad Society, 1889), Vol. VI, pp. 371 ff.
In Elizabeth's England a standing army was unknown. In 1558, 1570, and 1588 the entire force of the counties was called out. The national levy made in 1588 produced about 750 lancers (heavy-armed cavalry), 2,000 light horse, and 56,000 foot, besides 20,000 men employed in watching the coast.
Philip II's attempt to invade England in 1588 bears a close resemblance to Napoleon's plan of 1805. The Spanish fleet of 130 ships and 30,000 men, of whom 19,000 were soldiers, was concentrated at Lisbon and Corunna. It sailed up the English Channel, where it was to embark the legions of the Duke of Parma and transport them to England. The English fleet of 197 ships and 18,000 men, practically all of whom were seamen, had an overwhelming superiority of fire power. The Spanish fleet reached Calais without major losses. Here, in the shallow waters of the French coast, on August 7 (N.S.), 1588, Admiral Howard attacked with eight fire ships and next day struck with the full weight of his fleet so that every large ship of the Armada was "very much spoiled." In danger of being beached by the wind, the Spanish admiral, Medina-Sidonia, was glad to escape into the North Sea and return home by circumnavigating the British Isles. Parma had been bottled up by the English and the Dutch in Flanders, a hundred miles above Calais, and had

been unable to move. The Spanish loss has been estimated at 63 ships. The English lost no ships, and the Spaniards did not "even burn so much as one sheepcote in this land." J. B. Black, *The Reign of Elizabeth, 1588–1603*, pp. 339–352.

No. 24. *The Sailor to His Messmates.*

S. sh., 8¾ × 13½; one side, one column.
Bibl. Lind., No. 1546; tentative dating, August, 1803.
Brit. Mus. *Catalogue, s.v.* "Sailor"; dating, 1803.
Note the repeated mention of the year 1803 in the text.

The drama from which the sailor's declamation was extracted is thus criticized in the *Monthly Review* for August, 1803 (p. 442): *Bonaparte, or The Freebooter*, a Drama in three Acts by John Scott Ripon, Esq. It represents the Invasion, in which an old woman, after having knocked down 50 French soldiers with a poker, solicits the Duke of Y—— to grant, as a reward for her prowess, a poker for her armorial bearings. Bonaparte falls in single combat with a young English officer, and 40,000 of the French are slain, with the loss of only a few hundred English.— Genest, characterizing the piece as "a poor drama," lists it among plays not acted, in *Some Account of the English Stage*, Vol. X, p. 226. Ripon is a pen name for John Scott Byerley; see Baker's *Biographia Dramatica*, under that name.

No. 25. *A Second Dialogue between Buonaparte and John Bull.*

S. sh., 17½ × 21½; one side, one column.
Bibl. Lind., No. 1511; tentative dating, June, 1803.
Brit. Mus. *Catalogue, s.v.* "Bull (John)"; tentative dating, 1803.

Boyer, Pierre-François-Joseph (1772–1851). A French marshal who, volunteering in January, 1792, achieved rapid advancement. He was appointed major general in the Army of Italy on June 2, 1796, served in Germany, and was attached to Kléber's division of the Army of Egypt on May 5, 1798. Appointed general of brigade on March 29, 1801, he was arrested in Alexandria by General Destaing, on the order of Menou, and left for France with Reynier. Sent to Santo Domingo, he was taken prisoner by the English in May, 1803, but returned to France to serve in later campaigns. His name is inscribed on the Arc de Triomphe.

No. 26. *Another Confirmation of the . . . Mercies of Bonaparte.*

Dated July 25, 1803.
S. sh., 8 × 13½; one side, one column.
Bibl. Lind., No. 1531.
Brit. Mus. *Catalogue, s.v.* "Bull (John) *pseud.*"

The title of the book from which the broadside draws its extract is entered in the catalogue of the British Museum, under the name of William Wittman, as follows: "Travels in Turkey, Asia Minor, Syria, and across the desert into Egypt during the years 1799, 1800, and 1801, in company with the Turkish army and the British military mission. To which are annexed, observations on the plague, and on the diseases prevalent in Turkey, and a meteorological journal. London, 1803. 4to." Wittman's work is discussed at some length in the *Edinburgh Review* for July, 1803, pp. 330–337. The only quotation there adduced contains the passage cited in the broadside, a little more and a little less. Between the words in our text, ". . . Nation calling itself civilized" and "Indeed, I am sorry to add," the text as quoted in the *Review* has the following sentence, "It would give pleasure to the author of this work, as well as to every liberal mind, to hear these facts contradicted on substantial evidence." Quite evidently it gave pleasure to the author of the broadside to omit, as not pertinent to his purpose, this mitigating statement, and to insert the parenthesis "Bonaparte" in two places. The *Edinburgh* reviewer takes Dr. Wittman to task for not supporting his principal hearsay allegations with proper local evidence. Cf. No. 4, with its notes, and the testimony of a purported eyewitness, the soldier in No. 28.

No. 27. *Englishmen!*

S. sh., 17½ × 21½; one side, two columns.
Bibl. Lind., No. 1491; tentative dating, June, 1803.

Dumouriez, Charles-François (1739–1823). A French military officer and statesman. As commandant at Cherbourg in 1779 he drew up a plan for the capture of the Isle of Wight. Prominent during the Revolution as Minister of Foreign Affairs and as a commander in the field, his increasing Royalist tendencies so much embroiled him with authorities that he fled France and spent the rest of his life in exile (1793–1823). Having won the regard of Lord Nelson, he was called to England in October, 1803. Here he was soon engaged, not unreservedly under official auspices, in preparing an elaborate scheme of defense against the threatened invasion, the conviction having grown upon him that a victory of England over Napoleon was necessary to the ultimate salvation of France. His story is told at length by J. Holland Rose and A. M. Broadley, in *Dumouriez and the Defence of England against Napoleon* (London, 1909); for his plan of defense, see pp. 240 ff.

Various figures have been given for the size of the volunteer army at this time. According to Sidney J. Low and F. S. Pulling, in the *Dictionary of English History*, p. 731: "In 1803 the fear of French Invasion caused nearly half a million of men to enroll themselves in Volunteer regiments."

For a discussion of the militia in June, 1803, see *Cobbett's Annual Register* (1803), Vol. III, pp. 182–191. The military forces consisted of the regular army, the militia, and the volunteers. The official returns of the volunteer force made at the War Office are listed in the *Monthly Mirror* (November, 1803), Vol. XVI, p. 358, as: Infantry, 297,502; Cavalry, 31,600; Artillery, 6,207; total, 335,209, with the comment, "If we add to these our regular militia we, too, may boast of 500,000 fighting men." Desbrière, *Projets et tentatives*, Vol. III, p. 259, gives the number of British volunteers on December 1, 1803, as 463,001.

No. 28. *A Dialogue between a British Tar . . . and a Brave Soldier.*

S. sh., 10½ × 17½; one side, two columns.
Bibl. Lind., No. 1487; tentative dating, June, 1803.
Brit. Mus. *Catalogue, s.v.* "Dialogue"; tentative dating, 1803.
Portsmouth. The chief naval station of England.
"Our brave captain" is probably a reference to Nelson.

No. 29. *Britannia's Charge to the Sons of Freedom.*

S. sh., 8½ × 13½; one side, one column.
Brit. Mus. *Catalogue, s.v.* "Rowe, Nicholas"; tentative dating, 1803.
Rowe, Nicholas (1674–1718). Dramatist and editor (1709) of Shakespeare. According to the *Dictionary of National Biography*, Rowe's poem was published as a broadside in 1703.
Caius Cornelius Cethegus. A conspirator with Catiline, Cethegus suffered death by strangling at the order of the Roman Senate.
Lucius Sergius Catilina, commonly called Catiline (108–62 B.C.). The famous Roman who organized a conspiracy in 63 B.C. to overthrow the existing Roman government. Summoned by Cicero before the Senate, Catiline fled to Faesulae and soon afterward fell with the revolting troops.

No. 30. *Victorious Englishmen.*

Dated August 8, 1803.
S. sh., 9½ × 15½; one side, two columns.
Bibl. Lind., No. 1541.

No. 31. *Epitaph underneath a Gibbet.*

S. sh., 8½ × 12½; one side, one column.
Bibl. Lind., No. 1492; tentative dating, June, 1803.
Printed in full in Ashton's *English Caricature and Satire*, p. 177; also, with minor changes, in the *Spirit of the Public Journals for 1803*, pp. 366–367.
Hastings. A parliamentary and county borough, one of the Cinque

Ports on the Channel, in the county of Sussex. William the Conqueror landed here in 1066 and on October 14 of that year fought the famous battle seven miles northwest of the town.

No. 32. *Shakespeare's Ghost!*

S. sh., 17½ × 23½; one side, one column.

Bibl. Lind., No. 1513; tentative dating, June, 1803.

Printed in full in the *Gentleman's Magazine* (July, 1803), Vol. LXXIII, Pt. 2, p. 664, and there subscribed "L. H."

The Shakespearean declamation is a mosaic of several passages from the plays. "Be stirring . . . Let us to arms" is from *King John*, Act V, scene 1; "Now on you noblest English . . . For England! and King George" is from *King Henry V*, Act III, scene 1; "This England . . . to itself do rest but true" forms the conclusion of *King John*, Act V, scene 7. Note the substitution of "King George" for "Saint George" in the second passage; and the insertion of a hortatory "Britons," not found in the original, at two places in the broadside. Shakespeare contributed variously to the defense of England in the crisis. See the patriotic parody, "To arm, or not to arm?" in the *Gentleman's Magazine* (August, 1803), Vol. LXXIII, Pt. 2, pp. 760–761; further, William Boscawen's "Occasional Address to the Volunteers," spoken by Charles Kemble at a performance of *King Henry V*, in the number for December, p. 1160.

Alexander the Great (356–323 B.C.). One of the four great commanders of history (Alexander, Hannibal, Caesar, and Napoleon).

No. 33. *The Declaration of the Merchants . . . of London.*

Dated July 26, 1803.

S. sh., 13 × 20½; one side, one column.

Bibl. Lind., No. 1533.

Brit. Mus. *Catalogue*, *s.v.* "Bosanquet, Jacob." Two entries, as follows: first, "Address of Jacob Bosanquet, Esq., on Tuesday, the 26th of July, 1803, at the Royal Exchange, as chairman of a . . . meeting of merchants, etc. J. Barfield: London, 1803. *S. sh.* fol."; second, "Substance of the speech of Jacob Bosanquet, Esq., at the Royal Exchange, July the 26th, 1803. James Asperne: London [1803] *S. sh.* fol."

Bosanquet, Jacob (1756–1828), of Broxbournbury, Hertfordshire, was for forty-five years a director of the East India Company, and served as chairman of the Company in 1803. He was a grandson of David Bosanquet (1661–1732) of Lyons, who, after the revocation of the Edict of Nantes, came with his brother John to England. Various members of the family in the course of time became prominent in English affairs.

A correspondent subscribing himself "A Freeholder of the British Empire," writing under date of August, 1803, applauds the Declaration, with especial reference to the rights of nations, quoting the paragraph, "We fight for that Constitution . . . ," in the *Gentleman's Magazine* (August, 1803), Vol. LXXIII, Pt. 2, pp. 731–732. In the same periodical, for June, 1803, p. 550, may be found complimentary verses, one set addressed to the Bosanquet family, and the other to Jacob Bosanquet, both expressing recognition of high public service.

No. 34. *Union and Watchfulness.*

S. sh., 10½ × 15; one side, two columns.
Bibl. Lind., No. 1521; tentative dating, June, 1803.
One passage in this pious exhortation suggests the Miltonic Satan, the arch-invader of Eden.

No. 35. *The Duke of Shoreditch; or, Barlow's Ghost.*

S. sh., 10½ × 16¾; one side, one column.
Bibl. Lind., No. 1488; tentative dating, June, 1803.
Brit. Mus. *Catalogue, s.v.* "Barlow (   )"; tentative dating, 1803.
Various works of reference tell substantially the same story of Barlow: Practice with the long bow, famous in English military history, continued under royal favor and even under royal prescription long after this weapon had been superseded in battle by the crossbow. At one of the annual contests Henry VII (in some accounts, as in the broadside, Henry VIII) singled out an archer from Shoreditch, Barlow by name, for especial praise and by way of reward conferred upon him the title, Duke of Shoreditch. See Sir Walter Besant, *Survey of London* (London, 1904), Vol. IV, p. 355. Cf. the somewhat different version in the Honourable Daines Barrington's "Observations on the Practice of Archery in England," a letter read before the Society of Antiquaries, February 27, 1783, in *Archæologia; or Miscellaneous Tracts relating to Antiquity* (London, 1785), p. 66. Maps of Finsbury Fields and Shoreditch may be found in the *Survey of London*, Vol. III, p. 85.

It may be of interest to note that among the volunteers reviewed by the King in Hyde Park on October 26, 1803, were 294 effectives from Shoreditch; see the *Gentleman's Magazine* (October, 1803), Vol. LXXIII, Pt. 2, p. 977.

Shoreditch is a quarter of London north of "the City."

Spitalfields is an eastern district of London on the north side of the Thames. It is a great seat of silk manufacturing.

Finsbury is a part of London just north of "the City."

Clerkenwell is a district of London, county of Middlesex, one mile north of St. Paul's. It has a famous prison.

No. 36. *Freedom or Slavery.*

S. sh., 10½ × 17½; one side, one column.
Brit. Mus. *Catalogue, s.v.* "Freedom"; tentative dating, 1803.
The tune for "Rule Britannia" is to be found in Chappell, *Popular Music of the Olden Time*, p. 688.

No. 37. *Address to the People of Great Britain.*

S. sh., 11 × 17¾; one side, two columns.
Brit. Mus. *Catalogue, s.v.* "Denison, W. J."; tentative dating, 1803.
Denison, William Joseph (1770–1849), at various periods a member of Parliament, was a wealthy banker of Lombard Street. The *Dictionary of National Biography* characterizes his Address as "a patriotic poem of some merit on Napoleon's threatened invasion of 1803."
Caractacus. A British king, celebrated in verse and story, hero of his people in their battles against the Romans in the first century of the Christian era.
Wallace, Sir William (1272–1305). Scottish hero in the struggle against Edward I, whose greatest victory, at Stirling Castle in September, 1297, became a symbol of heroism for the Scots. Defeated, and in time betrayed, he was tried and executed in England.
Barons of Runnymede. The English barons who secured King John's signature to the Magna Charta, on June 15, 1215. Runnymede has its name from a meadow on the south bank of the Thames in Surrey.
Batavia. The Latin name for the Netherlands.
Nassau. William III (1650–1702), King of England. The great-grandson of William I, Prince of Orange, Count of Nassau. As William I had resisted Spain, William III resisted France.
Bruce, Robert (1274–1329). King of Scotland. Won Scottish independence at the Battle of Bannockburn (1314).
Duncan, Adam, Viscount Duncan (1731–1804). Commander-in-chief in the North Sea from 1795 to 1801, this able British admiral prevented the mutiny of 1797 from extending to his flagship and defeated the Dutch off Camperdown in the same year.
Jervis, John, Earl of St. Vincent (1735–1823). British admiral, who fought against the French at Quebec (1759), off Brest (1778), and in the West Indies (1793). His victory off Cape St. Vincent, on February 14, 1797, was a great triumph. With fifteen ships, he defeated twenty-seven Spanish ships.
Boyne, Battle of the (July 1, 1690). Driven from the throne by William III, in the Revolution of 1688, King James II, supported by his cousin the French king, Louis XIV, attempted to regain his position through

Ireland, most of which he conquered. William, with English and Dutch troops, gained a complete victory at the Boyne, in one of the decisive contests in Anglo-Irish history.

Calpe. Ancient name of Gibraltar, one of the Pillars of Hercules at the east end of the Strait of Gibraltar.

Denmark stood as guardian to the entrance of the Baltic, a chief supply house of naval stores for the English fleet and merchant marine. Latent maritime enmity between Britain and the Baltic countries led to the formation of armed-neutrality leagues in 1780 and 1800, composed of Denmark, Sweden, Prussia, and Russia. So grave a menace to British strength was averted in 1801 by the double blow of the assassination of the Czar Paul I of Russia (March 23) and Nelson's bombardment of Copenhagen (April 2). Alexander I abandoned the plans of Paul, and Nelson's blow removed the threat by the Danes, who were usually in Napoleon's camp.

Attila (d. 453). A king of the Huns, called the "Scourge of God," he ravaged the Eastern Empire during the years 445–450, then invaded the Western Empire and was defeated at Châlons in 451.

Ausonia. A name applied by poets to Italy, after the Ausones or Aurunci, an ancient Latin tribe.

No. 38. *Corporal Trim on the Invasion.*

S. sh., 10¼ × 17¾; one side, two columns.

Bibl. Lind., No. 1486; tentative dating, June, 1803.

Brit. Mus. *Catalogue, s.v.* "Trim"; tentative dating, 1803.

The pseudonymous author borrows his name and title from the past master of military science, Corporal Trim, in Sterne's *Tristram Shandy*.

With this technical discussion of defense measures may be compared Colonel Hope's "Instructions to . . . the Edinburgh Volunteers," in the *Gentleman's Magazine* (November, 1803), Vol. LXXIII, Pt. 2, pp. 1068–1070, and our broadside No. 3.

Our Egyptians. Veterans of the British campaigns in Egypt. Cf. the paragraph on the Army of Egypt in our broadside No. 49.

Suvarov (Suwarrow, Suvoroff), Aleksander Vasilyevich (1729–1800). A famous Russian general. As commander in northern Italy in the War of the Second Coalition (1798–1799), he drove the French out of upper Italy. His triple principle was *coup d'œil*, speed, attack, and he was never directly beaten. One of his favorite military maxims was: "The bullet is a fool; the bayonet is a good fellow."

Armée d'Angleterre. A French army organized specifically for the invasion of England. See Desbrière's *Projets et tentatives*, Vol. I, pp. 283 ff. Cf. "the real Army of England" mentioned toward the close of broadside No. 46.

No. 39. *Citizens of England*.

S. sh., 10¾ × 17¼; one side, one column.

Bibl. Lind., No. 1484; tentative dating, June, 1803.

Brit. Mus. *Catalogue, s.v.* "Napoleon I"; tentative dating, 1803.

This piece is printed, except for the last paragraph, in Ashton's *English Caricature and Satire*, pp. 202–203.

With the detailed preparations here recited may be compared Napoleon's orders, under date of March 11, 1803, affecting dispositions at Dunkirk and Cherbourg, in Desbrière, *Projets et tentatives*, Vol. III, p. 22. Similar aggressive activities at the various Channel ports of France and the Netherlands are set forth, *passim*, in the same volume.

Nature was Napoleon's first opponent in the invasion of the British Isles. The "invasion towns," or bases for invasion flotillas, Dunkirk, Calais, Boulogne, Le Havre, had shallow harbors which frequently were filled with silt. It was only the Continental harbors in the region of Antwerp and Rotterdam that could be counted on, and the century-long struggle of France to hold the ports of Belgium and Holland thus had a geographical foundation. Britain's numerous harbors were free from silt; but her interlocking system of inland river ports was so effective as even to delay roadbuilding. The broadsides emphasize that British local defense must withstand invading forces, because rapid concentration of troops at a point of danger was difficult without military roads, such as France possessed. France, without good harbors, but with good roads, could readily move her armies but not her fleet. England, in contrast, had mobility on sea and river but less on land.

Boulogne. This French city on the Strait of Dover is one of the coastal cities nearest England. It was a beehive of activity during the various invasion concentrations, and its shipbuilding works supplied to Napoleon many of his gunboats and flat-bottomed boats. Bruges, a Flemish town in Belgium, formerly a member of the Hanseatic League, served as a chief center for the transshipment of goods. Antwerp, on the Scheldt River, which had been the leading seaport of Europe in the reign of Charles V, declined during the civil wars in the Low Countries, and was a mere shell when Napoleon occupied it in 1803. He improved the harbor and the forts. He regarded Antwerp as a pistol pointing at the heart of England, and as a city which he hoped might rival London.

No. 40. *A Peep into Hanover*.

S. sh., 10½ × 17; one side, one column.

Bibl. Lind., No. 1507; tentative dating, June, 1803.

Printed, except for the verse, in Ashton's *English Caricature and Satire*, pp. 139–140.

The lines of verse are taken from a poem by John Pomfret (1667–1702) entitled "Cruelty and Lust, An Epistolary Essay." The entire poem may be read in Johnson's *Works of the English Poets* (London, 1790), Vol. XVII, pp. 65–79. A footnote there explains the title as follows: "This piece was occasioned by the barbarity of Kirke, a commander in the Western Rebellion, 1685, who debauched a young lady with a promise to save her husband's life, but hanged him the next morning." The broadside picks up the theme and even the wording in the title of the poem.

Aga. A Turkish official, here referring to the French commandant in Hanover.

Janissaries. Turkish infantrymen. The first Janizaries were personal slaves of the Sultan; later members of the troop were for the most part Christian slaves and miscellaneous conscripts. On their revolting in 1826, the organization was abolished. This term for Napoleon's soldiery, and the title of Sultan applied to him as their chief, fixed upon the French invaders the odium of despots.

Gottingen (Göttingen) is the famous German university town.

Hanover surrendered to General Mortier on June 3, 1803.

Cf. the exemplary story of atrocities told by the Hanoverian blacksmith in No. 63.

No. 41. *Parody*.

S. sh., 11 × 17½; one side, one column.

Keppel, Augustus, first Viscount Keppel (1725–1786). A British admiral, commander of the ships of the North American station in 1754, commander-in-chief of the grand fleet in 1778, and First Lord of the Admiralty in 1782.

Boscawen, Edward (1711–1761). A British admiral, who served first in the West Indies, and then in the East Indies during the war of the Austrian Succession. He fought in European and North American waters during the Seven Years' War, became admiral in 1758, and helped capture Louisburg in the same year. In 1759–1760 he was in command in the Mediterranean and on the western coast of France. His nephew, William Boscawen (1752–1811), educated at Eton and Westminster, was Commissioner of the Victualling Office in 1785. He published a translation of Horace and other works. For the meetings of the Literary Fund, which he considered as almost his own child, he made frequent contributions of occasional verse. See our notes on No. 6.

No. 42. *The Prophecy!*

S. sh., 13 × 14¾; one side, two columns.

This piece is more remarkable for patriotic energy than for metrical skill.

Old or Young Paines. No doubt a reference to Thomas Paine (1737–1809), American political writer, author of *The Rights of Man* and *The Age of Reason*, whose doctrines would scarcely appeal to an arch-conservative like the poet of "The Prophecy," to whom republics, at first pleasing a "delusive Fancy," end by affrighting mankind.

A hundred rich men. The Paris Papers of August 1, 1803, contained an account of the Debates on the English Army of Defense Bill, with a statement imputed to Mr. Windham that England would experience the fate of Carthage if France should prevail in the contest. The *Moniteur* observes: "No, Mr. Windham, no: we will chastise about one hundred oligarchical families, whose influence and counsels ever sway the Government itself, and which are responsible for all the blood which has been shed in Europe for some years past. We will permit the English to enjoy all the blessings of equality; and establish a permanent alliance, which shall secure the repose of Europe, the civilization of the two worlds, and the improvement of the human species!!!" Quoting this piece from the *Moniteur*, the *Gentleman's Magazine* (August, 1803), Vol. LXXIII, Pt. 2, p. 773, comments, "When the Moniteur threatens us with the destruction of an hundred of our principal families, one would almost suppose that Paper in the pay of the British government. . . . If anything will rouse our Nobility, this will. Here again we have the old cant of 'Peace to the Cottage, and destruction to the Palace.'—When the Sheep had given up their Dogs to the Wolves, we remember the consequences."

No. 43. *Address to Irishmen Residing in England*.

Dated August 8, 1803.

S. sh., 10½ × 17; one side, one column, except for the list of publications, which is in two-column measure.

Bibl. Lind., No. 1540.

On Sheridan as the model for Irishmen in England, see No. 16 and its notes.

Large numbers of Irishmen had emigrated to England as well as to America in the eighteenth century. The writer of the broadside undoubtedly knew the story of Edward Marcus Despard (1751–1803), a captain of engineers and ruler of the Mosquito Shore in Central America, who was suspended from office without a hearing in 1790, and imprisoned during the Rebellion of 1798. Subsequently, spies reported that he planned to seize the Tower and the Bank of England, and to assassinate the King. He and forty men, most of whom were Irishmen, were arrested on November 16, 1802. Although Nelson testified in his behalf, he was convicted and executed on February 21, 1803.

Robert Emmet's (1778–1803) insurrection in Ireland on July 23, 1803, followed Despard's execution. Emmet planned to seize Dublin Castle, Pigeon House Fort, and the person of the Viceroy. The Viceroy was killed, but the attack on the Castle by one hundred men was repelled. Tried on September 19, 1803, Emmet was hanged next day. His speech before sentence became a historical classic. News of Emmet's rebellion might have reached the writer of the broadside, dated August 8, 1803. Whether the two insurrections were related has not been determined.

No. 44. *Britons Triumph.* (Omitted, as a duplicate of No. 20.)

No. 45. *The Great Egyptian Gun.*

S. sh., 8 × 13½; one side, two columns, except for the last stanza.
At the top of the sheet there is a woodcut of the great gun.
St. James's Park. Developed from fields by Charles II in the fashion of Druid gardens. The piece of water in the Park is a relic of the course of the Tyburn stream which flowed into the Thames at Westminster. See Bird-cage Walk, in notes to No. 3.

No. 46. *Navy of Britain.*

Dated July 11, 1803.
S. sh., 10½ × 17½; one side, one column.
Bibl. Lind., No. 1525.
Brit. Mus. *Catalogue, s.v.* "Navy."
Bumboat. A scavenger's boat, or a provision boat. The term lends itself to punning, possibly not here intended.
Drake, Sir Francis (1540 ?–1596). One of Elizabeth's sea dogs. Knighted by the great queen in 1581, after his exploits in the West Indies and his circumnavigation of the globe, he was active in the defeat of the Spanish Armada. An investment of £1 in one of his voyages yielded a return of £47.
Rodney, George Brydges, first Baron Rodney (1719–1792). Made an admiral in 1778, Rodney relieved Gibraltar on his way to the West Indies, by a crushing victory over the Spanish at Cape St. Vincent. In 1782 he inflicted a decisive defeat upon the French fleet under De Grasse.
The Tower of London. The ancient fortress, palace, and prison, surrounded by a moat on the bank of the Thames at the southeast angle of the old walled city, was constructed by William the Conqueror and his successors, especially Henry III.
The "real army of England" is here placed in contrast to the French *Armée d'Angleterre* organized for the invasion of England. Cf. No. 38 and its note.
Publicola, the subscribed author, is presumably to be identified with the author of No. 1 and No. 49.

No. 47. *John Bull Turned into a Galley Slave.*

S. sh., 11 × 17; one side, one column.
Bibl. Lind., No. 1499; tentative dating, June, 1803.
Brit. Mus. *Catalogue, s.v.* "Bull (John)"; tentative dating, 1803.
The broadside to which this is a sequel is advertised in the list of publications under No. 43.
Austria. The Hapsburg monarchy, having fought a series of wars against the Revolutionary French and Napoleon, had just made the Peace of Lunéville (February 9, 1801). Austria reëntered the war in 1805. She drew strength from the migration of Germans from the Rhineland to Vienna, of whom Metternich was the most famous. Austria, next to England the most consistent enemy of France, was one of the four great powers which finally overwhelmed Napoleon and remapped Europe at the Congress of Vienna, 1814–1815.

No. 48. *English Mastiffs.*

S. sh., 11 × 17; one side, one column.
Bibl. Lind., No. 1489; tentative dating, June, 1803.
Brit. Mus. *Catalogue, s.v.* "English"; tentative dating, 1803.
Printed in full in John Ashton's *English Caricature and Satire,* pp. 149–150. A footnote there indicates that the text is extracted from "Mr. Stanhope's speech at a meeting of Yorkshire noblemen and gentlemen, at the castle, York, July 28, 1803, for the purpose of addressing the king on the situation of the country." Mr. Stanhope may possibly have been Charles Stanhope (1753–1829), third Earl of Harrington, who from July, 1803, to October, 1809, acted as second-in-command of the staff of the London district.
On the identification of Yorkshiremen with mastiffs, cf. the traditional honorific, "Yorkshire tike," employed to characterize the title personage in Carey's ballad opera, *The Honest Yorkshireman* (1736). See the *New English Dictionary, s.v.* "tyke."

No. 49. *Brave Soldiers, Defenders of Your Country!*

S. sh., 10½ × 17½; one side, one column.
Bibl. Lind., No. 1481; tentative dating, June, 1803.
Brit. Mus. *Catalogue, s.v.* "Publicola," presumably identical with the author of No. 1 and No. 46; tentative dating, 1803.
Printed in full in Ashton's *English Caricature and Satire,* pp. 141–143.

No. 50. *Invasion!*

Dated July 5, 1803.

S. sh., 10½ × 17¾; one side, one column.
Bibl. Lind., No. 1523.
Brit. Mus. *Catalogue, s.v.* "Bull (John)."
Regraters. On regrating, a forbidden middleman's practice corresponding to our modern "profiteering," see John Ashton, *The Dawn of the Nineteenth Century in England,* pp. 16 ff., where will be found also some comparative statistics relating to the cost of living in the period just before the invasion year.

No. 51. *English, Scots, and Irishmen.*

Dated July, 1803.
S. sh., 10 × 17; one side, two columns.
Brit. Mus. *Catalogue, s.v.* "Mayne (John) of Dumfries"; also with other pieces, *s.v.* "Songs. Loyal Songs"; tentative dating, 1803.
Printed in the *Gentleman's Magazine* (September, 1803), Vol. LXXIII, Pt. 2, p. 858, under the same title but with the added designation of the writer as "Author of *Glasgow,* a Poem."
John Mayne (1759–1836), a Scottish poet whom Sir Walter Scott held in rather high esteem. See the *Dictionary of National Biography.*

No. 52. *The Menaces of Bonaparte.*

S. sh., 10½ × 17; one side, one column.
Bibl. Lind., No. 1502; tentative dating, June, 1803.
Brit. Mus. *Catalogue, s.v.* "Napoleon I"; tentative dating, 1803.

No. 53. *Advice Suggested by the State of the Times.*

S. sh., 11 × 17½; one side, two columns.
Bibl. Lind., No. 1475; tentative dating, June, 1803.
Brit. Mus. *Catalogue, s.v.* "Wilberforce (William)"; tentative dating, 1803.
Wilberforce, William (1759–1833). Best known for his lifelong devotion to the abolition of the British slave trade and slavery, he was also the leading layman of the Evangelicals, commonly called the Clapham Sect. The ideas of this broadside are expressed in detail in his book, *A Practical View of the Prevailing Religious System of Professed Christians in the Higher and Middle Classes, Contrasted with Real Christianity.* Published in April, 1797, 7,500 copies were sold in the first six months. By 1824, fifteen editions had been published in England and twenty-five in America. Wilberforce, during his long Parliamentary career, controlled about forty votes of a group known as the Pious Party or The Saints. As a Pietist, he attempted to suppress Sunday newspapers, such as the *British Neptune* (Nos. 57, 63), but failed because most of these papers were sup-

porters of the government. For the career of Wilberforce see Reginald Coupland, *Wilberforce: A Narrative*, and Frank J. Klingberg, *The Anti-Slavery Movement in England: A Study in English Humanitarianism* (New Haven and London, 1926).

No. 54. *Freedom and Loyalty: with a New Song.*

Dated July 30, 1803.
S. sh., 11 x 17; one side, in part one column, in part two.
Bibl. Lind., No. 1537.
Brit. Mus. *Catalogue, s.v.* "Freedom."
The reference to the "Common People" at the beginning suggests comparison with No. 57, *The Ploughman's Ditty*, which expresses the poor man's point of view.

No. 55. *The Consequences of Buonaparte's Succeeding.*

S. sh., 10½ x 17; one side, one column.
Bibl. Lind., No. 1485; tentative dating, June, 1803.
Brit. Mus. *Catalogue, s.v.* "Napoleon I"; tentative dating, 1803.
These "Consequences" summarize the more forbidding elements in the entire series of broadsides.

No. 56. *The Antigallican Club. For Our Country.*

Dated August 23, 1803.
S. sh., 10¾ x 17½; one side, dialogue in two columns.
Bibl. Lind., No. 1545.
Brit. Mus. *Catalogue, s.v.* "Antigallican."
Antigallican. A term equivalent to Anti-French.
Oakland. The land of the (British) Oak.
The entire setting of the meeting of the club, the descriptive names of the members, and the punning dialogue suggest the rehearsal by the "rude mechanicals," in Shakespeare's *Midsummer Night's Dream*, Act I, scene 2, of their play of "Pyramis and Thisbe."
The name of the chairman, Crispin Heeltap, carries a reminder that the Battle of Agincourt, frequently mentioned in the broadsides, was fought on St. Crispin's Day; Shakespeare's *King Henry V*, Act IV, scene 3.
Caxon. A caxon was a kind of wig.
Manchet. An old term for wheaten bread of fine quality.
Tory-rory. The term implies boisterous conduct.
Mummies. Possibly a malapropism for "Mamelukes," a term applied derisively in several of the broadsides to Napoleon's troops.
Mungo. Probably a reference to a black slave in a farce by Isaac

Bickerstaffe, called *The Padlock*, in which the part of Mungo was played by Charles Dibdin.

The bag. To give one the bag to hold: to leave in the lurch.

Full bottoms, majors, brigadiers, ramilees, collyflowers, Brutuses. Wigs of various fashions.

Blocks. A block was a wooden head used in shaping a wig.

Meal-tub plot. *New English Dictionary:* "Meal-tub Plot, the pretended conspiracy of the Duke of Monmouth in 1679, the evidence for which consisted of papers found in a meal-tub."

Royal Brunswick Blacking. Presumably a trade name for a brand of varnish made of turpentine and asphalt or lampblack.

Naples and Otranto, Italy. At the beginning of the nineteenth century, the Kingdom of Naples comprised all of Italy south of the Papal States. British sea power in the Mediterranean made the position of Naples a bone of contention between Britain and France. By the Treaty of Amiens, French occupation of Naples was to end. The occupation of Naples and Otranto in the summer of 1803, together with the naval activity at Toulon and Genoa, left it doubtful whether Napoleon had determined to strike at London or resume his eastern adventures.

Lapstone. A stone which shoemakers laid in their laps to beat leather upon.

Dead men. A slang term applied sometimes to the baker himself, sometimes to an extra loaf smuggled out of the shop by the baker's boy, in a basket intended for customers.

Wooden walls. The British Fleet, the "hearts of oak."

The *European Magazine and London Review* (February, 1804), Vol. XLIV, p. 235, reviews an invasion miscellany under the title, *The Antigallican; or Standard of British loyalty, Religion, and Liberty: Including a collection of the principal Papers, Tracts, Speeches, Poems, and Songs that have been published on the threatened Invasion*.

No. 57. [Three songs.]

S. sh., 8½ × 11; both sides: recto, "The Ploughman's Ditty," two columns; verso, "The Island of Britain," and the "New God Save the King," two columns.

All three of the songs are taken from *The British Neptune*, under different dates.

57 a. *The Ploughman's Ditty*.

Brit. Mus. *Catalogue, s.v.* "Ploughman."

The tune "He that has the best wife" may be found in Chappell's *Popular Music of the Olden Time*, Vol. II, p. 557. The verse is by Hannah

More, English religious writer (1745–1833). See Wheeler and Broadley, *Napoleon and the Invasion of England*, Vol. II, pp. 301–303.

Printed in the *Gentleman's Magazine* (Suppl. for 1803), Vol. LXXIII, Pt. 2, p. 1238, and in *The Patriots' Vocal Miscellany*, Dublin, 1804.

The *Monthly Review* for 1803 notices, among other fast-day sermons preached on October 19, one entitled, "What has the Poor Man to lose in the Event of a successful Invasion?" The answer of the preacher is briefly indicated (*Mon. Rev.*, November, 1803, p. 331): The poor man would become a hewer of wood and a drawer of water. Consequences more dire are promised in an unsigned prose contribution to the *Gentleman's Magazine* (August, 1803), Vol. LXXIII, Pt. 2, pp. 729–730, entitled, "Advice to English Day Labourers concerning Buonaparte's Invasion": nothing less than shooting or poisoning, after the fashion of Jaffa.

57 b. *The Island of Britain. A Loyal Song.*

On the tune "Hearts of Oak" see the note to No. 15.

57 c. *New God Save the King.*

The Corse. The Corsican.

Brunswick's Royal Line. The House of Hanover.

The Patriotic Fund at Lloyd's. The following account of the inauguration of the fund appeared in the *European Magazine* (August, 1803), Vol. XLIV, p. 54: "A meeting of the subscribers to Lloyd's Coffee-House, held to consider a better way of rewarding the defenders of the Country, and relieving the relations of those who fall in battle, than took place during the last war, resolved, instead of raising a partial occasional fund, to raise one general fund for the purpose of rewarding the individuals who distinguish themselves in the defense of their country, and of relieving the relations of those who fall. For this purpose a general fund was opened; and the first act was, a vote to it from the Funds of the Society of Lloyd's Coffee-House of £20,000, three per cent. Consols. . . . The sum raised at the end of this month exceeded £150,000." In the number for October, 1803, *ibid.*, p. 289, especial mention is made of liberal contributions from "titled and untitled" women in all parts of the kingdom. Cf. Sir Walter Besant, *Survey of London*, Vol. VII, p. 48.

Lloyd's Coffee-House. Known as a popular place of refreshment toward the end of the 17th century, Lloyd's gradually became the resort of persons interested in marine insurance. By degrees, and through various changes in organization and control, the institution has reached its present commanding position in the field of shipping and insurance. Cf. the article, "Lloyd's," in the *Encyclopædia Britannica*.

The Poor. Time has effaced the memory of the severe blows struck by Pitt against the English sympathizers with the French Revolution. Burke began the crusade against France in his *Reflections on the French Revolution* (1790). The societies which advocated constitutional reform in England were all crushed by 1799. The leading champion of radicalism was Thomas Paine, whose *Rights of Man* was published in 1791 and 1792 as an answer to Burke. His plea was for full democracy and equality between man and man.

Paine advocated a reduction of taxation by cutting down administrative expenditure; provision for education of the poor and for the aged poor; family allowances; maternity grants; funeral allowances; a graduated income tax; and a limitation of armaments by international agreement. Two hundred thousand copies of this work were sold in 1793.

There were three main radical organizations in England. The Friends of the People, a group dominated by aristocratic Whigs, followers of Charles James Fox, was the most conservative. The Society for Constitutional Information, under Major John Cartwright and Horne Tooke, represented the middle-class radicals. The London Corresponding Society, the most extreme of the groups, represented the skilled workmen. Thomas Hardy, a shoemaker, was its secretary. All these societies were, before the outbreak of the war on February 1, 1793, in correspondence with the French Revolutionary clubs.

The British government sponsored its own organization, the Society for Preserving Liberty and Property against Republicans and Levellers. It published quantities of reading matter, held meetings, and intimidated owners of buildings so that radicals of the specifically English type could not hold meetings. The government brought to trial publishers, booksellers, and authors. The Habeas Corpus Act was suspended from 1794 to 1800. Whether persons were convicted or acquitted, the radical societies lost their members. The London Corresponding Society, the last survivor, was abolished by an Act of Parliament in 1799, which made this and similar organizations illegal and suppressed trade unionism as well. By 1800 the courts and Parliament had checked the reform movement in England.

However, in spite of agitation, the French Revolution found British workers in agriculture and industry in so disorganized a condition that neither agricultural nor urban revolution was possible. Enclosure was destroying the independence of the rural population, and, in industry, trade unionism had not yet taken root. The middle classes in England were asking for constitutional changes to give them a share in government, but they were not interested in revolution of the French type. Skilled artisans were rising into the middle class. In short, the soil of revolution was not ready in England, even had there been no repressive action by the government. The English aristocracy differed from that of France in that its members remained a race of country gentlemen, were happiest away from London, and kept in close contact with the people of their counties. Squire Western of *Tom Jones* might spend the night under the table if he spent the day in the saddle. The English gentry kept the tradition of independence and of participation in the county services. The Lord Lieutenant, the Sheriff, the Justices of the Peace, held offices of as much honor as was a seat in Parliament. This condition was in sharp contrast to the situation of France, where the nobles, having lost control both of the king and of local governments, were idly congregated in Paris. See Robert Birley, *The English Jacobins*, passim; G. D. H. Cole, *A Short History of the British Working Class Movement*, Vol. I, pp. 43-75; G. D. H. Cole and Raymond Postgate, *The British Common People, 1746-1938*, pp. 137-153. Philip Anthony Brown's *The French Revolution in English History* is a brilliant study by a young scholar, killed in action in 1915. Emphasis on the worker of England is given in J. L. and Barbara Hammond, *The Skilled Labourer, 1760-1832*; *The Village Labourer, 1760-1832*; and *The Town Labourer, 1760-1832*. These three volumes give a penetrating analysis of the age of transition from a rural economy to an industrial economy.

No. 58. *Fellow Citizens.*

S. sh., 11 × 17; one side, one column.
Bibl. Lind., No. 1493; tentative dating, June, 1803.
Printed in full in Ashton's *Dawn of the Nineteenth Century in England*, pp. 80-81.
On the British army's relation to the bayonet, cf. Suwarrow's maxim in the note to our No. 38.
The closing quotation is from Shakespeare's *King John*, Act V, scene 7.

No. 59. *A Word of Advice to the Self-Created Consul.*

Dated August 10, 1803.
S. sh., 11 × 17½; one side, one column.
Bibl. Lind., No. 1542.
With the dismal forecast of a defeated French army returning home to plunder its own people may be compared the similar prospect held out by General Dumouriez in No. 27.

No. 60. *A Relish for Old Nick.*

S. sh., 10¾ × 17¼; one side, one column.
The tune "Vicar and Moses" is to be found in Chappell's *Popular*

Music of the Olden Time, p. 602. A text of "The Vicar and Moses," with an illustration by Robert Cruikshank, appears in *The Universal Songster*, Vol. I, pp. 353–354.

No. 61. *A Dialogue between a British Tar . . . and a Brave Soldier.*

Omitted, as a duplicate of No. 28.

No. 62. *People of the British Isles.*

S. sh., 10½ x 17½; one side, one column.
Bibl. Lind., No. 1509; tentative dating, June, 1803.
Brit. Mus. *Catalogue, s.v.* "Volunteer"; tentative dating, 1803.
The references to the merchants and traders at the close of the broadside suggest comparison with No. 33.

No. 63. *Horrors upon Horrors.*

S. sh., 10¾ x 16¾; one side, narrative in two columns.
Bibl. Lind., No. 1495; tentative dating, June, 1803.
As for the substance of the piece, related allegations relative to the French occupation of Hanover will be found briefly set forth in No. 40. The emphasis upon Napoleonic atrocities runs as a pervasive undertone throughout the broadsides.

Harbourgh (Harburg), Hanover, is a town of Prussia on the river Elbe, six miles from Hamburg and twenty-three miles northwest of Lüneburg.

No. 64. *Substance of the Corsican Bonaparte's Hand-bills.*

S. sh., 10¾ x 17; one side, one column.
Bibl. Lind., No. 1515; tentative dating, June, 1803.
Marcoff (Markoff, Markov), Count Arcadi Ivanovitch (1747–1827). A Russian diplomat, who, on the accession of Alexander I, was appointed Minister Plenipotentiary to France in 1800. Marcoff was concerned variously in the negotiations between Whitworth and Talleyrand. See Oscar Browning, *England and Napoleon in 1803.*

Industrial towns. The rise of the northern industrial towns is sometimes spoken of as a covered-wagon migration of workers to the new industrial areas such as Manchester, Liverpool, Sheffield, and Leeds. Liverpool, often called the center of the slave trade, was also the shipping port for this industrial area. These new towns grew with a rapidity comparable only to that of our own cities of the Great Lakes.

No. 65. *Twenty Thousand Pounds Reward.*

S. sh., 10 x 16; one side, one column.
Bibl. Lind., No. 1520; tentative dating, June, 1803.

This broadside was issued with various headings for distribution in the severally designated counties.

Whitworth, Charles, Earl Whitworth (1752–1825). Great Britain was confronted by the menace of both Russia and France at the turn of the century. Whitworth spent twelve years as ambassador to Russia (1788–1800), where he worked against the Russian policy of expansion into Turkey and Poland. For this position his qualifications have been described in the *Cambridge History of British Foreign Policy*, Vol. I, p. 222: "Sir Charles Whitworth . . . a man of soldierly bearing and firmness of character withstood alike the craft of Catherine and the whimsical impulses of Paul I."

Trained and trusted by Pitt and Grenville, Whitworth was exactly the type of career diplomat needed by Addington and Hawkesbury to represent Great Britain in Paris after the very long break in diplomatic relations between the two countries, and to carry out the policy of the Addington administration of peace with France. Of this policy the *Cambridge History of British Foreign Policy* says (p. 320): "Much . . . could be urged in favor of Addington's waiting policy. Peace having been concluded, its author had to ensure for it a fair trial. . . . The sole hope for the preservation of peace in the spring of 1803 was that he should substitute reason for menace, and, admitting that his annexations and other proceedings had naturally alarmed Great Britain, should offer either to forget one or more of them or admit the justice of her claims to compensation, conceded in the negotiations at Amiens."

The epithetical use of Lord Whitworth's name in the broadside seems scarcely intended as a compliment to the late British ambassador at Paris. Perhaps there is an implied criticism of Whitworth's temporizing with Napoleon over Malta and other questions in dispute prior to the somewhat dilatory rupture of relations in May, 1803. If so, the writer evidently regarded Whitworth as an "appeaser." See Oscar Browning's *England and Napoleon in 1803*. For final attempts to preserve peace by persuading Napoleon to give up Malta, see C. L. Lokke, "Secret Negotiations to Maintain the Peace of Amiens," *American Historical Review* (October, 1943), Vol. XLIX, pp. 55–64.

On Napoleon as a fit subject for exhibition in a menagerie, see No. 69.

Ketch, Jack (d. 1686). From John Ketch, whose notorious barbarity from the time of his appointment as executioner in 1663 made his name the symbol of the office of executioner by 1702.

Vauxhall Gardens was a venerable pleasure ground, on the Surrey side of the Thames, long enough established to have been frequented by Samuel Pepys and his friends. Let Boswell describe the resort as it was some few years before our period: "Vauxhall Gardens . . . is peculiarly adapted to the taste of the English nation; there being a mixture of curious show,—gay exhibition, musick, vocal and instrumental, not too refined for the general ear;—for all which only a shilling is paid; and, though last, not least, good eating and drinking for those who choose to purchase that regale" (*Life of Johnson*, Anno 1778). Cf. Ashton, *Dawn of the Nineteenth Century*, pp. 358–359. A song celebrating the delights of Vauxhall may be found in *The Universal Musician* (London, 1738), Vol. I, p. 65.

No. 66. *Advice Suggested by the State of the Times.*

Bibl. Lind., No. 1474.

Omitted, as a duplicate of No. 53, except for variations in the imprint.

No. 67. *Men of England!*

S. sh., 11 x 17; one side, one column.

Bibl. Lind., No. 1501; tentative dating, June, 1803.

Printed in full in Ashton's *English Caricature and Satire*, pp. 144–145.

On the hint of "fifth column" sentiment in England, see No. 57a and its notes and the general note on "The Poor" under No. 57. See also No. 68.

The reference to divine institution and sanction of monarchical government suggests comparison with the earlier doctrine of the divine right of kings, as against the delusive French tenet of equality.

No. 68. *To the Infamous Wretch.*

S. sh., 11 x 17; one side, one column.

Bibl. Lind., No. 1518; tentative dating, June, 1803.

Printed in full in Ashton's *English Caricature and Satire*, pp. 146–147.

Another suggestion, as in No. 67, of "fifth column" leanings among certain elements of the population of Britain.

Denon, Dominique-Vivant (1747–1825). French artist, diplomat, and author who accompanied Napoleon on his Egyptian campaign and was later made director general of the museums of France by Napoleon. His *Voyage dans la basse et la haute Egypte*, widely read at the time, is reviewed in the *British Critic* (June, 1803), Vol. XXI, pp. 618–623, and Vol. XXII, pp. 18–19. The original French edition of Denon's *Voyage* is surveyed at length in the *Edinburgh Review* (January, 1803), Vol. I, pp. 320–345. The reviewer quotes (pp. 339–340) the passage cited in the broadside, in a translated form differing considerably from that presented in our text. Denon's work appears (p. 320) to have been published under sponsorship of the Institute at Cairo and under the patronage of the First Consul himself. The reviewer appraises the book in a tone which tends to justify the imputations of the maker of the broadside.

No. 69. *Most Wonderful Wonder of Wonders!!*

S. sh., 11 × 17; one side, one column, except for the list of publications in two columns.

Bibl. Lind., No. 1503; tentative dating, June, 1803.

Printed in full in Ashton's *English Caricature and Satire*, pp. 200–201. Cf., *ibid.*, pp. 193–194, the illustrated broadside entitled "Pidcock's Grand Menagerie, with an exact representation of Buonaparte, the little Corsican monkey, as he may probably appear at the above Receptacle of Foreign Curiosities, on, or before, Christmas, 1803."

Mrs. Hester Lynch Thrale Piozzi (1741–1821) in diary entries of July and August, 1803, makes several comments on the invasion. She inserts some verses written by a woman friend, entitled "The Mammoth": Ages ago a mammoth ranged the fields destroying man and beast until he was himself killed by the lion. His preserved carcase is now on exhibition in London. In these latter days a second mammoth, a Corsican, oppresses nations. Happily, the British Lion comes on the scene as an avenger and "a second mammoth dies." Mrs. Piozzi observes that in case of invasion either Britain or Napoleon will be undone; further, that Englishmen will fight to defend their own shores, but hardly to set up a king in France. See *Thraliana*, ed. Katherine C. Balderston (2 vols.; Oxford, 1942), Vol. II, pp. 1035 ff.

The appended caution to the "Corps Diplomatique" is probably an allusion to Napoleon's outburst against England in the presence of the British ambassador, Lord Whitworth, at a public reception held by the First Consul. See Oscar Browning, *England and Napoleon in 1803*, pp. 115–117.

Mufti. A Mohammedan priest or expounder of the laws.

No. 70. *Buonaparte and Talleyrand.*

S. sh., 10¾ × 17½; one side, dialogue in two columns.

Brit Mus. *Catalogue, s.v.* "Napoleon I"; tentative dating, 1803.

Printed in full in Ashton's *English Caricature and Satire*, pp. 221–223.

Talleyrand's apparently traitorous forecast upon the planned invasion probably reflects his fixed concern for the welfare of France even at the expense of his loyalty to the ambitions of Napoleon. In Ashton's *English Caricature and Satire*, pp. 210–214, appears a verse satire in which Talleyrand's opposition to the invasion is further illustrated.

GUIDE TO PERSONS, PLACES,
AND SOCIETIES

This list incorporates, in addition to the general record of names, annotations on names occurring in two or more of the broadsides. Annotations affecting only a single broadside, or the author of any one broadside, will be found in the Notes to the Broadsides, above. Numbers refer to broadsides, not pages.

GUIDE TO PERSONS, PLACES, AND SOCIETIES

Abercromby, Sir Ralph (1734–1801). Commanded the troops sent against the French West Indies (1795–1796), fought in Flanders, and at the Battle of Alexandria (March 21, 1801) defeated the army Napoleon had abandoned in Egypt in 1799. Fell in this battle. See note on Broadside 4, Broadside 9d and note, and Broadsides 37, 41, 49

Aboukir, Egypt. Nelson defeated the French in a night attack in Aboukir Bay at the "Battle of the Nile" on August 1, 1798, and bottled up Napoleon's army in Egypt. 5, 7 n., 9, 26, 37, 46

Acland, Lady Harriet (1750–1815). 11 and note

Acland, John Dyke (d. 1778). 11

Acon. 9d and note

Acre (also called, by the French, Ptolémaïs and St.-Jean-d'Acre). A seaport in Palestine, where, in 1799, the Turks under Yussuf Pasha, aided by the English under Sir Sidney Smith, held out for sixty days against Napoleon. "That miserable fort," as Napoleon called it, caused him to abandon his Syrian expedition and possible Oriental schemes. 2, 4 n., 7, 9d and note, 12, 21, 26, 46

Addington, Henry, first Viscount Sidmouth (1757–1844). 3 n., 16 n., 65 n.

Agincourt, Battle of (October 25, 1415). Henry V, with an army of 15,000 Englishmen, defeated the French army of 50,000. The light-armed English yeomen killed 10,000 Frenchmen, including 8,000 nobles, knights, and squires. 1, 3, 6, 26, 30, 32, 37, 49, 56 n.

Ajaccio, Corsica. 12 and note

Albanians. 7 and note

Alexander I, Tsar of Russia (r. 1801–1825). 37 n., 64 n.

Alexander the Great (356–323 B.C.). 32 and note

Alexandria, Battle of (March 21, 1801). *See* Abercromby, Sir Ralph. 4 n., 12, 21, 25, 26, 37, 45

Alfred, King of England (871–901). His stand against the Danish invaders made him a legendary as well as a historical character. His kingdom all but overrun, he nevertheless saved its heart, Wessex. 6, 37

Algiers. 4 n.

Allepins. 7 and note

Amiens, Peace of (March, 1802–May, 1803). Introduction, 3 n., 4 n., 12 n., 56 n.

Andréossy (Andreossi), Antoine-François (1761–1828). 4 and note

Anne, Queen of England (r. 1702–1714). 6 and note

Greenwich Hospital, England. 25

Grenville, William Wyndham, Baron Grenville (1759–1834). 65 n.

Halsewell Indiaman. 11 and note

Hampden, John (1594–1643). A cousin of Oliver Cromwell, he was one of the five members of Parliament whom Charles I, going to the House of Commons in person, attempted to arrest in January, 1642. Hampden raised a regiment for the Parliamentarians and was mortally wounded at Chalgrove Field. His stalwart resistance to Charles made him a hero, and Gray's *Elegy* immortalized him as a defender of the people's rights. 9, 37

Hannibal (?247–?183 B.C.). 32 n.

Hanover, Duchy of. The Georges were not only Kings of England but also Electors of Hanover in Germany. They found Hanover difficult to defend and impossible to abandon. Victoria's accession to the throne, in 1837, marks the final separation into independent royal lines. Both France and Prussia wished to annex Hanover. Annexed by Napoleon in June, 1803. 12, 22, 40 and note, 50, 54, 63 and note

Hanseatic League. 39 n.

Hapsburgs. 47 n.

Harbourgh (Harburg), Hanover. 63 and note

Hardy, Thomas (1752–1832). 57 n.

Harold the Saxon (r. 1066). 3 and note

Harry (Henry V). *See* Henry V. 9

Hastings, Battle of (October 14, 1066). 3 and note, 31 and note

Havre, France. 39 n.

Hawkesbury, Lord. *See* Jenkinson, Robert Banks

Haymarket Theater. 19 n.

Helvetia. A name often applied to Switzerland. 9, 59

Henry III, King of England (r. 1216–1272). 46 n.

Henry V, King of England (King Harry) (r. 1413–1422). His secret treaty with the Burgundians reopened the Hundred Years' War. At the Battle of Agincourt (1415) he defeated the French, and in 1419 he conquered Normandy. *See* Agincourt. 1, 2, 6, 9, 15, 32, 37, 49

Henry VII, King of England (r. 1485–1509). 35 n.

Henry VIII, King of England (r. 1509–1547). 35 and note

Hoche, Lazare (1768–1797). Introduction, 3 n.

Holland (and Belgium). The geographical position of Holland and Belgium, and their great resources in agriculture, industry, and shipping, make them of the greatest strategic importance on the continent of Europe for the people of Britain. A chief cause of the rupture of the Peace of Amiens was Napoleon's domination of this region. Britain,

The Romantic movement in England drew inspiration from the Swiss people and Swiss scenery. A visit to the Swiss mountains was a favorite English pastime. Napoleon's domination of a country so long free seemed an ominous extension of French power on the Continent during the Peace of Amiens. 3 n., 20 n., 21, 22 n., 30, 35, 40, 50, 54, 56, 59, 69

Sydney (Sidney), Algernon (1622–1683). Wounded at Marston Moor in 1644, when he took up arms against Charles I, Sydney was later nominated a commissioner for the trial of Charles but opposed the proceedings of the high court as invalid. Held aloof from the Protectorate after the dissolution of the Rump Parliament, but later became a member of the Council of State (1659) and chief of four commissioners who mediated between Sweden and Denmark at Elsinore in 1659–1660. He refused to give pledges to Charles II, vindicated himself from a charge of complicity in a Nonconformist plot, later discussed questions of insurrection with Whig leaders in January, 1683, and was sent to the Tower of London after discovery of the Rye House plot in June. He was executed on Tower Hill in December, 1683. 9, 37

Syracuse. 14 and note

Syria. Entering Syria from Egypt in February, 1799, Napoleon, in a vigorous campaign, captured Gaza, invested Jaffa, and by March 19 encamped outside Acre. The unexpected resistance offered here, together with war threats in Europe and the inroads of the plague, finally caused him to raise the siege and begin a retreat to Egypt. For the races of Syria see note to broadside No. 7. *See also* Gaza, Jaffa, Acre. 4 n., 8, 9, 22, 26 n., 70

Tallard, Camille de (1652–1728). 6 and note

Talleyrand-Périgord, Charles-Maurice de (1754–1838). A famous diplomatist, throughout a long life he had a genius for timing, for abandoning one regime and joining the next. His defense was that he had the interests of France alone at heart. Never fully trusted by Napoleon, his relations with England and Russia were obscure. He was Louis XVIII's representative at the Congress of Vienna. Talleyrand is known to Americans for his residence in Philadelphia (1794–1795), where he took an oath of allegiance to the United States (May 19, 1794), and for his attempt as Foreign Secretary to extort a tribute from Americans, known as the X.Y.Z. affair (1797–1798). He is unique in having wielded power under the *ancien régime*, the Revolution, Napoleon, and the Restoration. 3 and note, 4, 70 and note

Thersites. 14 and note

Timoleon (*ca.* 411–*ca.* 337 B.C.). Greek statesman and general. 14 and note, 27

BIBLIOGRAPHY

BIBLIOGRAPHY

I

FOR the lay reader, it may be interesting to note that Napoleon has a literature rivaled only by that of Martin Luther. In process of accumulation for nearly a century and a half, the stream shows no signs of diminishing. From this mass of scholarship a few titles may here be included for the convenience of the reader. The layman is fortunate in having available H. A. L. Fisher's *A History of Europe: The Liberal Experiment* (Boston, 1936), which covers this period in a quick survey. Three recent lives of Napoleon may be mentioned for ready reference: J. Holland Rose, *Life of Napoleon I*; August Fournier, *Napoleon I, a Biography*; and H. A. L. Fisher's small volume, *Napoleon*, which is a masterly condensation.

Standard for the history of Great Britain at this time are the two volumes of J. Holland Rose, *William Pitt and National Revival* (London, 1911) and *William Pitt and the Great War* (London, 1911). On the Navy, Alfred Thayer Mahan has written *The Influence of Sea Power upon the French Revolution and Empire, 1793–1812* (Boston, 1898), and his *Life of Nelson* (Boston, 1899) is the best biography of the famous admiral. The British army has been presented in a series of volumes by Sir John Fortescue, a work notable for interpretative detail. Briefer is Sir Charles Oman's *Wellington's Army, 1809–1814* (New York, 1912). This study has valuable information on all phases of the British army from military tactics to chaplains and pietism in the army.

Graham Wallas, in his *Life of Francis Place, 1771–1854* (New York, 1898), and G. D. H. Cole, in *The Life of William Cobbett* (New York, 1925), present the lives of two great propagandists. The social effects of the agricultural and industrial revolutions are told by J. L. and Barbara Hammond. Their *Town Labourer, 1760–1832*, will interest all readers. The shift of English opinion from sympathy to violent hostility is related in P. A. Brown, *The French Revolution in English History*. The overwhelming reactionary power of Edmund Burke's *Reflections on the Revolution in France* need only be mentioned in passing. Reginald Coupland's *Wilberforce, a Narrative* integrates the Evangelical group into the social order and politics of the time.

For England, and particularly Ireland, during the French Revolution, the volumes of W. E. H. Lecky, *History of England in the Eighteenth Century* (London, 1878–1890), are still the classic presentation. Two recent works by George Macaulay Trevelyan will give the reader a quick survey of British history: *History of England* (New York and London,

1926) and *English Social History: A Survey of Six Centuries, Chaucer to Queen Victoria* (New York, 1942).

A convenient record of diplomatic exchanges between England and Napoleon preceding the rupture of the Peace of Amiens may be found in the dispatches of Lord Whitworth, as presented by Oscar Browning in *England and Napoleon in 1803.*

For a French view of the various attempts at invasion in this general period, with information on defensive measures in England, see the abundantly documented treatment by Desbrière in his voluminous *Projets et tentatives de débarquement aux Îles Britanniques.*

Illuminating side lights on British reactions to the threat of invasion, particularly in the field of caricature, will be found in John Ashton's *Dawn of the Nineteenth Century in England* and *English Caricature and Satire on Napoleon I.*

II

Adams, William Forbes. *Ireland and Irish Emigration to the New World from 1815 to the Famine* (New Haven, 1932).

Antigallican, The; or Standard of British loyalty, Religion, and Liberty: Including a collection of the principal Papers, Tracts, Speeches, Poems, and Songs that have been published on the threatened Invasion (London, 1804).

Ashton, John. *Dawn of the XIXth Century in England* (London, 1906).

——. *English Caricature and Satire on Napoleon I* (London, 1888).

Assalini, Paolo. *Observations on the Disease called the Plague, on the Dysentery, the Ophthalmy of Egypt, and on the Means of Prevention.* . . . Translated from the French by Adam Neale (New York, 1806).

Barrington, The Hon. Daines. "Observations on the Practice of Archery in England," *Archæologia; or Miscellaneous Tracts relating to Antiquity* (London, 1785).

Besant, Sir Walter. *London City* (London, 1910).

——. *London in the Time of the Tudors* (London, 1904).

Birley, Robert. *The English Jacobins* (Oxford, 1924).

Black, J. B. *The Reign of Elizabeth, 1558–1603* (Oxford, 1936).

British Critic, and Quarterly Theological Review, The (London, 1803), Vols. XXI, XXII.

British Museum. *Catalogue of Printed Books* (London, 1881–1900; incl. *Supplement*, 1905).

——. *Catalogue of Printed Music Published between 1487 and 1800* (London, 1912).

——. *General Catalogue of Printed Books* (London, 1931——).

Brown, Philip Anthony. *The French Revolution in English History* (London, 1918).

Browning, Oscar (ed.). *England and Napoleon in 1803* (London and New York, 1887).

Bruun, Geoffrey. *Europe and the French Imperium, 1799–1814* (New York, 1938).

Burke, Edmund. "Reflections on the Revolution in France," Vol. V in *The Works of the Right Honourable Edmund Burke* (London, 1826).

Cambridge History of British Foreign Policy, 1783–1919, The (New York, 1922–1923), Vol. I.

Cambridge History of Poland from Augustus II to Pilsudski, 1697–1935, The (Cambridge, England, 1941).

Cambridge History of the British Empire, The (New York and Cambridge, England, 1929, 1940), Vols. I and II.

Chappell, William. *Popular Music of the Olden Time* (London, [1855–1859]).

Cobbett's Annual Register (London, 1803), Vol. III.

Cole, G. D. H. *A Short History of the British Working Class Movement* (New York, 1927).

Cole, G. D. H., and Postgate, Raymond. *The British Common People, 1746–1938* (New York, 1939).

Correspondance de Napoléon Ier (Paris, 1858–1870), 32 vols., Vol. V.

Coupland, Reginald. *Wilberforce, a Narrative* (Oxford, 1923).

Denon, Dominique-Vivant. *Voyage dans la basse et la haute Egypte pendant les campagnes du Général Bonaparte* (Paris, 1802), 2 vols.

Desbrière, Edouard. *Projets et tentatives de débarquement aux Îles Britanniques* (Paris, 1900–1902), 4 vols. in 5.

Deutsch, Harold C. "Napoleonic Policy and the Project of a Descent upon England," *Journal of Modern History*, Vol. II, pp. 541–568.

Dominian, Leon. *The Frontiers of Language and Nationality in Europe* (New York, 1917).

Edinburgh Review or Critical Journal, The (Edinburgh, 1803).

European Magazine and London Review, The (London, 1801, 1802, 1803), Vols. XL, XLII, XLIII, XLIV.

Fortescue, J. W. *British Statesmen of the Great War, 1793–1814* (Oxford, 1911).

Fournier, August. *Napoleon I, a Biography* (New York, 1915), 2 vols.

Frischauer, Paul. *England's Years of Danger* (New York, 1938).

Garrick, David. *Three Plays*, ed. Elizabeth P. Stein (New York, 1926).

Genest, John. *Some Account of the English Stage from the Restoration in 1660 to 1830* (Bath, 1832), 10 vols., Vol. VII.

Gentleman's Magazine, The (London, 1786, 1802, 1803), Vols. LVI, LXXIII, LXXIV, LXXVII.

Gooch, George Peabody. *The French Revolution* (London, 1920).

Grove, Sir George. *Grove's Dictionary of Music and Musicians* (New York, 1908–1910).

Hallam, Henry. *The Constitutional History of England from the Accession of Henry VII to the Death of George II* (New York, 1897).

Hammond, J. L. and Barbara. *The Skilled Labourer, 1760–1832* (London, 1920).

———. *The Town Labourer, 1760–1832* (London, 1925).

———. *The Village Labourer, 1760–1832* (London, 1924).

Hazlitt, William. *The Life of Napoleon Bonaparte* (New York, 1902), 3 vols.

Hume, David. *The History of England from the Invasion of Julius Caesar to the Abdication of James II, 1688* (Boston, 1849–1850), 6 vols.

Klingberg, Frank J. "Ideas That Did Not Migrate from England to America," *Pennsylvania Magazine of History and Biography*, Vol. LXIII, pp. 380–389.

———. *The Anti-Slavery Movement in England: A Study in English Humanitarianism* (New Haven and London, 1926).

———. "The Evolution of the Humanitarian Spirit in Eighteenth Century England," *Pennsylvania Magazine of History and Biography*, Vol. LXVI, pp. 260–278.

Low, Sidney J., and Pulling, F. S. *The Dictionary of English History* (London, 1911).

Maitland, Frederick W. *The Constitutional History of England* (Cambridge, England, 1908).

Massinger, Philip. *Plays*, ed. W. Gifford (London, 1805), 4 vols.

May, Sir Thomas Erskine. *The Constitutional History of England* (London, 1912), 3 vols.

Monthly Mirror, The (London, 1803), Vols. XV, XVI.

Monthly Review, The (London, 1803), Vols. XL–XLII.

Morier, John P. *Memoir of a Campaign with the Ottoman Army in Egypt from February to July, 1800: containing a description of the Turkish army, journal of its march from Syria to Egypt, general observations on the Arabs, and on the treaty of El-Arish, etc.* (London, 1801).

Paine, Thomas. *The Age of Reason* (London, 1796).

———. *The Rights of Man* (London, 1817).

Palmer, Robert R. "Ideas That Did Not Migrate from America to Europe," *Pennsylvania Magazine of History and Biography*, Vol. LXIII, pp. 369–379.

Pièces diverses et Correspondance relatives aux opérations de l'Armée d'Orient en Egypte (Paris, 1801).

Piozzi, Mrs. Hester Lynch Thrale. *Thraliana*, ed. Katherine C. Balderston (Oxford, 1942), 2 vols.

Purcell, Henry. *Orpheus Britannicus* (2d ed.; London, 1706–1712), 2 vols.

———. *Works* (Purcell Society, 1878———).

Rose, J. Holland. *Life of Napoleon I* (London, 1902; 10th ed., 1929), 2 vols. in 1.

Rose, J. Holland, and Broadley, A. M. *Dumouriez and the Defence of England against Napoleon* (London, 1909).

Roxburghe Ballads, The, ed. J. W. Ebsworth (Hertford, 1889), 9 vols.

Sheridan, Richard Brinsley. *The Speeches of the Right Honourable Richard Brinsley Sheridan, edited by a constitutional friend* (London, 1842), 3 vols.

Skalkowski, A. M. *Polacy na San Domingo, 1802–1809* (Poznan, 1921).

Spirit of the Public Journals for 1803, The (London, 1804).

Stein, Elizabeth P. *David Garrick, Dramatist* (New York, 1938).

Trevelyan, George Macaulay. *English Social History: A Survey of Six Centuries, Chaucer to Queen Victoria* (New York, 1942).

———. *History of England* (New York, 1926).

Universal Musician, The (London, 1738).

Universal Songster; or Museum of mirth: forming the most complete, extensive, and valuable collection of ancient and modern songs in the English language (London, [1834]), 3 vols.

Wheeler, H. F. B., and Broadley, A. M., *Napoleon and the Invasion of England* (London, 1908), 2 vols.

White, Andrew D. *Seven Great Statesmen* (New York, 1926).

Wilberforce, William. *A Practical View of the Prevailing Religious System of Professed Christians in the Higher and Middle Classes, Contrasted with Real Christianity* (London, 1797).

Wilson, Robert Thomas. *History of the British Expedition to Egypt: to which is subjoined, a Sketch of the present State of that Country, and its Means of Defence* (London, 1802).

Wittman, William. *Travels in Turkey, Asia Minor, Syria, and across the desert into Egypt during the years 1799, 1800, and 1801, in company with the Turkish army and the British military mission. To which are annexed, observations on the plague, and on the diseases prevalent in Turkey, and a meteorological journal* (London, 1803).